616.89 P9236b 2012
Preece, Emma L
Biological psychology

Biological Psychology

Psychology Express

D1279567

WITHDRAWN

The PsychologyExpress series

→ UNDERSTAND QUICKLY
→ REVISE EFFECTIVELY
→ TAKE EXAMS WITH CONFIDENCE

'All of the revision material I need in one place – a must for psychology undergrads.'
Andrea Franklin, Psychology student at Anglia Ruskin University

'Very useful, straight to the point and provides guidance to the student, while helping them to develop independent learning.'
Lindsay Pitcher, Psychology student at Anglia Ruskin University

'Engaging, interesting, comprehensive . . . it helps to guide understanding and boosts confidence.'
Megan Munro, Forensic Psychology student at Leeds Trinity University College

'Very useful . . . bridges the gap between Statistics textbooks and Statistics workbooks.'
Chris Lynch, Psychology student at the University of Chester

'The answer guidelines are brilliant, I wish I had had it last year.'
Tony Whalley, Psychology student at the University of Chester

'I definitely would (buy a revision guide) as I like the structure, the assessment advice and practice questions and would feel more confident knowing exactly what to revise and having something to refer to.'
Steff Copestake, Psychology student at the University of Chester

'The clarity is absolutely first rate . . . These chapters will be an excellent revision guide for students as well as providing a good opportunity for novel forms of assessment in and out of class.'
Dr Deaglan Page, Queen's University, Belfast

'Do you think they will help students when revising/working towards assessment? Unreservedly, yes.'
Dr Mike Cox, Newcastle University

'The revision guide should be very helpful to students preparing for their exams.'
Dr Kun Guo, University of Lincoln

'A brilliant revision guide, very helpful for students of all levels.'
Svetoslav Georgiev, Psychology student at Anglia Ruskin University

Biological Psychology

Emma Preece
University of Worcester

Series editor:
Dominic Upton
University of Worcester

Prentice Hall
is an imprint of

Harlow, England • London • New York • Boston • San Francisco • Toronto
Sydney • Tokyo • Singapore • Hong Kong • Seoul • Taipei • New Delhi
Cape Town • Madrid • Mexico City • Amsterdam • Munich • Paris • Milan

CUYAHOGA COMMUNITY COLLEGE
EASTERN CAMPUS LIBRARY

Psychology Express

Pearson Education Limited
Edinburgh Gate
Harlow
Essex CM20 2JE
England

and Associated Companies throughout the world

Visit us on the World Wide Web at:
www.pearsoned.co.uk

First published 2012

© Pearson Education Limited 2012

The right of Emma Preece to be identified as author of this Work has been asserted by her in accordance with the Copyright, Designs and Patents Act 1988.

All rights reserved. No part of this publication may be reproduced, stored in a retrieval system, or transmitted in any form or by any means, electronic, mechanical, photocopying, recording or otherwise, without either the prior written permission of the publisher or a licence permitting restricted copying in the United Kingdom issued by the Copyright Licensing Agency Ltd, Saffron House, 6–10 Kirby Street, London EC1N 8TS.

Pearson Education is not responsible for the content of third-party Internet sites.

ISBN 978-0-273-73722-3

British Library Cataloguing-in-Publication Data
A catalogue record for this book is available from the British Library

Library of Congress Cataloging-in-Publication Data
A catalog record for this book is available from the Library of Congress

10 9 8 7 6 5 4 3 2 1
15 14 13 12

Typeset in 9.5/12.5pt Avenir Book by 30
Printed in Great Britain by Henry Ling Ltd, at the Dorset Press, Dorchester, Dorset

CUYAHOGA COMMUNITY COLLEGE
EASTERN CAMPUS LIBRARY

Contents

Supporting resources

Visit www.pearsoned.co.uk/psychologyexpress *to find valuable online resources.*

Companion website for students

→ **Get help in organising your revision**: download and print topic maps and revision checklists for each area.

→ **Ensure you know the key concepts in each area**: test yourself with *flashcards*. You can use them online, print them out or download to an iPod.

→ **Improve the quality of your essays in assignments and exams**: use the sample exam questions, referring to the answer guidelines for extra help.

→ **Practise for exams**: check the answers to the Test your knowledge sections in this book and take additional tests for each chapter.

→ **Go into exams with confidence**: use the You be the marker exercises to consider sample answers through the eyes of the examiner.

Also: The companion website provides the following features:

● Search tool to help locate specific items of content.

● E-mail results and profile tools to send results of quizzes to instructors.

● Online help and support to assist with website usage and troubleshooting.

For more information please contact your local Pearson Education sales representative or visit www.pearsoned.co.uk/psychologyexpress

Acknowledgements

Author's acknowledgements

Thanks are due firstly to the editor Professor Dominic Upton for giving me the opportunity to write this text. Thank you to Dr Jonathan Catling for his support during the writing process and to Mr Lee Badham who designed most of the artwork. Special thanks are also due to my family, Angela Huddart, Michelle Hallard, Catherine Moreland, Charlotte Taylor, Helena Darby, Carole Hender, Gemma Taylor, Tracey Price, Laura Scurlock-Evans, Emma Jackson, Chris Leck, Daniel Kay and all other friends and colleagues for their support and encouragement.

Series editor's acknowledgments

I am grateful to Janey Webb and Jane Lawes at Pearson Education for their assistance with this series. I would also like to thank Penney, Francesca, Rosie and Gabriel for their dedication to psychology.

Dominic Upton

Publisher's acknowledgements

Our thanks go to all the reviewers who contributed to the development of this text, including students who participated in research and focus groups which helped to shape the series format.

Dr Paul Hitchcott, Southampton Solent University
Dr Minna Lyons, Liverpool Hope University
Dr Deaglan Page, Queen's University Belfast
Dr Jonathon Reay, Northumbria University
Dr Julia Robertson, Buckinghamshire New University
Dr Mark Scase, De Montfort University
Dr Sonia Tucci, University of Liverpool

Student reviewer:
Katie Towers, Psychology student at Anglia Ruskin University

Introduction

Not only is psychology one of the fastest growing subjects to study at university worldwide, it is also one of the most exciting and relevant subjects. Over the past decade the scope, breadth and importance of psychology have developed considerably. Important research work from as far afield as the UK, Europe, USA and Australia has demonstrated the exacting research base of the topic and how this can be applied to all manner of everyday issues and concerns. Being a student of psychology is an exciting experience – the study of mind and behaviour is a fascinating journey of discovery. Studying psychology at degree level brings with it new experiences, new skills and knowledge. As the Quality Assurance Agency (QAA, 2010) has stressed:

> psychology is distinctive in the rich and diverse range of attributes it develops – skills which are associated with the humanities (e.g. critical thinking and essay writing) and the sciences (hypotheses-testing and numeracy). (QAA, 2010, p. 5)

Recent evidence suggests that employers appreciate the skills and knowledge of psychology graduates, but in order to reach this pinnacle you need to develop your skills, further your knowledge and most of all successfully complete your degree to your maximum ability. The skills, knowledge and opportunities acquired during your psychology degree will give you an edge in the employment field. The QAA stresses the high level of employment skills developed during a psychology degree:

> due to the wide range of generic skills, and the rigour with which they are taught, training in psychology is widely accepted as providing an excellent preparation for many careers. In addition to subject skills and knowledge, graduates also develop skills in communication, numeracy, teamwork, critical thinking, computing, independent learning and many others, all of which are highly valued by employers. (QAA, 2010, p. 2)

This book is part of the comprehensive new series, Psychology Express, that helps you achieve these aspirations. It is not a replacement for every single text, journal article, presentation and abstract you will read and review during the course of your degree programme. It is in no way a replacement for your lectures, seminars or additional reading. A top-rated assessment answer is likely to include considerable additional information and wider reading – and you are directed to some of these in this text. This revision guide is a conductor: directing you through the maze of your degree by providing an overview of your course, helping you formulate your ideas, and directing your reading.

Each book within Psychology Express presents a summary coverage of the key concepts, theories and research in the field, within an explicit framework of revision. The focus throughout all of the books in the series will be on how you should approach and consider your topics in relation to assessment and exams. Various features have been included to help you build up your skills and knowledge ready for your assessments. More details of these features can be found in the guided tour for this book on page xii.

By reading and engaging with this book, you will develop your skills and knowledge base and in this way you should excel in your studies and your associated assessments.

Psychology Express: Biological Psychology is divided into nine chapters and your course has probably been divided up into similar sections. However we, the series authors and editors, must stress a key point: do not let the purchase, reading and engagement with the material in this text restrict your reading or your thinking. In psychology, you need to be aware of the wider literature and how it interrelates and how authors and thinkers have criticised and developed the arguments of others. So even if an essay asks you about one particular topic you need to draw on similar issues raised in other areas of psychology. There are, of course, some similar themes that run throughout the material covered in this text, but you can learn from the other areas of psychology covered in the other texts in this series as well as from material presented elsewhere.

We hope you enjoy this text and the others in the Psychology Express series, which cover the complete knowledge base of psychology:

- *Biological Psychology* (Emma Preece): covering the biological basis of behaviour, hormones and behaviour, sleeping and dreaming, and psychological abnormalities.

- *Cognitive Psychology* (Jonathan Ling and Jonathan Catling): including key material on perception, learning, memory, thinking and language.

- *Developmental Psychology* (Penney Upton): from pre-natal development through to old age, the development of individuals is considered. Childhood, adolescence and lifespan development are all covered.

- *Personality and Individual Differences* (Laura Scurlock): normal and abnormal personality, psychological testing, intelligence, emotion and motivation are all covered in this book.

- *Social Psychology* (Jenny Mercer and Debbie Clayton): covering all the key topics in Social Psychology including attributions, attitudes, group relations, close relationships and critical social psychology.

- *Statistics in Psychology* (Catherine Steele, Holly Andrews and Dominic Upton): an overview of data analysis related to psychology is presented along with why we need statistics in psychology. Descriptive and inferential statistics and both parametric and non-parametric analysis are included.

- *Research Methods in Psychology* (Steve Jones and Mark Forshaw): research design, experimental methods, discussion of qualitative and quantitative methods and ethics are all presented in this text.

- *Conceptual and Historical Issues in Psychology* (Brian M. Hughes): the foundations of psychology and its development from a mere interest into a scientific discipline. The key conceptual issues of current-day psychology are also presented.

This book, and the other companion volumes in this series, should cover all your study needs (there will also be further guidance on the website). It will, obviously, need to be supplemented with further reading and this text directs you towards suitable sources. Hopefully, quite a bit of what you read here you will already have come across and the text will act as a jolt to set your mind at rest – you do know the material in depth. Overall, we hope that you find this book useful and informative as a guide for both your study now and in your future as a successful psychology graduate.

Revision note

- *Use evidence based on your reading, not on anecdotes or your 'common sense'.*
- *Show the examiner you know your material in depth – use your additional reading wisely.*
- *Remember to draw on a number of different sources: there is rarely one 'correct' answer to any psychological problem.*
- *Base your conclusions on research-based evidence.*

Explore the accompanying website at www.pearsoned.co.uk/psychologyexpress
→ Prepare more effectively for exams and assignments using the answer guidelines for questions from this chapter.
→ Test your knowledge using multiple choice questions and flashcards.
→ Improve your essay skills by exploring the You be the marker exercises.

Guided tour

→ Understand key concepts quickly

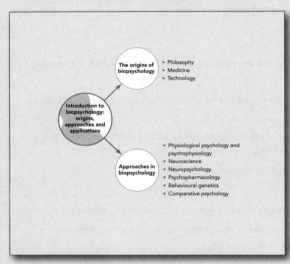

Start to plan your revision using the **Topic maps**.

Grasp **Key terms** quickly using the handy definitions. Use the flashcards online to test yourself.

Key terms

Humorism: An ancient school of thought concerned with the balance of the body's naturally produced substances: bile, blood and phlegm.

Cognitivism: A school of thought concerned with human cognition.

Behaviourism: A school of thought concerned with purely observable and measureable human and animal behaviour.

→ Revise effectively

KEY STUDY

The suprachiasmatic nucleus and circadian rhythms

Silver, LeSauter, Tresco and Lehman (1996) identified that surgical removal of the SCN of hamsters eradicated their circadian rhythms, suggesting that this structure may be the locus of the circadian clock. Furthermore, when SCN tissue was transplanted into the hamsters' third ventricles using small semi-permeable capsules, the circadian rhythms recommenced. However, the notable issue with this finding is that while chemicals and nutrients could pass through the capsule to replenish the SCN tissue, the tissue itself was not able to establish synaptic connections to the surrounding tissue due to the nature of the capsules. This suggests that the SCN may control circadian rhythms through chemicals rather than electrical signals although the nature of these chemicals is yet to be determined.

Quickly remind yourself of the **Key studies** using the special boxes in the text.

Test your knowledge

5.8   What are the physical dimensions of audition?

5.9   What are the perceptual dimensions of audition?

5.10   Where is the primary auditory cortex located?

Answers to these questions can be found on the companion website at: www.pearsoned.co.uk/psychologyexpress

Prepare for upcoming exams and tests using the **Test your knowledge** and **Sample question** features.

Compare your responses with the **Answer guidelines** in the text and on the website.

Answer guidelines

✳ Sample question   Essay

Compare and contrast two biological approaches to studying human emotion.

Approaching the question

This question is asking you to apply your understanding of human emotion and two different approaches in biological psychology to discuss how these approaches present similar or different interpretations. This can include any of the approaches described in Chapter 1 and any emotional state. You will also need to critically evaluate these perspectives.

Chapter 2: Perception

Home > Student Resources > Chapter 2: Perception > Chapter 2: Test your knowledge questions

Chapter 2: Test your Knowledge questions

The following are a copy of the Test your knowledge questions found in this chapter of your book.

Have a go at answering the question, referring to the 'Answer Guidelines' for extra help in how to frame

The Biology of the visual system

1. Name the image-forming structures of the eye.
   Q1: Answer Guidelines
2. What are the three types of retinal cells and what are their functions?
   Q1: Answer Guidelines
   Q2: Answer Guidelines
3. What does retinotopic mapping mean?
   Q2: Answer Guidelines
4. Describe the main types of cells in the V1 area.
   Q3: Answer Guidelines

Gestalt Theory

5. How did the Gestaltists suggest form is extracted?
   Q1: Answer Guidelines
6. Describe the law of Prägnanz.
   Q2: Answer Guidelines
7. What is figure-ground segregation?
   Q2: Answer Guidelines
8. List four shortcomings of Gestalt theory.
   Q3: Answer Guidelines

→ Make your answers stand out

Use the **Critical focus** boxes to impress your examiner with your deep and critical understanding.

CRITICAL FOCUS

The Mumby box

The Mumby box was developed by Mumby et al., (1989) in an attempt to test rats' ability to perform a delayed non-matching-to-sample task after lesions to the hippocampus. Rats were used because the location of their hippocampus means that only a small section of the parietal neocortex would also be damaged during the aspiration (suction) of this area, whereas in other animals the rhinal cortex would also be damaged.

During the experiment, a rat is placed in the middle of a box partitioned into three sections. One of the sliding doors is lifted to reveal a sample object which hides a food source. A trained, intact rat will run to the object and push it aside to obtain the food. The rat returns to the middle section while the first door is closed and the second door is lifted. The rat finds an object identical to the sample and a new object at the end of

Make your answer stand out

To make an answer stand out in this area you need to demonstrate that you have an understanding of the broader aspects of learning and memory which span across both biological and non-biological approaches and also across clinical and non-clinical samples. This will mean that you will need to be able to synthesise and critically evaluate a range of evidence while explicitly linking this to the essay question. For example, how can research with neurologically damaged patients correspond to research with healthy control subjects? You will also need to demonstrate that you are aware of (and understand) the theoretical and practical challenges directed towards neuropsychology.

Go into the exam with confidence using the handy tips to **make your answer stand out**.

Guided tour of the companion website

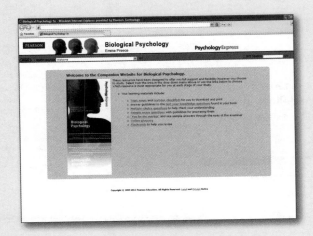

→ **Understand key concepts quickly**

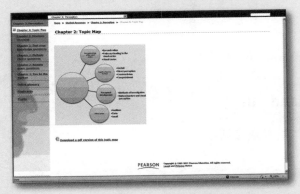

Printable versions of the **Topic maps** give an overview of the subject and help you plan your revision.

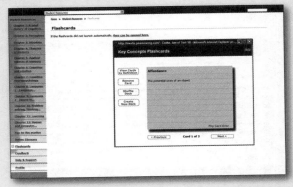

Test yourself on key definitions with the online **Flashcards**.

→ Revise effectively

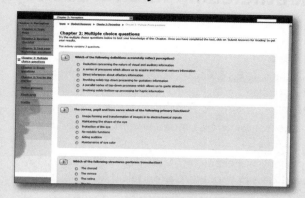

Check your understanding and practise for exams with the **Multiple choice questions**.

→ Make your answers stand out

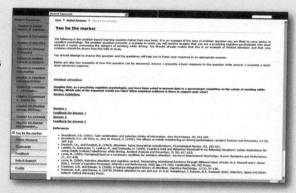

Evaluate sample exam answers in the **You be the marker** exercises and understand how and why an examiner awards marks.

Put your skills into practice with the **Sample exam questions**, then check your answers with the guidelines.

All this and more can be found at
www.pearsoned.co.uk/psychologyexpress

Key research studies

- Corkin, S., Sullivan, E. V., Twitchell, T. E., & Grove, E. (1981). The amnesic patient H. M.: Clinical observations and a test performance 28 years after operation. *Society of Neuroscience Abstracts, 7,* 235.

- Darwin, C. (1872/1965). *The expression of the emotions in man and animals.* Chicago: University of Chicago Press.

- Galton, F. (1865). Hereditary talent and character. *Macmillan's Magazine, 12,* 157–166. Available: http://psychclassics.yorku.ca/Galton/talent.htm.

- Hubel, D. H. & Wiesel, T. N. (1977). Functional architecture of macaque monkey visual cortex. *Proceedings of the Royal Society of London, 198,* 1–59.

- Lashley, K. S. (1930). Basic neural mechanisms in behaviour. *Psychological Review, 37* (1), 1–24. Available: http://psychclassics.yorku.ca/Lashley/neural.htm

- Madsen, P. L., Holm, S., Vorstrup, S., Friberg, L., Lassen, N. A. & Wildschiodz, G. (1991). Human regional cerebral blood flow during rapid-eye-movement sleep. *Journal of Cerebral Blood Flow and Metabolism, 11,* 502–507.

- Sperry, R. W. (1966). Brain bisection and consciousness. In J. Eccles (Ed.), *Brain and conscious experience.* New York: Springer-Verlag.

- Weiskrantz, I. (1987). Residual vision in the scotoma: A follow-up study of 'form' discrimination. *Brain, 110,* 77–92.

1

Introduction to biopsychology: origins, approaches and applications

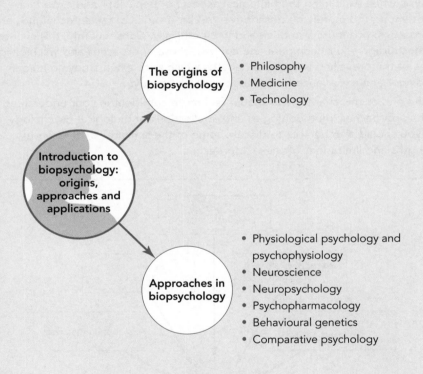

The origins of biopsychology
- Philosophy
- Medicine
- Technology

Introduction to biopsychology: origins, approaches and applications

Approaches in biopsychology
- Physiological psychology and psychophysiology
- Neuroscience
- Neuropsychology
- Psychopharmacology
- Behavioural genetics
- Comparative psychology

A printable version of this topic map is available from
www.pearsoned.co.uk/psychologyexpress

Introduction

This chapter will provide an overview of some of the main areas of biological psychology and will draw your attention to research techniques, theories and prominent research within these areas. Although you need to understand the general origins, nature and scope of biological psychology it is also important to remember that it consists of several significantly different approaches. These include physiological psychology, neuropsychology, cognitive neuroscience, behavioural genetics and psychopharmacology (see Figure 1.1).

Each of these approaches focuses on different levels of analysis and employs different techniques and interpretations. However, you should also understand that these approaches are applied and combined to provide several levels of analysis when examining the biological aspects of behaviour and experience. It is not enough to merely be descriptive and list a series of facts, techniques and approaches; you must also think and write critically. Consequently, this chapter will encourage you to compare and contrast these approaches and will highlight some of the prevailing issues and debates which arise when studying human behaviour and experience from a biological perspective.

By the end of this chapter you should feel more confident in your understanding of the approaches, methodologies and applications of biological psychology but you should also be able to discuss some of the similarities, differences, strengths and limitations of these approaches.

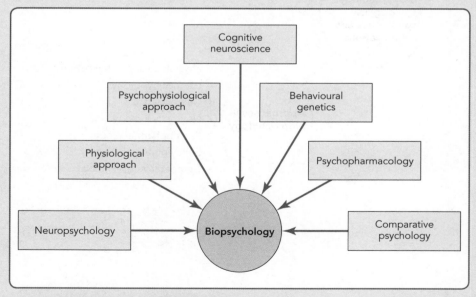

Figure 1.1 Approaches in biopsychology

Revision checklist

Essential points to revise are:

❑ How biopsychology originated and evolved

❑ What the main approaches in biopsychology are

❑ Which methodologies are used in biopsychology

❑ How biopsychology is applied to study phenomena

❑ What some of the continuing issues and debates are

Assessment advice

Essay questions for introductory biopsychology will usually ask you to compare and contrast two or more approaches or research techniques with reference to a specific phenomenon. For example, you may be asked to evaluate and compare neuropsychological and physiological approaches to studying perception. For questions like this you will need to understand the similarities, differences, techniques and principles of these approaches. You will also need to cite specific examples of these approaches in action.

Sample question

Could you answer this question? Below is a typical essay question that could arise on this topic.

✳ Sample question   *Essay*

To what extent has biopsychology contributed towards the understanding of human behaviour and experience? Discuss in relation to two approaches.

Guidelines on answering this question are included at the end of this chapter, whilst further guidance on tackling other exam questions can be found on the companion website at: **www.pearsoned.co.uk/psychologyexpress**

The origins of biopsychology

The biological psychology that we know today is the product of several theoretical shifts, centuries of research and numerous methodological adaptations (Carlson, 2004; Pinel, 2003). Indeed, biopsychology has links to philosophy, science, medicine and technology and can be tracked back as far as ancient Greece and humorism (Burton, 1989/1994). These influences have contributed towards the diversity of contemporary biopsychology. Indeed, the origins and development of biopsychology are also intertwined with the other schools of thought in psychology, such as cognitivism and behaviourism. As such, it is impossible to fully summarise the complete history of biopsychology in this book, but links to further reading are provided at the end of this section. A brief review of some of the contributions which have been made towards the origin and development of biopsychology is provided below.

Key terms

Humorism: An ancient school of thought concerned with the balance of the body's naturally produced substances: bile, blood and phlegm.

Cognitivism: A school of thought concerned with human cognition.

Behaviourism: A school of thought concerned with purely observable and measureable human and animal behaviour.

Philosophy

The mind–body problem

The philosophical origins of biopsychology are notably eclectic and incorporate several of the prominent and prevailing debates in psychology (Valentine, 1992). For example, the Critical Focus box below details how biopsychology is routed in the mind–body problem. This has been a common theme for debates since the origins of philosophy and features in religious scriptures that discuss the soul. The debate concerns the relationship between the mind (or, more generally, any incorporeal aspect) and the body. Contemporary biopsychology tends to adopt a dualist perspective, which argues that cognition and bodily responses are both relevant to human experience, rather than a monist perspective, which argues that there is only one reality and that is either physical (materialism) or psychological (idealism) in nature.

Key terms

Dualist/dualism: A perspective which states the mind and body both exist as separate entities which contribute toward the sense of reality.

Idealism: A perspective which states that the only reality is that created by the mind.

Materialism: A perspective which states that the only reality is that experienced by the body.

Mind–body problem: A philosophical debate concerning the relationship between and dominance of the mind and the body.

Monist/monism: A perspective which states that either the mind or the body exists independently. There is only one reality and that may be through the mind (idealism) or the body (materialism).

CRITICAL FOCUS

The mind–body problem

It is important that you can understand how the debates surrounding the mind–body problem have informed and influenced development and interpretation in biopsychology. For example, the monist perspective known as idealism states that the mind exists independent of the body, implying that bodily responses are irrelevant in determining behaviour and experience. In contrast, the monist perspective known as materialism states that only the physical reality is real, making all phenomena which cannot be observed and quantified irrelevant. This approach was endorsed by early behaviourism. In this case, it might be useful for you to consider the technological and methodological adaptations which have occurred since monist perspectives were widely endorsed. Can cognition and other previously unobservable (for example, physiological) phenomena now be quantified given the correct technology and measures?

Indeed, it is significant that branches of contemporary biopsychology tend to be founded on the assumptions of the dualist perspective known as interactionism. This states that there is a two-way relationship between the mind and the body. In this sense, bodily responses can influence thought and cognition can mediate bodily responses. For example, consider how chemical imbalances and negative thought patterns may interact in cases of depression to exacerbate the symptoms. Also consider how the perception of pain is relative rather than a universal. It is significant that both medication and thought processes (such as meditation) can reduce the perception of pain. However, can you think of any examples where this may not be the case? For example, in cases where 'blind-sight' individuals are able to reach for an object of which they are not consciously aware. This may support the dualist perspective known as parallelism, which states that there is a correlation between the mind and body rather than causation.

Functionalism and structuralism

The origins and current status of biopsychology are also intertwined with the debate between structuralism and functionalism (Valentine, 1992). For example, early structuralism attempted to study the structure and organisation of the mind based purely on conscious mental experience. This approach was linked to introspection and relied to a large extent on self-examination. However, several criticisms were levelled at this approach, including that it was subjective, unscientific and intrinsically linked to idealism.

In contrast, early functionalism attempted to understand behaviour and experience in terms of the functions which it served and how it facilitated or reflected reactions to the environment. As such, functionalism envisioned constant interaction between mental states, physiology and situational influences and is more representative of contemporary biopsychology. For example, in the case of evolutionary theories, behaviours are believed both to be determined by genetic predisposition and form a response to environmental factors. In this case, a behaviour, physiological response or mental state would serve the function of promoting survival (Lashley, 1930). Indeed, contemporary biopsychology attempts to identify which cerebral structures or physiological responses serve which specific functions.

Key terms

Evolutionary theories: Theories that behaviour and experience have developed through centuries of genetic mutation, evolution and survival of the fittest.

Functionalism: An approach which is concerned with identifying the functions which behaviour and experience serve.

Introspection: A technique developed by Wundt (1902) to study the subjective experience of patients based on their description of their thoughts and feelings.

Structuralism: An approach which is concerned with studying how the structure and organisation of the mind influence behaviour and experience.

Psychology as a science

You have probably already encountered the debate surrounding whether psychology can be considered to be a science. This debate has been ongoing since the emergence of early research and theorisation concerning the mind–body debate and is likely to continue due to the permanently evolving status of psychology (Hergenhahn, 2009; James, 1890; Valentine, 1992). For the purpose of this chapter it is important to note that biopsychology possesses more explicit links to science, medicine and technology than any other area of psychology. Indeed, while its origins are linked to philosophy, its development has been highly determined by scientific influences which are discussed later in this section. However, it is also important that you remember that biopsychology is also concerned with explaining phenomena which cannot always be observed and quantified. Sciences such as physics and biology have also experienced similar problems and technological advances have resolved several of these limitations.

Nature–nurture debate

The nature–nurture debate permeated psychology and refers to whether behaviour is determined by biological or environmental factors (Galton, 1865). However, in most cases the extremist views which arose as a product of monism have since been replaced by dualist perspectives (Valentine, 1992). Indeed, the most commonly endorsed perspective concerning the origins of mental illness is the diathesis–stress model. Proponents of this model argue that individuals may be predisposed to a condition due to genetic or physiological factors but that environmental factors can determine whether the condition manifests. For example, an individual may have low levels of the neurotransmitters serotonin and dopamine which would predispose them to depression, but the condition may not arise until a serious life event exacerbates these factors. It is also important to remember that cognitive factors, such as negative thoughts and worry, and social factors, including social norms and values, also influence human behaviour.

Key terms

Diathesis–stress: A theoretical model which states that behaviour and experience are produced by both biological and environmental factors.

Nature–nurture: A theoretical debate surrounding the topic of whether an individual's behaviour and experience are determined and inevitable due to biological factors, or undetermined and changeable due to environmental factors.

Neurotransmitter: A naturally occurring chemical produced in the body at the terminal buttons of neurons which facilitates the transmission of action potentials across synaptic gaps. The activation threshold and compatibility of the postsynaptic receptor cells will determine their efficiency. Neurotransmitters can have excitatory or inhibitory effects.

Medicine

Biopsychology also has explicit bases and links to medicine because both disciplines examine how biology influences behaviour. For example, in ancient Greece, humorism stated that imbalance between the body's humors (believed to be yellow bile, black bile, blood and phlegm) could result in both physical and mental illness (Burton, 1989/1994). Based on this assumption, techniques such as bloodletting and trepanning (drilling holes in the skull) were used for centuries to relieve imbalance and pressure respectively. Over the centuries several other medically based approaches have been adopted in the study of human experience and behaviour, including the use of medication to alter physiological states and the use of cerebral lesions to treat psychological impairments. While it is important to remember that many of these approaches would be reprehensible today, the general principles remain prevalent in both medicine and biopsychology. For example, cerebral lesions to areas of the brain are still occasionally performed to reduce the symptoms of severe unipolar depression and obsessive compulsive disorder. Therefore, it is important to remember that both early and contemporary biological psychology is concerned with how genetics, physiology and anatomy influence both normal and maladaptive behaviour (Burton, 1989/1994; Carlson, 2004; Galton, 1865; James, 1890; Lashley, 1930; Pinel, 2003). As such, the links between medicine and psychology are most pronounced in this area and these links are further strengthened by the contemporary reliance on technology.

Sample question *Essay*

To what extent has contemporary biopsychology been influenced by philosophy and medicine?

Key terms

Bloodletting: An ancient technique of releasing blood from the body in an attempt to restore balance.

Lesions: The severing of connections or damage to structures in the brain.

Obsessive compulsive disorder: A psychological condition in which individuals experience extreme anxiety, obsessive thoughts and compulsions to perform actions which they believe relieve the anxiety.

Trepanning: An ancient technique in which holes are drilled in the skull in an attempt to relieve pressure.

Unipolar depression: A psychological condition characterised by unusually low mood, lethargy, negative thoughts and negative emotions.

Technology

Biopsychology is highly influenced by and often dependent on technological advancement. Indeed, due to the association with medicine and the need to understand how both normal and impaired functions arise it has often utilised the tools of medicine. However, it is important to remember that technology is constantly evolving and contemporary biopsychology is significantly different from the rudimentary approaches discussed previously. For example, cognitive neuroscience relies on complex neuroimaging technologies such as positron emission tomography (PET) to understand which physiological processes and anatomical structures are associated with human behaviour and experience. In addition, neuropsychology adopts numerous technologies including conventional experimentation using computers, laboratory equipment and neuroimaging. These approaches are discussed in more detail in the following section, but it is important that you remember the development of biopsychology is highly dependent upon the tools and measures that are available.

Key term

Neuroimaging: A procedure in which neurological imaging technology is used to visualise and record the activity of the brain.

Sample question — *Essay*

To what extent is contemporary biopsychology dependent upon technological advancement?

Further reading The origins of biopsychology

Topic	Key reading
Mental health	Comer, R. J. (2007). *Abnormal psychology* (6th ed.). New York: Worth Publishers.
History of psychology	Hergenhahn, B. R. (2009). *An introduction to the history of psychology* (6th ed.). Belmont, CA: Wadsworth.
Theoretical origins of psychology	Valentine, E. R. (1992). *Conceptual issues in psychology* (2nd ed.). London: Routledge.

Test your knowledge

1.1 How has philosophy contributed towards the origins and development of biopsychology?

1.2 How has medicine contributed towards the origins and development of biopsychology?

1.3 To what extent has the emergence of biopsychology been subject to the rate of technological advancement?

1.4 Does contemporary biopsychology still resemble early biological psychology?

Answers to these questions can be found on the companion website at: www.pearsoned.co.uk/psychologyexpress

---

Approaches in biopsychology

There are several significant sub-disciplines within biopsychology. These approaches study human behaviour and experience using different but complementary levels of analyses and methodologies. Several also vary in the type of participants they examine. The following sections provide brief overviews of these approaches which you will need to know. Indeed, these approaches will form the basis of your understanding and reoccur throughout this revision guide. However, you should remember that the approaches are often combined, a practice known as converging operations, to study the same phenomenon at several different levels of analysis.

Key term

Converging operations: Combining two or more different approaches or techniques to study the same phenomenon at different levels of analysis.

Physiological psychology and psychophysiology

Physiological psychology attempts to identify the neural correlates of behaviour and experience, often through manipulating the brain using surgery and electrical stimulation. As such there is a tendency for this approach to rely on laboratory animals rather than human subjects due to the explorative and invasive nature of this research. For example, Anand and Brobeck (1951) performed bilateral electrolytic lesions to the lateral hypothalamus of rats and cats and observed that the animals ceased eating. This is a condition known as aphagia and demonstrates how areas of the brain correspond with behaviour.

Key terms

Aphagia: A condition in which a neurologically damaged individual ceases to eat.

Physiological psychology: An approach in psychology which attempts to identify the neural correlates of behaviour and experience, often in laboratory animals.

Psychophysiology: An approach in psychology which investigates the correspondence between physiological activity, behaviour and experience in human subjects.

In contrast, psychophysiology investigates the correspondence between physiological activity, behaviour and experience in human subjects. The procedures tend to be significantly less invasive than those used in physiological psychology (Pinel, 2003). For example, an electroencephalogram (EEG) can be used to detect electrical activity produced by the brain using electrodes attached to the surface of the scalp. As such, the participant is usually able to remain mobile and measures are taken throughout their daily routine. For example, EEG can be used to identify the cerebral origins of seizures in cases of epilepsy. The methodologies used in physiological psychology (see Table 1.1) and psychophysiology (see Table 1.2) are significantly diverse and a list is provided at the end of this section to guide your further reading. Please note that this list is by no means complete and methodology is constantly advancing.

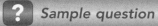 **Sample question**   *Essay*

Compare and contrast physiological psychology and psychophysiology.

Table 1.1 **Measures used in physiological psychology**

Technique	Description
Cryogenic blockade	This is an alternative to lesions and involves applying a coolant to the cerebral area under investigation to temporarily cease activity.
Lesions	This can include aspiration, radio-frequency lesions or knife cutting. Parts of the brain are damaged, destroyed or completely removed.

Table 1.2 **Measures used in psychophysiology**

Technique	Description
ECG	**Electrocardiogram**: Measures the electrical signal produced by the heart using electrodes placed on the chest.
EEG	**Electroencephalogram**: Measures the electrical signals produced by the brain using electrodes placed on the scalp.
EMG	**Electromyography**: Measures muscle tension using electrodes placed on the skin near the respective muscle.
EOG	**Electrooculography**: Measures the electrical signal associated with eye-movements using electrodes placed around the eye.

However, several criticisms have been levelled at physiological psychology and psychophysiology. These include:

- There are significant issues in generalising findings from laboratory animals to humans.
- While physiological measures are more direct than behavioural measures, there is still a delay between the event and measurement, implying that other changes may be involved in the behaviour.
- Physiological approaches are reductionist and tend to ignore complex cognition and behaviour.

Further reading Physiological psychology

Topic	Key reading
Synthesising neuroscience and psychophysiology	Davidson, R. J. (2003). Affective neuroscience and psychophysiology: Towards a synthesis. *Psychophysiology*, 40, 655–665.

Neuroscience

Cognitive neuroscience attempts to identify the neural correlates of cognition using a combination of physiological measures (see Tables 1.1 and 1.2), neuroimaging techniques (see Table 1.3), conventional laboratory experiments

Table 1.3 **Neuroimaging techniques**

Technique	Description
CT	X-ray computed tomography is used to visualise the structures of the brain.
fMRI	Functional magnetic resonance imaging is used to produce a 3D computer-generated image of the brain reflecting blood and oxygen flow (cerebral activity).
MEG	Magnetoencephalography is used to measure changes in magnet field (cerebral activity) from the surface of the scalp.
MRI	Magnetic resonance imaging measures the waves produced by hydrogen atoms activated by radio-frequency waves in the magnetic field and produces a 2D or 3D image.
PET	Positron emission tomography is used to measure glucose metabolism (reflecting cerebral activity) in the brain using a low dose of radioactive 2-deoxyglucose.
X-ray	Contrast x-rays produce an image of the brain after a substance has been injected into the respective area which absorbed x-rays more or less than the surrounding tissue.

and information technology (Bear, Connors & Paradiso, 2007; Cabeza & Nyberg, 2000; Gazzaniga, 2003). It occasionally also employs computer models to simulate the human brain. This facilitates practices and investigations which would otherwise be unethical and inhuman. For example, a connectionist (computational) network can be used to simulate the micro-structure of the human brain and allows researchers to mimic learning processes and cognition and to map the effects of brain damage. This is a useful technique which permits researchers to investigate the nature of phenomena which occur infrequently or those which could otherwise not be studied. However, criticisms of cognitive neuroscience include:

● Biological approaches are reductionist and as such reduce complex behaviour to physiological responses.

● Neuroimaging techniques are not always time-sensitive and elements of the response can be lost in this interval.

● While techniques are usually non-invasive, they may still cause distress and this can influence physiology and confound results.

● The brain is highly interconnected and as such any effect seen in one cerebral region may have originated from or contributed towards the processing of another. Hence, these regions may also be associated with the form of processing which is being investigated.

Key terms

Connectionist: A computational model used to simulate human performance and neural activity.

Neuroscience: An approach in psychology which attempts to identify the neural correlates of cognition using a combination of physiological, experimental and computational measures.

Reductionist/reductionism: Attempting to explain a higher order function based on lower order processes.

Sample question — Problem-based learning

You aim to investigate which areas of the brain are associated with human memory. How would you go about designing and conducting an experiment in neuroscience? You will need to consider who your participants will be, which technique you would need to use, what measures you would obtain and any strengths and weaknesses of your approach.

Further reading Neuroscience

Topic	Key reading
General neuroscience	Bear, M. F., Connors, B., & Paradiso, M. (2007). *Neuroscience: Exploring the brain* (3rd ed.). Baltimore, MD: Lippincott Williams & Watkins.
Cognitive neuroscience	Cabeza, R., & Nyberg, L. (2000). Imaging cognition II: An empirical review of 275 PET and fMRI studies. *Journal of Cognitive Neuroscience, 21*(1), 1–47.
Cognitive neuroscience	Gazzaniga, M. (2003). *Cognitive neuroscience: The biology of the mind* (3rd ed.). New York: W. W. Norton & Co.

Neuropsychology

Researchers in neuropsychology attempt to identify how cerebral structures contribute towards cognitive processing by studying what happens when the cerebral region has been damaged. In other words, it attempts to identify how cerebral structures influence both normal and impaired functioning. Neuropsychology primarily draws upon case studies of individuals who have suffered brain damage or infection which resulted in a significant and notable change in cognitive function (Crawford & Garthwaite, 2002). However, group studies and computer simulations are also conducted (Cohen, Johnstone & Plunkett, 2002; Robertson, Knight, Rafal & Shimamura, 1993). This is a significant example of how converging operations can be employed in psychology to better understand a phenomenon (see Table 1.4). Indeed, a single case or group study can utilise a range of techniques including traditional experimentation, observation, neuroimaging, interviews and computer simulations.

The most reliable evidence in neuropsychology is obtained from the observation of double dissociation, in which one patient exhibits one form of impairment after damage to one region and another exhibits alternative impairment after damage to another region. A significant example of this is demonstrated by aphasia. Indeed, while damage to Broca's area in the brain can result in impaired speech production, damage to Wernicke's area can result in impaired language comprehension. However, it is important that you remember there are limitations in generalising findings from impaired cognition to normal functioning.

Key terms

Aphasia: A deficit in language usually produced through brain damage.

Double dissociation: Observed when one brain-damaged patient shows one pattern of impairment while another shows a different pattern of impairment. Potentially due to the damage of different cerebral structures.

Neuropsychology: An approach in psychology which attempts to identify both normal and impaired human function, usually through studying the effects of brain damage.

The limitations of this approach include:

- Case studies do not contain a baseline measure of how well the individual would perform the task before the incident.
- The individual may display idiosyncratic tendencies which are not representative of others. As such, any measures may reflect this rather than actual impairment due to brain damage.
- The brain is highly interconnected, which hinders researchers' abilities to establish localisation of function.
- There is always a period of rehabilitation in which specialism of function may be reorganised within the brain. Other structures may compensate for impairment.
- The experience of brain damage is traumatic and research may be seen as an invasion of privacy.

Table 1.4 **Techniques in neuropsychology**

Technique	Description
Case study	The detailed study of an individual who has experienced brain damage or infection, resulting in deficits for memory, perception, attention etc. Tends to be longitudinal and can extend to how well the brain can demonstrate reorganisation and plasticity during the period of rehabilitation.
Cohort study	The study of groups of individuals who are matched on all other possible factors except the variable under investigation.
Lesions	Lesions can be inflicted on laboratory animals to identify which cerebral structures may explain the symptoms exhibited by humans.
Cognitive neuroscience	Neuroimaging techniques and computer simulations can be used to further explore how brain damage can impair performance.

Further reading Neuropsychology

Topic	Key reading
Neuropsychology and neuroscience	Cohen, G., Johnstone, R. A., & Plunkett, K. (Eds.) (2002). *Exploring cognition: Damaged brains and neural networks – Readings in cognitive neuropsychology and connectionist modelling*. Hove: Psychology Press
Neuropsychology methodology	Robertson, L. C., Knight, R. T., Rafal, R., & Shimamura, A. P. (1993). Cognitive neuropsychology is more than single-case studies. *Journal of Experimental Psychology: Learning, Memory and Cognition, 19*(3), 710–717.
Neuropsychology methodology	Crawford, J. R., & Garthwaite, P. H. (2002). Investigation of the single case in neuropsychology: Confidence limits on the abnormality of test score and test score differences. *Neuropsychology, 40*(8), 1196–1208.

Psychopharmacology

Psychopharmacology investigates the effects of drugs on physiological activity, behaviour and experience (Coull, 1998; Meyer & Quenzer, 2004; Vitiello, 2007). The majority of research in this field is conducted in medicine with an applied focus of improving quality of life and reducing maladaptive behaviours. For example, psychopharmacology is prevalent in abnormal psychology which will be discussed in more detail in Chapter 9. Medications can be used to reduce the severity of symptoms in cases of anxiety, depression and schizophrenia, and also in some personality disorders. Trials in psychopharmacology attempt to identify the beneficial and potentially harmful effects of substances, the best method for administration, drug metabolism, correct doses and suitable applications. However, the regulation and testing of psychopharmacology products continue after the trials and previously unobserved side-effects are regularly reported even after the use of the drug has been approved. Clinical trials are highly regulated and are usually longitudinal. As such, research normally begins in a laboratory setting with cultures of tissue and laboratory animals and will only proceed to human volunteers if maximum safety has been ensured. However, occasionally errors do occur and can have disastrous consequences.

Some of the general limitations of psychopharmacology include:

- It is an expensive procedure which requires numerous experts, funding bodies, ethics committees and organisations.
- It is a time-consuming process which can span several years.
- Significant ethical issues arise both in the use of animals and in administering drugs to humans in clinical trials.
- Many medications have serious side-effects and restrictions of use.
- Several medications were designed for use in one specific condition and the administration in other cases is often explorative. Discoveries that a medication reduces symptoms in other disorders are often serendipitous.

Key terms

Anxiety disorder: A psychological condition characterised by high levels of stress and anxiety, usually elicited by an external stimuli but also influenced by internal processes.

Clinical trial: The procedure by which medications are tested and legalised.

Psychopharmacology: An approach in psychology which is concerned with the effects of medication on behaviour and experience.

Serendipitous: Findings which were observed but were not originally the subject of the investigation.

Schizophrenia: A severe condition in which sufferers experience hallucinations, delusions, speech impairment, irrationality, unusual motor activity and impairment in most aspects of their lives.

Further reading Psychopharmacology

Topic	Key reading
Psychopharmacology, attention and arousal	Coull, J. T. (1998). Neural correlates of attention and arousal: Insights from electrophysiology, functional neuroimaging and psychopharmacology. *Progress in Neurobiology*, *55*(4), 343–361.
Psychopharmacology	Meyer, J. S., & Quenzer, L. F. (2004). *Psychopharmacology: Drugs, the brain and behavior*. Sunderland, MA: Sinauer Associates Inc.
Child and adolescent psychopharmacology	Vitiello, B. (2007). Research in child and adolescent psychopharmacology: Recent accomplishments and new challenges. *Psychopharmacology*, *191*(1), 5–13.

Behavioural genetics

Behavioural genetics attempts to identify what proportion of the variance in a trait or behaviour can be attributed to genetics and to the environment (Plomin, 1988; Stabenau & Pollin, 1993; Zuckerman, 1991). This relationship is referred to as heredity and is a prominent aspect of several areas of biopsychology research. Indeed, you may be aware that research has often investigated if there are genetic components to personality traits, intelligence and mental illness. However, it is important to remember that there is a constant interaction between genes and the environment (Jaffee et al., 2005). For example, a genetic predisposition can determine which environments we seek while environmental factors can also determine whether a gene pool survives (Darwin, 1859). This is in accordance with evolutionary theories that behaviour tends to serve the purpose of promoting survival, but also incorporates the principle of diathesis–stress which states that both biology and environment influence behaviour.

Contemporary behavioural genetics often relies on techniques such as twin studies, adoption studies and family studies (Table 1.5) and employs a variety of parametric tests. Indeed, you may already be aware that monozygotic twins share the same DNA, while dizygotic twins only share around half of their DNA. Therefore, if genes are influential in determining behaviour, monozygotic twins are more likely to share the same traits and behaviours. However, adoption studies can also be used to investigate heredity. For example, by comparing monozygotic and dizygotic twins who have been raised either together or apart, researchers can calculate the proportion of the variance in a trait which can be explained by the environment and genetics. While behavioural genetics can contribute towards our understanding of how genetics and environment contribute towards determining our behaviour, there are several significant limitations with this approach:

- Behavioural genetics have previously been used to support prejudiced views and discrimination.
- Ethical issues arise surrounding related topics such as eugenics (the argument that intelligent individuals should have more children).
- Behavioural genetics can be seen as a deterministic perspective in which the individual is passive.
- The genetic code is extremely complex and it is unlikely that a trait will arise solely due to one chromosome.
- The environment is constantly changing and as such so are the influences on our behaviour.
- Behavioural genetics often focuses on the extremes of a given trait because these are more observable.
- Parametric tests are not infallible and vary considerably in reliability and validity.
- The distinction between normal and abnormal behaviour is culturally and temporally relative.

Table 1.5 Techniques in behavioural genetics

Technique	Description
Twin study	Investigates the extent to which scores on a trait correlate between monozygotic and dizygotic twins reared together. A test of heredity.
Adoption study	Investigates the extent to which scores on a trait correlate between monozygotic and dizygotic twins reared either together or apart. A test of heredity.
Family study	Investigates the prevalence of a trait or type within a family.
Targeted mutation	Intended genetic mutations are produced in a laboratory and injected into laboratory animals to produce the desired mutation.
Genetic engineering	The manipulation or cloning of the genome within laboratory settings.

Key terms

Adoption study: The comparison of siblings reared together or apart to assess heredity.

Behavioural genetics: An approach in psychology which attempts to identify what proportion of the variance in a trait or behaviour can be attributed to genetics and to the environment.

Dizygotic twins: Non-identical twins who only share half of their DNA.

Eugenics: A school of thought in which intelligent people are encouraged to reproduce in an attempt to improve the species.

Family study: A research technique in which the prevalence of a trait or type within a family is assessed in regards to heredity.

Genetic engineering: The manipulation or cloning of the genome within laboratory settings.

Heredity: The proportion of variance in a given trait or type which can be accounted for by genetics and the environment.

Monozygotic twins: Identical twins who share the same DNA.

Targeted mutation: Intended genetic mutations are produced in a laboratory and injected into laboratory animals to produce the desired mutation.

Twin study: The comparison of siblings on a specific measure to assess heredity.

KEY STUDY

Plomin (1988)

Plomin (1988) reanalysed the vast amount of literature concerning the heredity of intelligence derived from twin, adoption and family studies and identified the following findings:

- the IQ scores of identical twins reared apart correlated at 0.74
- the IQ scores of identical twins reared together correlated at 0.87
- the IQ scores of non-identical twins reared together correlated at 0.53

This suggests that genetics contributed 68 per cent of the variance in IQ, whereas the environment explained only 19 per cent. However, it also means that 13 per cent of the variance in scores was not explained by either genetics or the environment. Interesting results were also obtained for unrelated children living together (0.23) and between unrelated children and their adoptive parents (0.20). This suggests that the environment explained 20–25 per cent of the variance in intelligence scores.

Further reading	Behavioural genetics
Topic	Key reading
Nature–nurture	Jaffee, S. R., Caspi, A., Moffitt, T. E., Dodge, K. A., Rutter, M., Taylor, A., & Tully, L. A. (2005). Nature x nurture: Genetic vulnerabilities interact with physical maltreatment to promote conduct problems. *Developmental Psychopathology, 17*(1), 67–84.
Schizophrenia and heredity	Stabenau, J., & Pollin, W. (1993). Heredity and environment in schizophrenia, revisited: The contribution of twin and high-risk studies. *Journal of Nervous and Mental Disease, 181*(5), 290–297.
Personality and heredity	Zuckerman, M. (1991). *Psychobiology of personality.* Cambridge: Cambridge University Press.

Comparative psychology

Comparative psychology is concerned with the general biology of behaviour and performs comparisons across species (Dewsbury, 1990). However, while there are similarities between comparative psychology and behavioural genetics, in that both attempt to identify genetic components of behaviour, there are also significant differences. Indeed, practitioners in comparative psychology are influenced by the evolutionary perspective to a greater extent than those in behaviour genetics. For example, they often believe that humans have evolved from other organisms and share some degree of their genetics, biology and behaviour with other animals (Darwin, 1859). In contrast, behavioural genetics is primarily concerned with how human DNA influences their behaviour and traits. There has also been an extension of comparative psychology to animal cognition, demonstrating influences of cognitive psychology (Wasserman, 1993). However, it is important for you to remember that although a large amount of research occurs in laboratory settings, animals are also studied in their natural environment. This is called ethological research and forms a significant proportion of contemporary research in comparative psychology.

Key terms

Comparative psychology: An approach in psychology which is concerned with the general biology of behaviour and performs comparisons across species.

Ethological research: A research technique in which animals are studied in their natural environment with little intervention by the researcher.

Some of the limitations of this approach include:

- interpretation issues in understanding animal behaviour
- ethical considerations in laboratory experiments with animals (e.g. pain and distress)
- ethical considerations in ethological research (e.g. invasion or damage of habitat)
- generalisation across species is problematic – while some features are similar there are also significant differences
- several aspects of evolutionary theory have been discounted.

CRITICAL FOCUS

Comparative psychology

While comparative approaches were prominent areas of research during the early days of biological psychology, its influence has subsequently declined and few studies are currently conducted in this area (Carlson, 2004; Darwin, 1859; Pinel, 2003). This may be due to technological advances, which allow us to study human behaviour in much more detail than was previously possible, and changes in ethical guidelines concerning research with laboratory animals. It may also be due to theoretical shifts towards including environmental factors in the equation for behaviour. For example, the nature–nurture debate has undermined several aspects of biological comparative approaches (Jaffee et al. 2005). Indeed, the majority of contemporary comparative research is accomplished through cross-cultural studies rather than cross-species comparisons. These studies usually adopt a very different perspective from that of biological approaches. For example, contemporary cross-cultural studies tend to assume that the environmental differences between cultures give rise to different behaviours and attitudes. This is in direct contrast to biological comparative psychology which argues that genetics is responsible for behavioural differences and similarities. However, it is significant that cross-cultural studies also once assumed that these differences were due to genetic factors, demonstrating significant developments in theory and practice.

Key term

Cross-cultural study: The study and comparison of groups of people from different cultural backgrounds.

Further reading Comparative psychology

Topic	Key reading
Comparative approaches	Dewsbury, D. A. (1990). *Contemporary issues in comparative psychology*. Sunderland, MA: Sinauer Associates Inc.
Comparative psychology and animal intelligence	Wasserman, E. A. (1993). Comparative cognition: Beginning the second century of animal intelligence. *Psychological Bulletin, 113*(2), 211–228.

Test your knowledge

1.5 What are the similarities and differences between cognitive neuropsychology and neuroscience?

1.6 What are the applications of psychopharmacology?

1.7 What are the issues and limitations which arise in behavioural genetics?

1.8 Can neuropsychology contribute towards understanding normal functions?

1.9 What are the strengths and limitations of psychophysiology?

Answers to these questions can be found on the companion website at: www.pearsoned.co.uk/psychologyexpress

Chapter summary – pulling it all together

→ Can you tick all the points from the revision checklist at the beginning of this chapter?

→ Attempt the sample question from the beginning of this chapter using the answer guidelines below.

→ Go to the companion website at www.pearsoned.co.uk/psychologyexpress to access more revision support online, including interactive quizzes, flashcards, You be the marker exercises as well as answer guidance for the Test your knowledge and Sample questions from this chapter.

Answer guidelines

 Sample question   *Essay*

To what extent has biopsychology contributed towards the understanding of human behaviour and experience? Discuss in relation to two approaches.

Approaching the question

Like most questions you will receive in this area, this question is asking you to review the extent to which two biological psychological approaches have contributed towards understanding human behaviour and experience.

Important points to include

You should begin your essay by providing a detailed summary of the two approaches you have chosen to describe and evaluate. This should clearly describe the principles and techniques which are used by each approach. You should also incorporate a critical evaluation of evidence concerning how each of these approaches has been applied to study a human behaviour and experience. It would be useful to provide examples from two or three areas of study (e.g. memory, language and perception). However, you should make sure that you write critically and evaluate all of the evidence you cite with reference to the question. For example, how does the evidence you are including demonstrate that biopsychology has contributed towards understanding these phenomena? Are there any aspects of these phenomena which one or both of these approaches is unable to explain? Your essay should finally draw conclusions concerning how well each of these approaches can explain and test human behaviour and experience with specific reference to their strengths and limitations.

Make your answer stand out

To make your answer stand out in this area you must demonstrate that you have drawn on a variety of information from a range of sources and that you have critically evaluated both the theories and the evidence you have cited to reach a coherent and balanced conclusion. It is not enough to simply list facts and figures; you must synthesise these ideas to establish an academic debate.

Explore the accompanying website at www.pearsoned.co.uk/psychologyexpress

→ Prepare more effectively for exams and assignments using the answer guidelines for questions from this chapter.

→ Test your knowledge using multiple choice questions and flashcards.

→ Improve your essay skills by exploring the You be the marker exercises.

Notes

Notes

Notes

2

Structure and function of the central and peripheral nervous systems

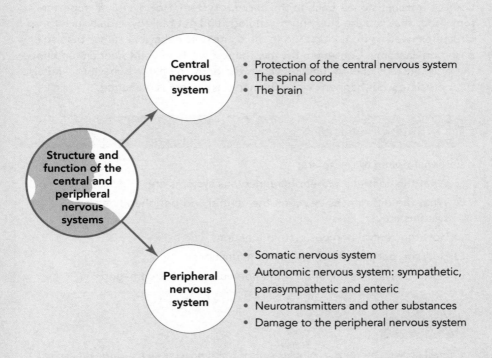

Central nervous system
- Protection of the central nervous system
- The spinal cord
- The brain

Structure and function of the central and peripheral nervous systems

Peripheral nervous system
- Somatic nervous system
- Autonomic nervous system: sympathetic, parasympathetic and enteric
- Neurotransmitters and other substances
- Damage to the peripheral nervous system

A printable version of this topic map is available from
www.pearsoned.co.uk/psychologyexpress

Introduction

This chapter will provide you with a summary of the structures and functions of the central nervous system (CNS) and the peripheral nervous system (PNS). In regards to the CNS, this includes the brain and spinal cord. However, you should remember that some texts also include the retinas – whether these are included in this system will depend on your course. The PNS includes all of the nerves, neurons, muscles and organs which are located beyond the central nervous system. The endocrine system, which is responsible for releasing and regulating hormones and related chemicals, is covered in Chapter 3. Together, these structures form the main regulatory and control systems responsible for facilitating all forms of cognition, experience and movement. They also play a large role in regulating bodily functions through a complex system of neurons which either send signals from the nervous system to trigger responses in the body or transmit signals back to the nervous system. However, it is important to remember that you are studying psychology and not biology and as such these structures need to be understood in the context of behaviour rather than solely based on anatomy. Consequently, this chapter will help you to understand how the brain and spinal cord function within the body to enable behaviour, and also to appreciate what happens when the nervous system is damaged.

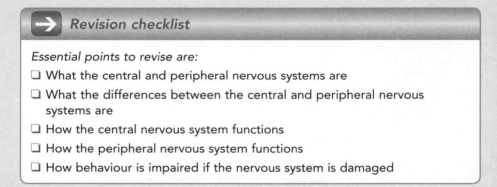

→ *Revision checklist*

Essential points to revise are:
- ❑ What the central and peripheral nervous systems are
- ❑ What the differences between the central and peripheral nervous systems are
- ❑ How the central nervous system functions
- ❑ How the peripheral nervous system functions
- ❑ How behaviour is impaired if the nervous system is damaged

Key terms

Central nervous system: A complex system which governs all top-down processes and consists of the brain and the spinal cord.

Endocrine system: The network of glands and organs which release and regulate hormones.

Hormones: Endogenous substances produced by the glands of the body.

Peripheral nervous system: A complex system which governs all bottom-up processes and consists of all of the nerves, muscles and organs beyond the CNS.

Assessment advice

Essay questions concerning the nervous system will often ask you to discuss how one of these vital systems enables behaviour and experience. For example, you may be asked to evaluate the extent to which the central nervous system determines perception. Although this question would not explicitly mention the peripheral nervous system, it would be prudent to consider multiple influences and establish an academic debate in your essay. This implies that it would be a good idea to consider whether the peripheral nervous system and non-biological factors complement, counteract or override the functions of the central nervous system. Alternatively, you could be explicitly asked to compare and contrast the structures and functions of the peripheral and central nervous systems in regards to one or two specific behaviours. For questions like these you will need to understand the structures, functions, research techniques for investigating these systems and the prominent findings which have been provided by research. You will also need to cite specific examples from the literature. Any essays in this area will also need to demonstrate that you can draw appropriate conclusions based on the evidence and correct interpretation of the nervous system.

Sample question

Could you answer this question? Below is a typical essay question that could arise on this topic.

 Sample question   *Essay*

To what extent does the central nervous system determine the course of human behaviour? Discuss with reference to at least two aspects of behaviour (for example, perception and memory).

Guidelines on answering this question are included at the end of this chapter, whilst further guidance on tackling other exam questions can be found on the companion website at: **www.pearsoned.co.uk/psychologyexpress**

The central nervous system

The central nervous system consists of the brain and the spinal cord. Although some texts include the retinas, there isn't a consensus concerning this inclusion. As such, they are not included in this revision guide, but you should consult your course text to determine whether your module includes these aspects. You should remember that the central nervous system is responsible for all forms of cognition including perception, attention and memory in addition to reflexes, compilation of somatosensory information and prompting motor movement.

> **Key term**
>
> **Somatosensory**: Information derived from the bodily senses.

Protection of the central nervous system

The importance of the central nervous system in evolutionary terms can be demonstrated by the level of protection provided by surrounding tissue. Indeed, the central nervous system is protected by three layers of tissue, called meninges:

- **Dura mater** is the outermost layer and can be described as thick, tough and flexible but not stretchable.
- **Arachnoid mater** is a soft, spongey and spiderweb-like tissue which forms the middle protective layer. The area between the arachnoid matter and following layer is called the subarachnoid space and is filled with cerebrospinal fluid (CSF) which cushions the central nervous system. CSF reduces the weight of the brain to just 80 grams and reduces the pressure at the base.
- **Pia mater** forms the final layer of protective tissue. This is closely connected to the brain and spinal cord and contains a network of blood vessels.

The spinal cord

Structure and organisation

The spinal cord is a long and relatively thin bundle of nervous tissues and support cells which begins at the occipital bone and extends from the brain via the medulla oblongata. It continues through the conus medullaris which is located near the first or second lumbar vertebra and ends with a fibrous extension known as a filum terminale. It also contains motor and sensory neurons demonstrating the connection of the central and peripheral nervous systems.

> **Sample question**   *Essay*
>
> Critically discuss the structures and functions of the brain and the spinal cord.

Further reading The structure of the spinal cord

Topic	Key reading
Cervical spinal cord	Wheeler-Kingshott, C. M., Hickman, S. J., Parker, J. M., Ciccarelli, O., Symms, M. R., Miller, D. H., & Barker, G. (2001). Investigating cervical spinal cord structure using axial diffusion tensor imaging. *Neuroimage*, *16*(1), 93–102.
General	Carlson, N. R. (2004). *Physiology of behavior* (8th ed.). New York: Pearson Education Inc.

Normal function

The primary function of the spinal cord is to transmit neural signals between the brain and the rest of the body including the somatosensory system, muscles and glands. However, it is important to remember that it also has some autonomy and can function independently as demonstrated by reflexes.

 Sample question   *Essay*

How would injury to the spinal cord impair normal functions in humans?

Damage to the spinal cord

Damage to the spinal cord can arise through trauma in the forms of stretching, laceration, bruising, excessive pressure, severing or shattering (Carlson, 2004; Pinel, 2003). This can result in the loss of feeling for corresponding parts of the body or complete bodily paralysis, known as quadriplegia. It can also result in muscle weakness, impaired motor function and muscle atrophy (decay). However, it is important to remember that while the effects of major trauma may be permanent, the duration of less severe impairments varies considerably across individuals and will depend upon the location and extent of the injury in addition to the rehabilitation and adaptability of the patient. Psychological factors such as determination, motivation, personality type, mood and the degree of social support available to the patient would also significantly influence the outcome.

Key term

Atrophy: The decay or wasting of a structure, organ or system.

Further reading The functions of the spinal cord

Topic	Key reading
Spinal cord injury	McDolald, J. W., & Sadowsky, C. (2002). Spinal-cord injury. *Lancet*, *359*(9304), 417–425.
Spinal cord injury	Proctor, M. R. (2002). Spinal cord injury. *Critical Care Medicine*, *30*(11), 489–499.

Test your knowledge

2.1 What are the names given to the three levels of spinal meninges?

2.2 In addition to the meninges, which other structures and substances protect the spinal cord?

2.3 What substance is contained within the subarachnoid space?

2.4 How might trauma to the spinal cord occur and what are the consequences?

Answers to these questions can be found on the companion website at: www.pearsoned.co.uk/psychologyexpress

---

The brain

The brain is the most important organ in the human body and is the subject of study in most areas of psychology. It is also by far the most complex structure in the human body. The brain plays a role in regulating other organs and largely determines our ability to think, move, use language, perceive the world, maintain consciousness, interact with each other and experience the world around us. Several theorists also believe that the brain stores our intelligence and personality and as such determines who we are. It is vitally important that you can understand both the normal structure and functions of this organ and also appreciate what happens when it is damaged. While it is impossible to fully cover this complex organ in the scope of this revision guide, it will provide you with a coherent and concise summary to guide your revision and test your understanding.

Structure and organisation

The brain can be described as a fragile, soft, jelly-like organ which is highly interconnected with millions of neurons. While it displays a significant degree of plasticity in childhood, this adaptability declines in adulthood. However, some ability to adapt to physical trauma and rearrange connections does remain throughout life. The importance of the brain was established during evolution and is replicated during the development of the central nervous system in all healthy embryos, children and adults. For example, in addition to the three levels of meninges, the brain is also protected by the skull, cerebrospinal fluid (CSF) and the blood–brain barrier. The skull forms a hard barrier between the brain and the external world while the cerebrospinal fluid cushions the brain and reduces the pressure at its base. The brain also contains four chambers (known as ventricles) which are filled with CSF and further protects the central nervous system. Indeed, this substance is constantly extracted from the bloodstream and projected into the ventricles by the choroid plexus before it flows through the central nervous system and is subsequently reabsorbed into the bloodstream. However, the blood–brain barrier prevents any chemicals which may be hazardous in the brain from being transmitted from the bloodstream, providing another level of defence.

Sample question   *Essay*

Critically review the extent to which the central nervous system is protected by biological factors.

The brain could simply be split along the corpus callosum and divided into two hemispheres where the right side of the brain synthesises information and the left side of the brain analyses information. However, several other attempts have been made to group regions of the brain according to structures which share commonalities in regards to either their location or their function. For example, Table 2.1 demonstrates how the brain can be divided into those falling in the forebrain, midbrain and hindbrain regions. Secondly, the brain can also be organised according to more specialised structures, such as those summarised in Figure 2.1 in addition to the specifications provided in Table 2.2.

Key term

Corpus callosum: A bundle of neural fibres connecting the left and right hemispheres of the brain.

 Sample question   *Essay*

To what extent has the brain been organised according to specialism and localisation of function?

Table 2.1 Broad breakdown of the areas of the brain

Area	Incorporated structures
Forebrain	Lateral ventricle, telencephalon, cerebral cortex, basal ganglia, limbic system, third ventricle, diencephalon, thalamus and hypothalamus. However, you should also remember that the cerebral cortex is also divided into regions called the lateral, parietal, temporal and occipital lobes.
Midbrain	Cerebral aqueduct, mesencephalon, tactum tegmentum.
Hindbrain	Fourth ventricle, metencephalon, cerebellum, pons, myelencephalon, medulla.

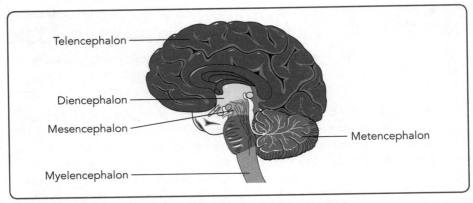

Figure 2.1 **The organisation of the brain according to encephalon**

Table 2.2 **Breakdown of the areas of the brain according to encephalon**

Area	Incorporated structures
Telencephalon	Cerebral cortex, primary visual cortex, primary auditory cortex, primary somatosensory cortex, insular cortex, primary motor cortex, the limbic system (hippocampus, amygdala, fornix and basal ganglia).
Diencephalon	Thalamus, hypothalamus, pituitary gland.
Mesencephalon	Superior colliculus, inferior colliculus, tegmentum, reticular formation, periaqueductal grey matter, red nucleus and substantia nigra.
Metencephalon	Cerebellum and pons.
Myelencephalon	Medulla.

Further reading The structure of the brain	
Topic	Key reading
Neuropsychology and neuroscience	Cohen, G., Johnstone, R. A., & Plunkett, K. (Eds.) (2002). *Exploring cognition: Damaged brains and neural networks – Readings in cognitive neuropsychology and connectionist modelling.* Hove: Psychology Press.
Blood–brain barrier	Smith, R. (2003). A review of blood–brain barrier transport techniques. *Methods of Molecular Medicine, 89*(3), 193–208.
Central nervous system	Brodal, P. (2010). *The central nervous system: Structure and function* (4th ed.). New York: Oxford University Press.

Function

Several factors may determine which regions of the brain specialise in which function. Biological factors can include evolution, genetics and anatomical predisposition. However, you should also remember that experience will determine the strength of connections in the brain, how well certain functions are performed and it can also result in the redistribution of functions in a manner which is not conventionally seen. You should also remember that the brain is highly interconnected. As such, while it may appear that certain areas are dominant in performing certain functions this may actually result from activity in other areas of the brain, or be due to the connections between regions. Table 2.3 provides an overview of some of the regions which have been consistently associated with certain functions. You should remember that this list is not exhaustive so consult further reading accordingly. Figure 2.2 should also help you to visualise where these structures are located in the brain and their proximity to other regions.

Table 2.3 Functions of the brain according to specialised structures

Structure	Function
Basal ganglia	Associated with the control of movement and balance.
Limbic system	Associated with emotion, language, memory and motivation.
Thalamus	Receives information from the cerebral cortex.
Hypothalamus	Associated with the regulation of the autonomic nervous system (part of the peripheral nervous system) and the pituitary gland. Also associated with species-typical behaviour and linked to hormones and the endocrine system.
Superior colliculus	Associated with vision.
Inferior colliculus	Associated with audition (hearing).
Reticular formation	Associated with arousal, attention, reflexes, movement and sleep.
Periaqueductal grey matter	Associated with pain perception.
Red nucleus and substantia nigra	Associated with motor systems.
Cerebellum	Receives visual, auditory, vestibular and somatosensory information. It is also associated with movement and balance.
Pons	Associated with sleep, arousal and the relay of information from the cerebral cortex to the cerebellum.
Medulla	Control of vital functions such as the cardiovascular system. Also associated with skeletal muscle tonus.
Amygdala	Associated with emotion and memory.
Cerebral cortex	Associated with most of the higher order functions such as cognition.

Damage to the brain

You should already be aware that brain damage can seriously impair an individual's ability to function normally from the discussion in Chapter 1. Brain damage can destroy specific structures in the brain or the connections between these structures, so it is important to remember that deficits observed after brain damage may arise either due to the impairment of a specific structure or due to the inability of structures to communicate (Belmonte et al., 2004; Cohen, Johnstone & Plunkett, 2002; Liddle, Laurens, Kiehl & Ngan 2006). Brain damage can impair memory, language, perception, emotional responses, attention, social skills, reasoning and personality. Indeed, you should remember that the brain may essentially be the seat of everything that we are and as such serious injury or infection may completely change an individual. However, you should also remember that the brain retains some ability to reorganise its processes and compensate for deficits, suggesting that less severe impairment may not be permanent.

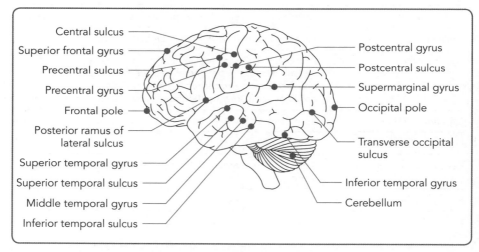

Figure 2.2 A diagrammatic representation of some of the specialised structures of the brain

Further reading The functions of the brain	
Topic	Key reading
Abnormal brain activity in schizophrenia	Liddle, P. F., Laurens, K. R., Kiehl, K. A., & Ngan, E. T. (2006). Abnormal function of the brain system supporting motivated attention in medicated patients with schizophrenia: An fMRI study. *Psychological Medicine*, *38*(8), 1097–1108.
Autism	Belmonte, M. K., Allen, G., Beckler-Mitchener, A., Boulanger, L. M., Carper, R. A., & Webb, S. J. (2004). Autism and abnormal development of brain connectivity. *The Journal of Neuroscience*, *24*(42), 9228–9231.

Test your knowledge

2.5 How many ventricles are there in the brain?

2.6 What is the primary difference between the left and right hemispheres?

2.7 Which functions does the hypothalamus perform?

2.8 Which structures are included in the telencephalon?

2.9 Which structures are included in the mesencephalon?

Answers to these questions can be found on the companion website at:
www.pearsoned.co.uk/psychologyexpress

The peripheral nervous system

The peripheral nervous system includes all of the cranial, spinal, motor and sensory neurons, organs and neurotransmitters located beyond the central nervous system. Hormones also play a role in the peripheral nervous system but are covered in greater detail in Chapter 3. The peripheral nervous system is responsible for transmitting signals to the central nervous system from the body though the afferent neurons (with the exception of visual information which is transmitted directly via the optical nerve) and also receives feedback from the central nervous system via the efferent neurons. You should also remember that there is constant interaction and communication between these systems and the rest of the body, including the glands and muscles which receive signals from the efferent neurons. There are also 12 pairs of cranial nerves which serve the function of transmitting sensory information from the head and neck back to the central nervous system. Somatosensory information from the peripheral nervous system is typically received by the central nervous system via unipolar neurons. However, the structure and functions of the peripheral nervous system are easier to understand when considered in the various subdivisions of this nervous system.

Somatic nervous system

The somatic nervous system is a division of the peripheral nervous system which is responsible for monitoring and interacting with the external world. You should remember that this system co-ordinates bodily movement and receives information concerning external stimuli via the somatosensory system. For example, it regulates the movements which are under voluntary control via the efferent neurons which are connected to skeletal muscles, skin and sense organs throughout the body. These messages are transmitted along the efferent neurons as action potentials (electrical signals) which stimulate the release of the neurotransmitter acetylcholine by the terminal buttons at the end of each neuron where they cross the synapse and are absorbed by nicotinic receptors.

The action potential is subsequently transmitted to the neuromuscular junctions of skeletal muscles where acetylcholine is released again to facilitate the contraction of muscle fibres.

Key terms

Action potential: An electrical signal which is transmitted along neurons.

Somatic nervous system: A division of the peripheral nervous system which is responsible for monitoring and interacting with the external world.

Autonomic nervous system: sympathetic, parasympathetic and enteric

The autonomic nervous system (ANS) is responsible for governing responses which are largely beyond conscious control. In contrast to the somatic nervous system it is concerned primarily with the internal world although its functions can be influenced by the perception of external stimuli. The autonomic nervous system can be divided into three subdivisions which all have different structures and functions. These are the sympathetic nervous system, parasympathetic nervous system and enteric nervous system. You should remember that together the sympathetic and parasympathetic nervous systems are responsible for the stress response, while the enteric system is responsible for maintaining the vital gastrointestinal system. Figure 2.3 should help you to understand which organs and functions are associated with the parasympathetic and sympathetic divisions of the autonomic nervous system.

Key terms

Autonomic nervous system: A division of the peripheral nervous system which is responsible for governing responses which are largely beyond conscious control.

Enteric nervous system: A division of the autonomic nervous system which is responsible for maintaining the gastrointestinal system.

Parasympathetic nervous system: A division of the autonomic nervous system which promotes the conservation of resources.

Stress response: The physiological, cognitive and behavioural response to threat and anxiety characterised by action readiness for 'fight-or-flight'.

Sympathetic nervous system: A division of the autonomic nervous system which promotes action readiness.

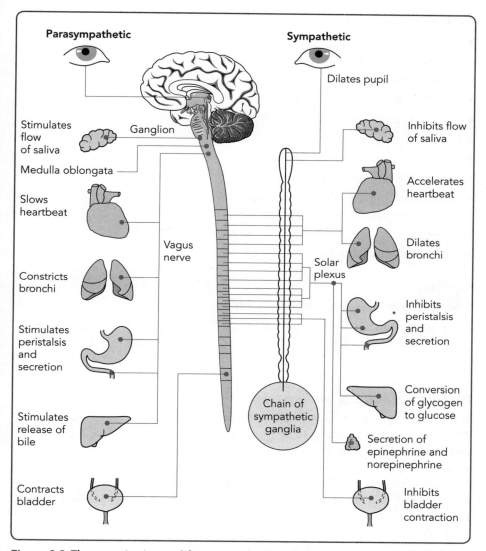

Figure 2.3 The organisation and functions of the autonomic nervous system

Sympathetic nervous system

The cell bodies of the sympathetic nervous system are located in the grey matter of the thoracic and lumbar regions of the spinal cord and form the sympathetic ganglion system which connects to the rest of the peripheral nervous system including most of the bodily organs and glands. The sympathetic nervous system generally promotes a state of readiness. The functions of this system are as follows:

- dilates pupils
- inhibits salivation
- dilates bronchioles in the lungs
- expands airways
- speeds heart rate
- stimulates sweating
- stimulates glucose release
- constricts blood vessels in the skin
- inhibits the digestive system
- stimulates secretion of the catecholamine hormones epinephrine and norepinephrine by adrenal medulla
- relaxes bladder
- stimulates sexual arousal.

 Sample question   *Essay*

Compare and contrast the structures and functions of the sympathetic and parasympathetic branches of the peripheral nervous system with reference to stress.

Parasympathetic nervous system

The parasympathetic branch of the autonomic nervous system has a similar structure to the sympathetic branch but originates from cells in the cranial and sacral regions. One of the main features of this system is the vagus nerve which regulates thoracic and abdominal cavities through efferent fibres. The parasympathetic system can be characterised as a system which counteracts the functions of the sympathetic nervous system. As a result its primary functions are to conserve energy and restore homeostasis. The functions of this system are as follows:

- constricts pupils
- stimulates salivation
- constricts airway
- slows heart rate
- stimulates digestive systems
- contracts bladder
- stimulates ejaculation.

Key term

Homeostasis: The naturally balanced state of the body. This is the ideal state and the parasympathetic nervous system strives to restore this equilibrium when physiology is imbalanced.

However, it is important to remember that while the central and peripheral nervous systems are discrete structures, they also interact. For example, if you consider the stress response, the peripheral nervous system may trigger the fight-or-flight response but the central nervous system would produce the assessment of stimuli and facilitate reflexes.

CRITICAL FOCUS

The stress response

The fight-or-flight theory of stress is concerned with how bodily responses create states of readiness which promote either combating the cause for the stress or escaping the stressor (Carlson, 2004; Selye, 1975). This frequently manifests in anxiety disorders, which are covered in Chapter 9, and can be seen in differential functions of the sympathetic and parasympathetic branches of the ANS. Indeed, the sympathetic branch creates a state of readiness for escape while the parasympathetic branch attempts to restore equilibrium and provide energy for combating the threat. Long-term states of stress can have serious medical and psychological complications (Carlson, 2004). However, the majority of early research in this area was conducted with laboratory animals. While it appears to be largely transferable to humans there are several other factors which should be considered. This especially includes cognitive appraisal of the stimuli or situation. For example, it stands to reason that different individuals will perceive different situations as threatening and that the manifestation of their stress and anxiety will vary according to social desirability, coping mechanisms, social norms, available escape routes, reasoning and learning from any previous experiences with the stimuli (LeDoux, 1995). It is also significant that the amygdala in the central nervous system is involved in fear responses. This demonstrates that the functions of the peripheral nervous system during the stress response may also be mediated by the central nervous system.

Enteric system

The enteric system is responsible for controlling the gastrointestinal system and operates autonomously from the other branches of the nervous system. Indeed, it continues to function even when the vagus nerve is severed. This is potentially due to the vital nature of the gastrointestinal system for survival. The enteric system contains efferent, afferent and inter-neurons and utilises the neurotransmitters acetylcholine, dopamine and serotonin.

Further reading The enteric nervous system

Topic	Key reading
The central nucleus and conditioned responses	LeDoux, J. E. (1995). Emotion: Clues from the brain. *Annual Review of Psychology, 46,* 209–235.
The enteric nervous system	Furness, J. B. (2006). *The enteric nervous system.* Malden, MA: Wiley-Blackwell.
Homeostasis	Pichon, A., & Chapelot, D. (2010). *Homeostatic role of the parasympathetic nervous systems in human behavior.* New York: Nova Science Publishers.

Neurotransmitters and other substances

Electrical signals within the body are transmitted as action potentials within neurons (see Figure 2.4). However, when these signals reach a gap between neurons (known as a synapse) a chemical must be released at the terminal buttons of the first neuron to carry the signal on to the receptor cells of the second neuron. These chemicals are naturally occurring compounds called neurotransmitters. You should remember that the type and proportion of neurotransmitter released will depend on the nature of the neurons and the strength of the signal. You should also remember that neurotransmitters can exert either an inhibitory or excitatory influence. Whether the neurotransmitters bind to the receptor cells will also depend on the compatibility between the receptor cell and neurotransmitter, the activation threshold of the cells and whether any other compounds are currently blocking the receptors. Figure 2.5 should help you to understand how synaptic transmission occurs. This image demonstrates how neurotransmitters are released from the terminal buttons of the first neuron and are transported across the synapse where they bind with the receptor sites of the next neuron.

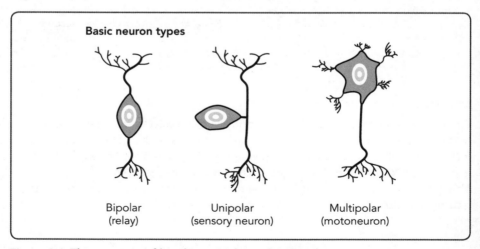

Basic neuron types

Bipolar (relay)   Unipolar (sensory neuron)   Multipolar (motoneuron)

Figure 2.4 The structure of bipolar, unipolar and multipolar neurons

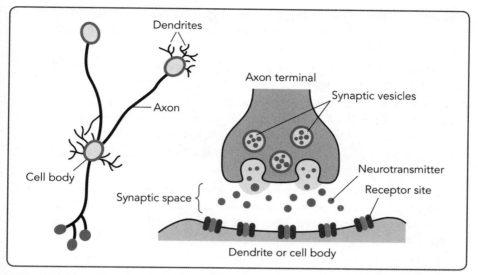

Figure 2.5 **Neural transmission between two neurons**

Table 2.4 provides an overview of some of the neurotransmitters you will need to know during your undergraduate degree, in addition to brief summaries concerning their primary functions. However, it is important for you to remember that this list is not exhaustive and neurotransmitters serve multiple functions.

? Sample question   *Problem-based question*

You must present a report to a mental health charity on the topic 'neurotransmitters and depression'. You should draft a report which includes some of the main findings, strengths and limitations of research in this area. Remember that your audience may not have expert knowledge of psychology.

Table 2.4 **The roles of neurotransmitters**

Neurotransmitter	Function
Norepinephrine and epinephrine	Operate in arousal and reward systems (Carlson, 2004).
Dopamine	Operates in reward, mood, cognition, endocrine, nausea and motor systems (Spanagel & Weiss, 1999).
Serotonin	Operates in mood, satiety, temperature and sleep systems (Owens & Nemeroff, 1994).
Acetylcholine	Operates in movement, learning, short-term memory, arousal and reward systems (Pinel, 2003).

However, you should remember that neurotransmitters are not the only chemicals which are active in the nervous system and that there are several subdivisions of influential substances:

- **Neurotransmitters:** These are endogenous (naturally occurring) chemicals which transport signals between neurons.
- **Hormones:** Endogenous chemicals produced mostly by the endocrine system (covered in Chapter 3). Hormones including steroids, testosterone and androgen can be influential in behaviour, mood and cognition.
- **Amino acids:** These include glutamate, GABA and glycine. All of these chemicals are influential in behaviour.
- **Monoamines:** These are biogenic amines which include dopamine, norepinephrine, epinephrine, histamine and serotonin. These substances are influence in reward mood/emotion, learning, motivation, behaviour and cognition.
- **Neuroactive peptides:** These chemicals often function in conjunction with neurotransmitters.

Further reading Neurotransmitters

Topic	Key reading
Monoamine hypothesis	Hirschfeld, R. M. A. (2000). History and evolution of the monoamine hypothesis of depression. *Journal of Clinical Psychiatry*, 61(6), 4–6.
Mood and neurotransmitters	Castrén, E. (2005). Is mood chemistry? *Nature Reviews Neuroscience*, 6, 241–246.

Damage to the peripheral nervous system

Damage to nerves through injury, infection, alcoholism, other medical conditions or nutritional deficiencies can have a detrimental effect on the performance of the peripheral nervous system. Indeed, this can impair the ability of nerves to carry signals along the peripheral nervous system which would hinder the normal functions of these systems and their ability to carry signals back to the central nervous system. This means that motor movements, the somatosensory system and the ability to regulate bodily organs would be impaired. For example, in the case of peripheral neuropathy the nerves which stimulate muscles to move are damaged and can result in muscle atrophy and facial palsy. Damage to the nerves responsible for sensation may hinder the ability to perceive temperature, pain or touch. Furthermore, damage to the nerves which serve the autonomic nervous system can result in incontinence, dizziness, impotence and fainting. Nerve damage can be permanent and treatment for these deficits tends to revolve around coping strategies, compensating for deficits and preventing further damage.

Key term

Peripheral neuropathy: A condition in which the nerves that stimulate muscles to move are damaged and can result in muscle atrophy and facial palsy.

Test your knowledge

2.10 What are the divisions of the autonomic nervous system and how do they differ?

2.11 What are the functions of the somatic nervous system?

2.12 What is the primary function of the enteric system?

2.13 How do neurotransmitters function?

Answers to these questions can be found on the companion website at: www.pearsoned.co.uk/psychologyexpress

Chapter summary – pulling it all together

→ Can you tick all the points from the revision checklist at the beginning of this chapter?

→ Attempt the sample question from the beginning of this chapter using the answer guidelines below.

→ Go to the companion website at www.pearsoned.co.uk/psychologyexpress to access more revision support online, including interactive quizzes, flashcards, You be the marker exercises as well as answer guidance for the Test your knowledge and Sample questions from this chapter.

Answer guidelines

 Sample question   *Essay*

To what extent does the central nervous system determine the course of human behaviour? Discuss with reference to at least two aspects of behaviour (for example, perception and memory).

Approaching the question

This question is asking you to evaluate the extent to which the central nervous system determines, monitors and regulates human behaviour. It also asks you to choose two areas of study to contextualise your response using the literature.

Important points to include

Your essay should begin with a description of the central nervous system and the two areas of research you have chosen to draw upon. This should ideally include two significantly different areas with varying influences of the nervous system to enable you to establish a clear and coherent academic debate. You should clearly define all of the technical and anatomical terms you use in this essay. You should subsequently critically evaluate the evidence provided by the literature which states the central nervous system determines these behaviours. However, you should also review the influences of other systems such as the peripheral nervous system, endocrine system and non-biological factors. You should then draw appropriate conclusions based on the strength of this evidence.

Make your answer stand out

It would be useful to choose two areas of study which are differentially influenced by the central nervous system. For example, if you were to select one behaviour which is primarily governed by the central nervous system (such as language production) and one which is primarily governed by peripheral nervous system (such as pain perception) this will demonstrate that you can write critically and consider different influences on behaviour. You can also make your essay stand out by incorporating non-biological factors which may influence these behaviours.

Explore the accompanying website at www.pearsoned.co.uk/psychologyexpress
→ Prepare more effectively for exams and assignments using the answer guidelines for questions from this chapter.
→ Test your knowledge using multiple choice questions and flashcards.
→ Improve your essay skills by exploring the You be the marker exercises.

Notes

Notes

Notes

3

The endocrine system: hormones and behaviour

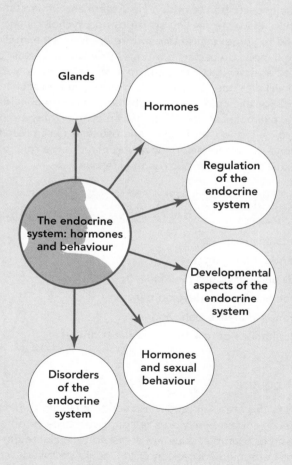

A printable version of this topic map is available from
www.pearsoned.co.uk/psychologyexpress

Introduction

This chapter will provide you with an overview of the structures and functions of the endocrine system and how it influences human behaviour and experience. The endocrine system is a series of cells, glands and organs that produce and release hormones which consequently circulate throughout the body. You should remember from the previous chapter that hormones are naturally occurring chemicals which influence bodily functions, physical development and emotions. This chapter will be primarily concerned with how the endocrine system influences sexual behaviour, although it can also influence other vital motivations such as eating and sleeping. By the end of this chapter you should be able to correctly describe the endocrine system and understand how certain hormones function. However, as you are studying psychology and not biology you will also need to contextualise this with reference to the implications for behaviour. For example, do certain hormones predispose certain behaviours? Are they released as a product of a behaviour or are they involved in performing the action? You will also need to put aside many of your misconceptions about hormones. For example, despite substantial anecdotal evidence there are few scientific examples of hormones determining any aspect of male and female gender roles. Indeed, androgens and estrogens are present in everyone regardless of gender. Hormones do, however, play a large role in determining physical and sexual development across the lifespan.

> **→ Revision checklist**
>
> *Essential points to revise are:*
> ❑ What the endocrine system is
> ❑ How glands and hormones function
> ❑ How hormones influence development
> ❑ How hormones influence behaviour
> ❑ What the limitations of research in this area are

Assessment advice

Essay questions in this area will usually ask you to evaluate the extent to which hormones influence certain behaviours or contribute towards differences between groups. For example, you may be asked to evaluate the extent to which hormones determine aggression or you could be asked to discuss whether hormones contribute towards gender typical behaviour. With questions like these you will need to demonstrate that you can synthesise evidence from various sources and critically evaluate the strength of this evidence. You must also consider other possible influences for these behaviours and differences. For example, this can include other biological factors, cognition, social factors, personality or intelligence. You will also need to consider whether the evidence suggests there is a causal relationship between hormones and behaviour or just a relationship between them (in which case behaviour could also result in the release of the hormone). Any essays in this area should include a balanced consideration of all possible sides of the argument and your conclusions should be based on a critical evaluation of this evidence.

Sample question

Could you answer this question? Below is a typical essay question that could arise on this topic.

 Sample question   *Essay*

To what extent can hormones be said to determine gender typical behaviour?

Guidelines on answering this question are included at the end of this chapter, whilst further guidance on tackling other exam questions can be found on the companion website at: **www.pearsoned.co.uk/psychologyexpress**

Glands

It is important to remember that there are two forms of glands. Endocrine glands secrete hormones directly into the bloodstream. This means that they can take effect almost immediately. In contrast exocrine glands firstly secrete chemicals into ducts. From the ducts they proceed from cell to cell by the process of diffusion and are excreted on the surface of the body as sweat. You should be able to make this distinction and appreciate that these glands perform significantly different functions. In humans the main endocrine glands and their functions are as follows:

- **Pineal body:** Secretes melatonin and is involved with regulating the body's natural rest–active cycles.
- **Pituitary gland:** Produces prolactin, growth hormone, luteinising hormone, follicle-stimulating hormone and adrenocorticotropic hormone. Regulates the growth of tissue and bone, controls the amount of water reabsorbed by the kidney, protects the body from physiological stress and stimulates the thyroid.
- **Hypothalamus:** Exerts control over the endocrine system, especially the pituitary gland. Also produces thyrotropic-releasing hormone, gonadotropin-releasing hormone, growth hormone-releasing hormone, corticotropin-releasing hormone, somatostatin and dopamine.

- **Thyroid gland:** Releases thyroxin and calcitonin. Regulates the rate of growth, metabolism and calcium levels in the blood.
- **Parathyroid gland:** Releases parathormone and promotes the homeostasis of calcium.
- **Thymus:** Releases thymosins and T-lymphocytes which promote the development of the immune system.
- **Adrenal glands:** Release epinephrine, norepinephrine, aldosterone and cortisol. Mediate the conversion of proteins into sugars and are involved in the stress response.
- **Pancreas:** Secretes insulin, glucagon and somatostatin to regulate sugar metabolism.
- **Ovaries:** The female gonads produce estrogens and progesterone to promote the development of external, physical, female characteristics. Fluctuations in gonadal hormones can also result in fluctuations in mood.
- **Testes:** The male gonads produce testosterone and promote external, physical, male characteristics. Fluctuations in gonadal hormones can also result in fluctuations in mood.

Key terms

Endocrine glands: Glands which secrete hormones directly into the bloodstream having fast-acting and concentrated effects.

Exocrine glands: Glands which secrete substances into ducts, from which they pass from cell to cell through diffusion.

Further reading Glands

Topic	Key reading
Hypothalamus–pituitary–adrenal axis	Ehlert, U., Gaab, J., & Heinrichs, M. (2001). Psychoneuroendocrinological contributions to the etiology of depression, posttraumatic stress disorder, and stress-related bodily disorders: The role of the hypothalamus–pituitary–adrenal axis. *Biological Psychology*, 57, 141–152.
Immunity, stress and the endocrine system	Glaser, R., & Kiecolt-Glaser, J. K. (Eds.) (1994). *Handbook of human stress and immunity*. San Diego, CA: Academic Press.
Stress and the endocrine system	Yehuda, R. (2001). Biology of posttraumatic stress disorder. *Journal of Clinical Psychiatry*, 62 (Supplement 17), 41–46.

Test your knowledge

3.1 Which glands secrete their chemicals directly into the bloodstream?

3.2 What are the functions of the adrenal gland?

3.3 What are the functions of the pituitary gland?

3.4 What chemicals are produced by the pancreas?

Answers to these questions can be found on the companion website at:
www.pearsoned.co.uk/psychologyexpress

Hormones

You may be aware that hormones are chemicals which arise naturally in the body and are associated with moods, behaviour and development (Carlson, 2004; Pinel, 2003). Hormones can be divided into three categories consisting of amino acid derivatives, peptides and proteins and finally steroids. A summary of these types of hormones is provided in Table 3.1 to help you refresh your memory.

Table 3.1 **Types of hormone**

Type of hormone	Characteristics
Amino acid derivatives	These substances are synthesised from epinephrine and are involved in the synthesis and transmission of peptides, proteins and neurotransmitters.
Peptides and proteins	These hormones are short and long chains of amino acids and facilitate physiological, biochemical and growth processes.
Steroids	These hormones are synthesised from cholesterol and play a large role in sexual development. Unlike other hormones they can bind to receptors and penetrate cell membranes allowing them to alter the manifestation of genetic characteristics. Effects are long-lasting. The sex steroids also include androgen, estrogen and progesterone which prepare the females for reproduction and parenting.

It is also important to remember that abuse of artificial substances which simulate the effects of steroids or natural imbalances of these substances can have serious consequences for health and wellbeing. For example, they can result in testicular atrophy, sterility, mood swings and gynecomastia (growth of breasts) in men. In women they can result in amenorrhea, sterility, mood swings, hirsutism (male pattern hair growth in women), abnormal male body shape, deepening of the voice, baldness, shrinking of the breast and growth of the clitoris. This demonstrates how hormones can significantly alter physical growth and impair health.

Sample question   *Essay*

Critically discuss the belief that steroids significantly influence sexual development.

 Sample question   *Problem-based learning*

One of your colleagues would like to investigate whether the injection of testosterone and estrogen into human female and male foetuses will result in stereotypically male and female behaviour respectively. They have asked for your advice concerning the ethical and practical implications of this research. What advice and evidence would you provide?

Further reading Hormones

Topic	Key reading
Steroids and sexual behaviour	Mani, S. K., Allen, J. M. C., Clark, J. H., Blaustein, J. D., & O'Malley, B. W. (1994). Convergent pathways for steroid hormone- and neurotransmitter-induced rat sexual behavior. *Science, 265*(5176), 1246–1249.

Test your knowledge

3.5 Which type of hormone is derived from cholesterol?

3.6 What are the main functions of steroids?

3.7 What are the main functions of amino acids?

3.8 What are the effects of steroid abuse?

Answers to these questions can be found on the companion website at: **www.pearsoned.co.uk/psychologyexpress**

Regulation of the endocrine system

Hypothalamus-releasing hormones play a large role in the regulation of the endocrine system which you should be aware of. Indeed, hormones tend to be topic which means that they stimulate or inhibit the release of other hormones (Carlson, 2004; Schommer, Hellhammer & Kirschbaum, 2003). For example, hormones from the hypothalamus trigger the release of thyrotropin-releasing hormones from the anterior pituitary which in turn stimulate the thyroid to release its hormones. Gonadotropin-releasing hormones also stimulate the release of follicle-stimulating hormone (FSH) and luteinising hormone (LH), which facilitate ovulation.

Key term

Topic: The term assigned to hormones which stimulate or inhibit the release of other hormones.

There are significant gender differences in the regulation of the endocrine system by the hypothalamus. For example, while the level of hormones in males remains relatively stable across time, female gonadal hormones are cyclical (Carlson, 2004; Kirschbaum, Kudielka, Gaab, Schommer & Hellhammer, 1999; Pinel, 2003). This cycle is on average 28 days and you will probably know that it stimulates the menstrual cycle including the development and release of an ovum and menstruation in the absence of conception. However, during pregnancy and for a brief time after birth there is a period of amenorrhoea in which menstruation is suspended, allowing time for the uterus to recover. The process can also be controlled with hormonal birth control which simulates the natural gonadal hormone progesterone. Regulation of the endocrine system can be also performed by the central nervous system, peripheral nervous system and other biological chemicals such as glucose, calcium and sodium.

Further reading Regulation of the endocrine system

Topic	Key reading
Hypothalamus–pituitary–adrenal axis	Kirschbaum, C., Kudielka, B. M., Gaab, J., Schommer, N. C., & Hellhammer, D. H. (1999). Impact of gender, menstrual cycle phase, and oral contraceptives on the activity of the hypothalamus–pituitary–adrenal axis. *Psychosomatic Medicine*, 61, 154–162.
Dissociation of endocrine system	Schommer, N. C., Hellhammer, D. C., & Kirschbaum, C. (2003). Dissociation between reactivity of the hypothalamus–pituitary–adrenal axis and the sympathetic-adrenal-medullary system to repeated psychosocial stress. *Psychosomatic Medicine*, 65, 450–460.

Test your knowledge

3.9 Which structures and substances are involved in the regulation of the endocrine system?

3.10 What characteristic of hormones means that they can be called topic?

3.11 What is the main difference between the levels of hormones in males and females?

3.12 How can the endocrine system be regulated by engineered substances?

Answers to these questions can be found on the companion website at: www.pearsoned.co.uk/psychologyexpress

Developmental aspects of the endocrine system

You have probably already realised that steroids such as androgen, estrogen, testosterone and progesterone play a large role in sexual development and behaviour (Escobar, Obregón & Rey, 2004; Handwerger & Freemark, 2000). Indeed, we have already identified that steroids are able to penetrate cell membranes and influence gene expression (how characteristics manifest). These chemicals are also involved with the production of sperm and ova by the male and female gonads respectively. This facilitates the production of a zygote at conception which will eventually grow into a foetus influenced by all of these hormones. In females, progesterone also prepares the uterus for carrying a baby and facilitates breast feeding.

> **?** *Sample question*   *Essay*
>
> Which hormones can result in sex differences?

Up to six weeks after conception, all foetuses have the same primordial gonads with the potential to develop ovaries or testes (Carlson, 2004; Pinel, 2003). However, at this point ovaries automatically develop and the male Y chromosome triggers the synthesis of the protein H-Y antigen which stimulates the development of testes. External genitalia develop from the second month of pregnancy although there are recursors from the glands, urethral folds, lateral bodies and labioscrotal swellings. You should also be aware that at six weeks after conception all foetuses have two sets of reproductive ducts. These are the male Wolffian system and the female Müllerian system. However, at the third month of foetal development the testes release testosterone and a Müllerian-inhibiting hormone which promote the development of the Wolffian system while inhibiting further development of the Müllerian system. The development of the precursors are all triggered by hormones and are listed below:

- **Glans:** Head of penis in males or the clitoris in females.
- **Urethral folds:** Fuse in males, enlarge and become the labia minora in females.
- **Lateral bodies:** The shaft of the penis in males or hood of the clitoris in females.
- **Labioscrotal swellings:** Scrotum in males or labia majora in females.

In addition to the sexual differences which arise due to hormones there are also differences in male and female brains. For example, you should know that the male brain is on average 15 per cent larger than the female brain and there are structural differences in the hypothalamus, corpus callosum, anterior commissure, thalamus and cerebral cortex. These changes are believed to arise due to hormones in the form of perinatal androgens occurring near the time of birth. However, it is important to remember that all sex steroids are derived from cholesterol and can be converted to other sex steroids via a process called aromatisation. This process may be responsible for the differences observed between male and female brains.

> **Key term**
>
> **Aromatisation**: The process by which sex steroids derived from cholesterol are converted into other sex steroids.

After foetal development the next significant stage in physical sexual development occurs during puberty. The secondary sexual characteristics develop during this time and include hair growth, body shape, voice deepening in males and breast growth in females. This growth spurt is stimulated by the release of hormones from the anterior pituitary gland and results in an increase in gonadal hormones, the maturation of the sexual organs and development of secondary sexual characteristics.

Therefore, it is important that you remember that hormones and the endocrine system play a significant role during physical development (García-Aragón et al., 1992; Pinel, 2003; Reiter, 1991). However, you should also remember that many other factors influence the rate and nature of physical development. These can include:

- nutrition
- mother's wellbeing
- social norms and culture
- other health conditions of the child
- premature birth
- socioeconomic status.

> **? Sample question** *Essay*
>
> To what extent is sexual development the product of the endocrine system?

Further reading Developmental aspects of the endocrine system

Topic	Key reading
Central nervous system development	Chan, S, & Kirby, M. D. (2000). Thyroid hormone and central nervous system development. *Journal of Endocrinology*, 165(1), 1–8.
Thyroid hormones and foetal brain development	Escobar, G. M., Obregón, M. J., & Rey, F. E. (2004). Maternal thyroid hormones early in pregnancy and fetal brain development. *Clinical Endocrinology and Metabolism*, 18(2), 225–248.
Foetal development	Handwerger, S., & Freemark, M. (2000). The roles of placental growth hormone and placental lactogen in the regulation of human fetal growth and development. *Journal of Pediatric Endocrinology and Metabolism*, 13, 343–356.

Test your knowledge

3.13 How does the endocrine system influence the development of a foetus?

3.14 How does the endocrine system influence development in adolescence?

3.15 How would steroids influence gene expression?

3.16 What other factors may influence physical development?

Answers to these questions can be found on the companion website at:
www.pearsoned.co.uk/psychologyexpress

Hormones and sexual behaviour

The previous belief that sex steroids promote male and female stereotypical behaviour is not held in contemporary psychology due to a notable lack of evidence (Carlson, 2004; Orwoll & Klein, 1995; Pinel, 2003). Indeed, all of these substances are present in both males and females although the evolutionary role of the hormones may not be transparent. It is important to remember that early research linked the perinatal hormones to animal reproductive behaviour. For example, injections of testosterone near the time of birth were believed to masculinise and defeminise female copulation behaviour of the offspring. However, it is important to remember that this research makes the assumption that the behaviour would not have been masculine without testosterone injections and that the findings may not be generalised from laboratory animals to humans. Indeed, a significant degree of the research conducted with laboratory animals has investigated the effects of pheromones on the menstrual cycle and sexual behaviour. Pheromones are chemicals released by an animal which are perceived by another via smell or taste. Research has demonstrated that these chemicals can indicate when a female is likely to conceive. In females, pheromones can stimulate ovulation. However, it is important to remember that this research is not directly applicable to humans who do not rely on these substances. Table 3.2 will refresh your memory concerning some of the effects of pheromones observed in laboratory animals.

Key term

Pheromone: A chemical substance transmitted from one animal to another via smell or taste, usually to signal receptivity, availability, challenge or threat.

Table 3.2 **The effects of pheromones**

Effect	Description
Lee–Boot effect	The slowing and cessation of the menstrual/estrous cycle if all female animals are housed together. It is caused by a pheromone carried in urine.
Whitten effect	The synchronisation of the menstrual/estrous cycle of a group of females triggered by the pheromones in the urine of a male.
Vanderbergh effect	The early onset of puberty in female rats housed with a male.
Bruce effect	The termination of pregnancy triggered by the pheromones in the urine of a mouse that did not impregnate the female mouse.

The removal of the testes (known as an orchidectomy) reduces sexual interest and behaviour (Carlson, 2004; Pinel, 2003). However, you should also remember that levels of testosterone do not reliably predict the sex drive of healthy adults when within normal parameters and that the effects of castration are considerably variable. Furthermore, while removal of the ovaries (known as an ovariectomy) in rats was originally believed to reduce receptivity towards a male rat, there is no evidence for this in humans. Indeed, while changes in the levels of female gonadal hormones can relate to the level of sexual interest, human copulation itself is not restricted by ovarian hormones. For example, it is important to remember that human copulation can occur at any point in the menstrual cycle and sexual interest does not always predict sexual behaviour. You should also remember that there are no significant differences in the levels of gonadal hormones of heterosexual and homosexual people despite different sexual practices and occasionally different degrees of gender stereotypical behaviour (Carlson, 2004; Pinel, 2003). This demonstrates that hormones may not reliably predict human sexual behaviour and suggests that factors other than gonadal hormones may be involved.

You may also be interested to know that lesions to the medial preoptic area of the hypothalamus in mammals cease male sexual behaviour and reduce the amount of time females spend with a sexually active partner (Pinel, 2003). You should also know that the ventromedial nucleus of the hypothalamus contains several neural circuits which are vital for female sexual behaviour. This suggests that the hypothalamus may play a significant role in sexual behaviour due to either the hormones it releases or physiological activity.

 Sample question *Essay*

Critically evaluate claims that sexual orientation is determined by the levels and functions of hormones.

Test your knowledge

3.17 How does removal of the ovaries influence human sexual behaviour?

3.18 How does removal of the testes influence human sexual behaviour?

3.19 What are the main limitations of early studies investigating the effects of hormones on sexual behaviour?

3.20 What are the main hormonal differences between heterosexual and homosexual people?

Answers to these questions can be found on the companion website at: www.pearsoned.co.uk/psychologyexpress

Disorders of the endocrine system

Disorders of the endocrine system are common and are usually detected by imbalanced levels of hormones, observable physical indications or when examining other illnesses (Counsell & Ruddell, 1994; Guzick, 2004; Legro, Kunselman, Dodson & Dunaif, 1999; Manolagas, 2000; Orwoll & Klein, 1995). Table 3.3 provides a summary of some of these conditions. However, it is important to remember that these conditions can co-occur and often also result in psychological distress such as depression and anxiety.

Table 3.3 **Disorders of the endocrine system**

Disorder	Description
Diabetes	This is one of the main disorders of the endocrine system and arises due to the failure of the pancreas to produce sufficient amounts of the hormone insulin or due to the body's inability to use insulin correctly. If undiagnosed, consequences can be severe due to the body's reliance on insulin to convert sugars and starch to energy.
Osteoporosis	This is a disorder in which bones become fragile and easily breakable. It can result from abnormally low levels of estrogen or testosterone. Diagnosis is often prompted by recurrent injuries.
Growth disorders	As the endocrine system regulates growth imbalances, impaired function or damage to this system can result in excessive or deficient growth.
Thyroid disorders	There are numerous types of thyroid disorders including hyperthyroidism (excessive amount of hormones), hypothyroidism (insufficient hormones), thyroid nodules and thyroid cancer. These conditions also significantly reduce autoimmunity and often result in weight changes.
Polycystic ovary syndrome (PCOS)	PCOS is also a very common disorder of the endocrine system which results in numerous cysts developing on the ovaries. This disrupts the menstrual cycle, can cause infertility and is often characterised by hirsutism (excessive hair growth), acne, diabetes and hypertension.

This table only provides a summary of the disorders which can arise due to the malfunction or impairment of the endocrine system. You should also remember that many other conditions can arise though the imbalance of hormones and that these conditions can result in or co-occur with other health complaints.

? Sample question   Essay

To what extent can the deficits or malfunction of endocrine system result in poor physical health?

Further reading Disorders of the endocrine system

Topic	Key reading
PCOS	Guzick, D. S. (2004). Polycystic ovary syndrome. *Obstetrics and Gynecology*, *103*(1), 181–193.
Diabetes and PCOS	Legro, R. S., Kunselman, A. R., Dodson, W. C., & Dunaif, A. (1999). Prevalence and predictors of risk for type 2 diabetes mellitus and impaired glucose tolerance in polycystic ovary syndrome: A prospective, controlled study in 254 affected women. *The Journal of Endocrinology and Metabolism*, *84*(1), 165–169.
Osteoporosis	Manolagas, S. C. (2000). Birth and death of bone cells: Basic regulatory mechanism and implications for the pathogenesis and treatment of osteoporosis. *Endocrine Reviews*, *21*(2), 115–137.

Test your knowledge

3.21 How can deficits of the endocrine system result in diabetes?

3.22 What are the main forms of thyroid disorder?

3.23 What are the main symptoms of polycystic ovary syndrome?

3.24 How does osteoporosis develop due to deficits in the endocrine system?

Answers to these questions can be found on the companion website at: www.pearsoned.co.uk/psychologyexpress

Chapter summary – pulling it all together

→ Can you tick all the points from the revision checklist at the beginning of this chapter?

→ Attempt the sample question from the beginning of this chapter using the answer guidelines below.

→ Go to the companion website at www.pearsoned.co.uk/psychologyexpress to access more revision support online, including interactive quizzes, flashcards, You be the marker exercises as well as answer guidance for the Test your knowledge and Sample questions from this chapter.

Answer guidelines

 Sample question   *Essay*

To what extent can hormones be said to determine gender typical behaviour?

Approaching the question

This question is asking you to discuss critically the factors which may result in male and female stereotypical behaviour. More specifically it is asking you to determine whether differences in the hormones of men and women result in different behaviours.

Important points to include

Your essay will begin with a summary concerning what gender typical behaviours are. This will usually include a brief summary of the debate concerning whether any behaviour can be considered to be typically male or female. It will also briefly summarise whether gender typical behaviours arise due to biological factors. Your essay should subsequently evaluate the evidence concerning whether hormones influence behaviour and result in gender differences. It would also be useful to consider both older and contemporary studies. For example, while earlier research tended to assume that testosterone was a male hormone and progesterone was a female hormone, more recent research has indicated that this is not the case. Your essay should also include a critical review of other factors which may influence behaviour including anatomy, social factors and cognition. For example, biological factors may predispose certain gender typical behaviours but social norms, upbringing and how individuals perceive themselves will influence how this manifests. Your conclusions should be based on your evaluation of this evidence and link explicitly back to the essay question.

Make your answer stand out

To make an answer stand out in this area you should write critically throughout your response. This means that you will evaluate not only the research evidence but also the key terms (such as 'gender typical') and theoretical accounts. This will include drawing on both traditional and contemporary evidence, evaluating research techniques, identifying assumptions and exposing misinterpretations or limitations in studies.

Explore the accompanying website at www.pearsoned.co.uk/psychologyexpress

→ Prepare more effectively for exams and assignments using the answer guidelines for questions from this chapter.

→ Test your knowledge using multiple choice questions and flashcards.

→ Improve your essay skills by exploring the You be the marker exercises.

Notes

Notes

4

Biological basis of language

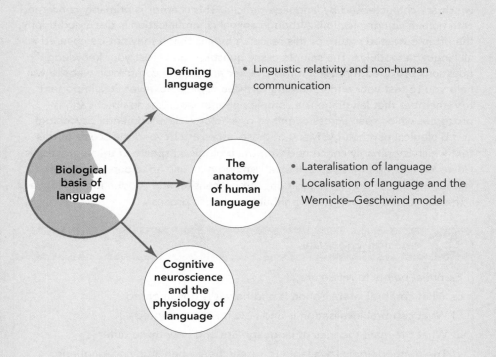

- Defining language
  - Linguistic relativity and non-human communication

- Biological basis of language

- The anatomy of human language
  - Lateralisation of language
  - Localisation of language and the Wernicke–Geschwind model

- Cognitive neuroscience and the physiology of language

A printable version of this topic map is available from
www.pearsoned.co.uk/psychologyexpress

Introduction

This chapter will provide you with an overview concerning how the structures and functions of the human body enable language acquisition, comprehension and production. You should remember that language acquisition, comprehension and production are some of the most complex processes which have generated a considerable amount of research and theoretical debate. Indeed, the ability to acquire, produce and comprehend language is often cited as one of the factors which differentiate humans from other animals (Gaskell, 2007; Harley, 2007). The initial sections of this chapter will provide a general overview of the features and nature of language to refresh your memory of these topics. These sections will guide your revision of the components and processes of language and communication. The latter sections will discuss the issues of cerebral lateralisation, cerebral localisation, methodologies and several disorders which are characterised by language deficits. This chapter is primarily concerned with human communication. Although animal communication is discussed briefly, the often outdated nature of this research means that it may not be covered in all language modules. The sample essay questions and 'Test your knowledge' questions provided throughout this chapter and on the companion website will help you to test your understanding of these topics. However, it is important to remember that language is a complex phenomenon made up of various processes which span across cognitive psychology, developmental psychology and biological psychology. Many of these issues are beyond the scope of this text which is primarily concerned with the biological aspects of these processes. However, it is vital that you can establish and maintain an understanding of various influences on the acquisition, comprehension and production of language – the suggested further reading should begin this process.

> ### → Revision checklist
>
> *Essential points to revise are:*
> ❑ What cerebral lateralisation is and how it is documented
> ❑ What cerebral localisation is and how it is documented
> ❑ What the main theories of language are and how these differ
> ❑ The methodologies available to researchers when studying language
> ❑ Key findings in the development of an understanding of language

Assessment advice

Essay questions in this area will usually ask you to evaluate the extent to which nature and nurture determine language development or the extent to which language is dependent on biological factors. For example, you may be asked to evaluate the extent to which anatomy and experience determine an individual's language acquisition, comprehension and production. You would need to consider physiology, anatomy, genetics, evolution, upbringing and exposure to stimuli. With questions like this you will need to demonstrate that you can synthesise evidence from various sources and critically evaluate the strength of this evidence to establish an academic debate. You must also consider a variety of possible influences on these behaviours. For example, it may be useful to compare verbal and non-verbal communication, possibly citing examples of the similarities and differences associated with human and animal communication. Any essays in this area should include a balanced consideration of all possible sides of the argument and your conclusions should be based on a critical evaluation of this evidence.

Sample question

Could you answer this question? Below is a typical essay question that could arise on this topic.

 Sample question   *Essay*

To what extent do biological and environmental factors determine language?

Guidelines on answering this question are included at the end of this chapter, whilst further guidance on tackling other exam questions can be found on the companion website at: **www.pearsoned.co.uk/psychologyexpress**.

Defining language

Language is a complex system which allows those who understand it to communicate, share thoughts, express feelings and desires, persuade and entertain (Gaskell, 2007; Harley, 2007). However, there are several established definitions which you will need to know in detail and be able to critically evaluate. For the purpose of this text the most prominent, broad definition of language was provided by Hockett (1960) in the theory of linguistic universals:

- Broadcast transmission means that messages are projected in all possible directions and can be received by any who are listening.
- Arbitrariness means that there is no correspondence between the symbols used in language and the objects they refer to.
- Cultural transmission means that language acquisition occurs through exposure to the culture.

- Displacement means that the messages are not restricted to a specific time.
- Discreteness means that there is a notable range of speech sounds within a language.
- Duality of structure means that phonemes can be combined or recombined in a potentially infinite number of ways.
- Productivity means that novel messages can be created using the rules and symbols of the language.
- Interchangeability means that those who share the language are both producers and receivers of messages.
- Semanticity means that meaning can be transmitted through the symbols.
- Total feedback means that the speaker has immediate auditory feedback.
- Specialisation means that the sounds of the language are distinct from other sounds in that they convey meaning.
- Transitoriness means that the messages fade quickly after they have been uttered.
- Vocal–auditory channel refers to the transmission of language using these two sensory modes.

Key term

Linguistic universals: The 13 principles of language which Hockett (1960) argued could be observed across all languages.

However, you should also remember that this definition suffers from several limitations, including its failure to consider non-verbal forms of communication such as sign language, gestures and written communication (Carlson, 2004; Harley, 2007). It should not have escaped your notice that written communication is significantly longer lasting than verbal communication although verbal communication itself may be long-lasting if recorded. It also fails to define and differentiate the units of language, which can be found in Table 4.1.

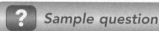

? Sample question   *Essay*

Critically evaluate Hockett's (1960) linguistic universals.

Table 4.1 Units of language

Unit/process	Description
Lexicon	The complete set of morphemes (see below) available within the language. Usually conceptualised as a store in memory.
Morpheme	The smallest unit of language which possesses meaning on its own through a combination of phonemes.
Phoneme	The smallest unit within a language which forms the building blocks of other utterances.
Semantics	The meaning carried by the symbols of the language.
Syntax	The rules for creating longer utterances. This includes the order in which words should be placed in a sentence.

The contemporary definition of language is that it must be a meaningful, symbolic, rule-based and shared system which can be acquired, comprehended and produced by members of the language community (Gaskell, 2007; Harley, 2007). You might be surprised to learn that there are 6909 recognised languages in the world today (Lewis, 2009). While these differ in their composition and expression due to cultural exposure, the biological prerequisites and corresponding biological activity appear to be universal (Gaskell, 2007; Harley, 2007).

Linguistic relativity and non-human communication

The linguistic relativity hypothesis refers to how thought and language are believed to influence each other and interact. In its strongest version, proponents argue that language determines and constrains the ability to think, whereas proponents of the weaker version argue that language influences cognition but that there is not a direct causal effect (Gaskell, 2007; Harley, 2007; Tohidian, 2009). However, today most psychologists who believe language and thought are related tend to adopt the weaker version due to very little evidence for the strong linguistic relativity hypothesis. While this topic is covered in more detail in the cognitive psychology text of this series, you should be aware of how this theory influences the view of non-human communication. For example, if non-human animals are able to communicate using a shared system, could they also think in a way which is similar to humans? Indeed, several animal species including birds, dolphins and monkeys appear to communicate with each other in a series of complex sounds and gestures which others in their species understand (Carlson, 2004; Harley, 2007; Pinel, 2003). Interestingly, despite possessing significantly different physiological, anatomical and genetic make-up, some non-human animals have also been able to acquire elements of human language (Carlson, 2004; Harley, 2007; Pinel, 2003). A collection of these cases is presented in Table 4.2.

Table 4.2 Cases of non-human animal communication

Species	Description
Dolphins	Dolphins were able to discriminate between meaningful sequences of gestures and random meaningless combinations of gestures. They also responded appropriately (Herman, Kuczaj & Holder, 1993).
Gorilla	The gorilla Koko was trained to understand over 300 American Sign Language gestures (Patterson, 1978, 1981).
Parrot	The African grey parrot Alex could identify 50 different objects, count to six, distinguish seven colours and differentiate five shapes. Alex also possessed a vocabulary of over 100 words and could combine these words to form new utterances (Pepperberg, 2006a, 2006b).
Chimpanzee	The chimpanzee Sarah was trained to communicate through the use of coloured plastic chips representing words. Language-trained chimpanzees also appeared to have various problem-solving abilities which non-trained chimpanzees did not (Premack, 1983).
Chimpanzee	The chimpanzee Lana was trained to use a computer-based sign language to form short meaningful sentences (Savage-Rumbaugh, Rumbaugh & McDonald, 1985; Savage-Rumbaugh, McDonald, Sevcik, Hopkins & Rupert 1986).
Bonobo	The bonobo Kanzi learnt to communicate using a sign board by observing another ape being trained (Gardner, Gardner & Van Contfort, 1989; Savage-Rumbaugh et al., 1985, 1986).
Chimpanzee	Nim Chimpsky lived with a human family from birth and was able to understand over 100 American Sign Language gestures (Terrace, 1979).

These cases should inspire you to wonder whether human language is as unique and advanced as we often believe it to be. The decision on that debate is still to be determined. However, you should keep in mind that verbal and physical communication rely on different biological factors and cognitive processes (Carlson, 2004; Gaskell, 2007; Harley, 2007; Pinel, 2003).

Further reading Defining language

Topic	Key reading
Psycholinguistics	Gaskell, M. G. (2007) (Ed.). *The Oxford handbook of psycholinguistics*. Oxford: Oxford University Press.
Introductory text	Harley, R. (2007). *The psychology of language: From data to theory* (3rd ed.). Hove: Psychology Press.
Linguistic relativity	Tohidian, I. (2009). Examining the linguistic relativity hypothesis as one of the main views on the relationship between language and thought. *Journal of Psycholinguistic Research, 38*(1), 65–74.

Test your knowledge

4.1 What are Hockett's (1960) linguistic universals?

4.2 What is the smallest unit of language?

4.3 Which other animals have been able to acquire elements of human language?

4.4 What is a morpheme?

4.5 Meaning is created through which aspect of language?

Answers to these questions can be found on the companion website at: www.pearsoned.co.uk/psychologyexpress

The anatomy of human language

It is undeniable that anatomical structures and biological mechanisms make human verbal communication possible (Harley, 2007; Pinel, 2003). Indeed, air is forced up by the lungs and passes over the vocal cords, causing them to vibrate at certain frequencies based on the force of the air and the position of the vocal cords. These frequencies can then be modified by the lips, tongue, teeth and soft palate to reduce some frequencies and enhance others. This demonstrates how the human vocal tract provides the basis of human speech. However, while you will need to be aware of how these anatomical structures make speech possible, you must remember that you are studying psychology and not biology. As such, biological psychology focuses on how the brain makes these processes possible and facilitates language acquisition, comprehension and production. The following sections will guide your revision of these topics.

Lateralisation of language

Theories which argue that language is a lateralised function are essentially arguing that the left hemisphere of the brain is the locus of these functions (Carlson, 2004; Harley, 2007; Pinel, 2003). As you should remember from the earlier chapters, the hemispheres can indeed be dominant in certain functions and serve minor roles in others. However, while this means that the left hemisphere appears to exert the greatest influence in the acquisition, comprehension and production of language, you should remember that language is extremely complex, activity is widely dispersed in the brain and the right hemisphere still shows levels of activity during language processes (Harley, 2007; Pinel, 2003). Indeed, although language is the most lateralised of all human functions, it is not even absolute in this case (Harley, 2007; Pinel, 2003). You should also remember that the hemispheres of a cerebrally intact individual are able to communicate via the corpus callosum and cerebral commissures which connect these structures. However, hemispheres do vary in their specialism which is most apparent when this communication is prevented. The left hemisphere tends to be dominant in vision for words, audition for language sounds, complex movement, ipsilateral movement, verbal memory, meaning in memories, speech, reading, writing and arithmetic. In contrast, the right hemisphere is usually dominant in vision for faces, audition for non-speech sounds, emotional expression, processing tactile patterns, mental rotation and spatial awareness. Several experimental techniques have been devised to assess the degree of cerebral lateralisation of language and a range of these techniques are discussed below.

Sodium amytal test

In a sodium amytal test this substance is injected into the neck to anaesthetise one hemisphere at a time. This allows the researchers to test the performance of the other hemisphere by asking the participant to perform a verbal task. When the left hemisphere is anaesthetised the participant is usually unable to speak, but can speak when the right hemisphere is anaesthetised (Carlson, 2004; Pinel, 2003). This should suggest to you that the left hemisphere is indeed dominant in speech production.

Dichotic listening

A dichotic listening test is a non-invasive technique in which participants are presented with two separate, distinctive auditory messages. One is presented to the left ear (right hemisphere) and the other is presented to the right ear (left hemisphere). The participant is then asked to recite both of the messages. Most participants are only able to recite the message presented to the right ear which sends signals to the left hemisphere (Carlson, 2004; Harley, 2007; Pinel, 2003). This should suggest to you that the left hemisphere is dominant in speech perception and memory for language.

Handedness, gender and neuropsychological case studies

You should already know that there is considerable debate surrounding the issue of whether left-handed (sinestral) and right-handed (dextral) individuals differ in lateralisation of language (Gaskell, 2007; Harley, 2007; Pinel, 2003). However, it is now widely accepted that the left hemisphere is dominant for most sinestral *and* dextral individuals. In two classic publications, Russell and Espir (1961) and Penfield and Roberts (1959), it was documented that 60 per cent of dextral and 30 per cent of sinestral individuals with left-hemisphere lesions presented with deficits in language. This compared to 2 per cent of dextral and 24 per cent of sinestral individuals who suffered right-hemisphere lesions. This suggests that while some left-handed individuals may have right-hemisphere dominance for language, most left- and right-handed individuals have left-hemisphere dominance. Neuropsychology has also identified that there are gender differences in lateralisation, with males who suffer a unilateral stroke being three times more likely to develop deficits in language than females. This suggests that men's language functions are more lateralised than females (Carlson, 2004; Pinel, 2003).

Split-brain studies

You should already be aware that split-brain studies form the majority of evidence for the lateralisation of language abilities. In these studies, the two hemispheres have been surgically separated in attempts to reduce medical problems such as epilepsy through the severing of the corpus callosum (Carlson, 2004; Penfield & Roberts, 1959; Pinel, 2003; Somers et al., 2011). Both hemispheres are able to function independently but communication between these two structures is severely limited and often impossible. This means that each hemisphere retains the processes for which it was dominant but is unable to integrate functions and processes which required the use of both hemispheres. These studies produce very interesting insights into the lateralisation of language which you will need to understand in your assessments.

- When words are presented to the right visual field and left hemisphere, patients are able to tell the experimenter what they are viewing or reach with their right hand. Performance is at chance when using the left hand, suggesting that performance is no better than if they were guessing the answer.

- When words are presented to the left visual field and right hemisphere, patients claim that nothing was presented although the left hand is still able to reach for and identify the object.

- There appears to be a degree of cross-curing (indirect communication between hemispheres) because when the left hemisphere is wrong the right hemisphere appears to provide suitable bodily cues which encourage the left hemisphere to re-evaluate. For example, the left hemisphere may provide an incorrect verbal response while the right hemisphere triggers a frown or shake of the head and the left hemisphere will trigger an alternative response (Carlson, 2004; Pinel, 2003).

- There is even a 'helping-hand' phenomenon in which the left hand (controlled by the right hemisphere) will reach out and grab the correct object even when the left hemisphere is providing the incorrect answer (Carlson, 2004; Pinel, 2003).

- For most split-brain patients the left hemisphere controls most daily activities and the right hemisphere has no ability to act with obvious intention. However, in some patients the right hemisphere remains active and can produce impulsive, socially unacceptable, obstinate, mischievous and disturbing gestures. In such cases, patients often report hatred towards their left side and right hemisphere because their left hemisphere is unable to understand what is happening (Pinel, 2003).

Key terms

Dextral: Right-handed.

Dichotic listening test: A task in which dual messages are presented to the left and right ear and participants must try to recite both messages.

Lateralisation: The theory that one hemisphere of the brain is dominant in a given process while the other serves only minor roles.

Localisation: The theory that specialised structures of the brain facilitate specific functions.

Sinestral: Left-handed.

Sodium amytal test: A test in which one hemisphere of the brain is anaesthetised to test the performance of the other hemisphere.

Split-brain study: A study which examines the performance of people who have had their hemispheres surgically separated.

Theories of lateralisation

There are three main interpretations concerning the function of lateralisation. However, you should be aware that there is evidence which both supports and refutes these perspectives (Gaskell, 2007; Harley, 2007; Soares & Grosjean, 1981).

- The first perspective is that the left hemisphere has evolved to be more logical and analytic while the right hemisphere has evolved to serve the function of synthesising information.

- The second perspective is that the left hemisphere has evolved to control fine motor skills of which speech is only one example.

- The final perspective forms the linguistic theory and proponents argue that the left hemisphere's primary function is language in all of its various forms.

The debate surrounding these theories is ongoing and I recommend that you direct your further reading accordingly. However, the contemporary view is that the early lateralisation and concept of hemispheric dominance is too simplistic to account for the complex phenomenon which is human language (Gaskell, 2007; Harley, 2007; Pinel, 2003; Pinel & Dehaene, 2010).

 Sample question   *Essay*

To what extent can language be considered a product of the left hemisphere? Discuss with reference to at least two experimental techniques.

Further reading Lateralisation of language

Topic	Key reading
Critique of lateralisation	Pinel, P., & Dehaene, S. (2010). Beyond hemispheric dominance: Brain regions underlying joint lateralization of language and arithmetic to the left hemisphere. *Journal of Cognitive Neuroscience, 22*(1), 48–66.
Classic study on handedness and lateralisation	Russell, W. R., & Espir, M. L. E. (1961). *Traumatic aphasia.* Oxford: Oxford University Press.
Evaluation of neuroimaging techniques and lateralisation	Somers, M., Neggers, S. F., Diederen, K. M., Boks, M. P., Kahn, R. S., & Sommer, I. (2011). The measurement of language lateralization with functional transcranial Doppler and functional MRI: A critical evaluation. *Frontiers in Human Neuroscience, 5*(1), 1–8.

Test your knowledge

4.6 What is the sodium amytal test?

4.7 How does dichotic listening differentiate the activity of each hemisphere?

4.8 How does handedness relate to the lateralisation of language?

4.9 What are the structural differences between the left and right hemispheres?

Answers to these questions can be found on the companion website at: www.pearsoned.co.uk/psychologyexpress

Localisation of language and the Wernicke–Geschwind model

In contrast to lateralisation, localisation is the principle that language functions and processes are the result of activity in specific cerebral structures rather than due to the activity of one hemisphere (Carlson, 2004; Pinel, 2003). To a large extent, this approach is based on findings from cognitive neuropsychology. You should remember from the first chapter that cognitive neuropsychology is concerned with the study of how brain damage impairs cognitive functions. This approach has provided insights which suggest that language may be the product of several specialised structures. Some of these insights include:

- Damage to Broca's area impairs speech production but not language comprehension. Patients produce stunted speech. Broca's aphasia is also known as expressive aphasia.

- Damage to Wernicke's area impairs language comprehension but not speech production. Patients produce fluent but meaningless speech. Wernicke's aphasia is also known as receptive aphasia.

- Damaging the connection between Broca's and Wernicke's areas can cause conduction aphasia in which individuals struggle to repeat words they have heard.
- Damage to the angular gyrus can result in an inability to read (alexia) and an inability to write (agraphia).

A comprehensive list of language deficits which can arise due to damage to specific regions of the brain can be found in Table 4.3 and also in the Glossary at the end of this book. You should remember that if a function is impaired after damage to a cerebral structure that structure may be the locus of the function or may be part of the pathway responsible for the function.

Table 4.3 Disorders and deficits of language

Condition/term	Description
Agrammatism	Deficits in understanding or employing grammatical devices.
Aphasia	A deficit in language comprehension or production caused by brain damage.
Apraxia of speech	Deficits in the ability to programme movements of the lips, tongue and throat to produce normal speech sounds.
Anomia	Deficits in remembering an appropriate word.
Autotopagnosia	The inability to name and identify body parts.
Broca's aphasia	A deficit in language production caused by damage to Broca's area in the prefrontal cortex. Characterised by anomia, agrammatism and difficulties in articulation. Also known as expressive aphasia.
Conduction aphasia	Inability to repeat words which are heard, while still being able to speak normally. Caused by damage to the arcuate fasciculus which connects Broca's area and Wernicke's area.
Direct dyslexia	The ability to read words despite lacking an understanding of them.
Orthographic dysgraphia	A writing disorder in which individuals are unable to spell irregularly spelled words while still being able to spell regularly spelled words.
Phonological dysgraphia	A writing disorder in which individuals are unable to sound out words and write them phonetically.
Phonological dyslexia	Ability to read familiar words but deficits in the ability to read unfamiliar words and pronounceable non-words.
Pure alexia	Inability to read without the loss of the ability to write produced by brain damage.
Pure word deafness	The ability to speak, hear, write and read without being able to comprehend the meaning of speech. Caused by damage to Wernicke's area and the disruption of auditory input.

Surface dyslexia	Ability to read words phonetically but deficits in the ability to read irregularly spelled words.
Transcortical sensory aphasia	Deficits in comprehending and producing meaningful spontaneous speech while being able to repeat speech. Caused by damage to the posterior region of Wernicke's area.
Wernicke's aphasia	Deficits in the ability to comprehend speech and/or the production of fluent but meaningless speech. Produced by damage to Wernicke's area in the auditory association cortex in the left temporal lobe. Also known as receptive aphasia.
Word form dyslexia	An individual is only able to read words after spelling out the individual letters. Also known as spelling dyslexia.

? Sample question   Problem-based learning

A patient has been referred to you with deficits in the ability to comprehend and produce meaningful spontaneous speech but they appear to be able to repeat the phrases you produce when instructed. How would this patient's condition be diagnosed and how is it different from other disorders of language? You will need to prepare a report which discusses this form of impairment and differentiates it from other conditions.

Geschwind (1970) utilised the insights provided by the early neuropsychologists and devised the Wernicke–Geschwind model of language. In this model, language is learnt, comprehended and produced through a complex circuit which runs through several cerebral structures. These include the primary visual cortex, angular gyrus, primary auditory cortex, Wernicke's area, arcuate fasciculus, Broca's area and the primary motor cortex, although the involvement of structures depends on the nature of the task (Carlson, 2004; Pinel, 2003). The functions which Geschwind (1970) assigned to this structures are listed below:

- The angular gyrus translates visual forms of words into auditory codes.
- The primary motor cortex controls the muscles of articulation.
- Wernicke's area is the centre of comprehension.
- The primary auditory cortex perceives spoken words.
- Broca's area is the centre of articulation.
- The primary visual cortex perceives written words.
- The left arcuate fasciculus carries signals between Broca's and Wernicke's area.

However, you should remember that this model employs serial processing which is restrictive and may not accurately reflect the complex nature of human language. Indeed, it is unclear how certain structures would be bypassed in a serial chain of processes while still successfully completing a task. The model is also susceptible to the limitations of cognitive neuropsychology. Some of the issues which you should keep in mind include:

- Brain damage is rarely localised, which makes drawing inferences about structures and their functions difficult.
- It is difficult to generalise findings from neuropsychological patients to the rest of the population.
- Performance may reflect compensation, idiosyncrasies or reorganisation of function rather than the results of brain damage per se.
- Performance may reflect damage to connections rather than to specific structures.
- There are no baseline measures meaning that we cannot compare current performance with performance prior to injury.
- Complete removal of Broca's area without damaging surrounding areas does not produce aphasia contrary to this model (Pinel, 2003).
- It is difficult to damage or remove Wernicke's area without damaging surrounding structures due to its location, but when this has been accomplished it does not always impair language comprehension (Pinel, 2003).
- Aphasias are usually more complicated than the model predicts with islands of ability remaining intact.
- Cognitive neuroscience has largely replaced this model in contemporary psychology.

? Sample question   Essay

Critically evaluate the Wernicke–Geschwind model of language.

Further reading The anatomy of language

Topic	Key reading
Conduction aphasia	Ardila, A. (2010). A review of conduction aphasia. *Current Neurology and Neuroscience Reports*, *10*(6), 499–503.
Aphasia	Bernal, B., & Ardila, A. (2009). The role of the arcuate fasciculus in conduction aphasia. *Brain*, *132*(9), 2309–2316.
Broca's aphasia	Rogalsky, C., & Hickok, G. (2011). The role of Broca's area in sentence comprehension. *Journal of Cognitive Neuroscience*, *23*(7), 1664–1680.
Semantic errors	Schwartz, M. F., Kimberg, D. Y., Walker, G. M., Faseyitan, O., Brecher, A., Dell, G. S., & Coslett, H. B. (2010). Anterior temporal involvement in semantic word retrieval: Voxel-based lesion-symptom mapping evidence from aphasia. *Brain*, *132*(12), 3411–3427.
Broca's aphasia	Thompson, C. K., & Lee, M. (2009). Psych verb production and comprehension in agrammatic Broca's aphasia. *Journal of Neurolinguistics*, *22*(4), 354–369.

Test your knowledge

4.10 What is Broca's aphasia?

4.11 What is Wernicke's aphasia?

4.12 How does localisation differ from lateralisation?

4.13 How does conduction aphasia arise?

Answers to these questions can be found on the companion website at: www.pearsoned.co.uk/psychologyexpress

Cognitive neuroscience and the physiology of language

In contrast to the earlier approaches you should remember that cognitive neuroscience is concerned with identifying the physiological activity associated with phenomena as measured through neuroimaging techniques. This approach is based on the ideas that larger processes can be broken down into constituent cognitive processes with corresponding physiological activity and that structures serve multiple functions (Bavelier et al., 1997; Bi et al., 2009; Carlson, 2004; Pinel, 2003). As opposed to the Wernicke–Geschwind model, the processing of language is parallel, complex and distributed throughout the brain. Indeed, Bavelier et al. (1997) monitored physiological activity during silent reading using functional magnetic resonance imaging and revealed that patterns of activation were patchy, variable, widespread, across both hemispheres and extending far beyond the structures cited in the Wernicke–Geschwind model. In addition, Damasio and colleagues have also identified that patterns of cerebral activity vary considerably according to the different categories of objects and tasks used (e.g. Damasio, Grabowski, Tranel, Hichwa & Damasio, 1996; Damasio, Tranel, Grabowski, Adolphs & Damasio, 2004). You should also remember that these areas also extended far beyond those of the earlier model. These studies suggest that the corresponding cerebral activity which is observed during the processing and production of language varies considerably and cannot be explained by lateralisation or simple localisation.

 Sample question *Essay*

Compare and contrast the insights gained from cognitive neuropsychology and cognitive neuroscience towards an understanding of human language.

> **Further reading** The cognitive neuroscience approach to studying language
>
> | Topic | Key reading |
> |---|---|
> | Neuroimaging | Damasio, H., Tranel, D., Grabowski, T., Adolphs, R., & Damasio, A. (2004). Neural systems behind word and concept retrieval. *Cognition*, *92*(1–2), 179–229. |

Test your knowledge

4.14 What are the constituent processes of language according to cognitive neuroscience?

4.15 Is it true that structures in the brain specialise in only one function?

4.16 How does cognitive neuroscience differ from other approaches to language?

Answers to these questions can be found on the companion website at: www.pearsoned.co.uk/psychologyexpress

Chapter summary – pulling it all together

→ Can you tick all the points from the revision checklist at the beginning of this chapter?

→ Attempt the sample question from the beginning of this chapter using the answer guidelines below.

→ Go to the companion website at www.pearsoned.co.uk/psychologyexpress to access more revision support online, including interactive quizzes, flashcards, You be the marker exercises as well as answer guidance for the Test your knowledge and Sample questions from this chapter.

Answer guidelines

 Sample question   *Essay*

To what extent do biological and environmental factors determine language?

Approaching the question

This question is asking you to discuss, compare, contrast and evaluate the contributions of nature and nurture towards determining language acquisition, comprehension and production.

Important points to include

Your essay should begin with a brief explanation and definition of language and an overview of the structure and content of your response. This is likely to include a statement concerning the stance you will adopt, such as whether you believe nature or nurture contributes more towards language. The main section of your essay should discuss and critically evaluate the biological and non-biological factors which make language possible. This will include a consideration of cerebral lateralisation, localisation, the insights from cognitive neuropsychology and the identification of environmental factors which may interact with these influences. It may also be useful to include a consideration of whether animals are able to communicate in a similar manner to humans despite different anatomy. However, it is vital that you take an evidence-based approach and support your arguments with evidence from the literature. Your essay should also contain a clear and concise conclusion which is based on your evaluation of the evidence and explicitly states whether biological and/or environmental factors contribute towards the ability to acquire, produce and comprehend language.

Make your answer stand out

To make an answer stand out on this topic you need to be able to demonstrate an awareness and understanding of the broader literature concerning language acquisition, production and comprehension. This will mean also considering the cognitive, social and developmental aspects of language to establish a critical and comprehensive academic debate.

Explore the accompanying website at www.pearsoned.co.uk/psychologyexpress
→ Prepare more effectively for exams and assignments using the answer guidelines for questions from this chapter.
→ Test your knowledge using multiple choice questions and flashcards.
→ Improve your essay skills by exploring the You be the marker exercises.

Notes

Notes

Mechanisms of perception and sensation

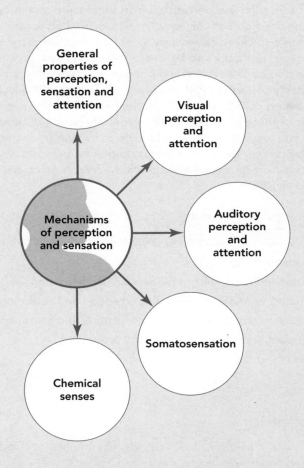

A printable version of this topic map is available from
www.pearsoned.co.uk/psychologyexpress

Introduction

This chapter will provide you with an overview of the biological structures, mechanisms and processes which underlie human perception, sensation and ultimately attention. Special attention will be paid to the general properties of perception and sensation, visual perception, auditory perception, somatosensory systems and the chemical senses. However, it is important to remember that additional information which is relevant to this topic was covered in Chapters 1–3. You should also remember that perception, sensation and attention are intrinsically linked. For example, we must perceive a stimulus in order to allocate our attention to this item. Our attention also facilitates the experiences of sensation and perception. You should also remember that the structures of the brain do not only serve one function. Perception, sensation and attention are also linked to memory, consciousness, language and social interaction. You will probably also be aware that while these processes are linked they can also be dissociated and operate independently. However this chapter is primarily concerned with the biological factors which facilitate or are observed during perception and sensation. The cognitive mechanisms and social functions of these phenomena are beyond the scope of this text but it is advisable that you expand your understanding to include other non-biological influences on behaviour. By the end of this chapter, you should be able to recall some of the physiological, neural and anatomical factors associated with human perception and sensation.

> → *Revision checklist*
>
> *Essential points to revise are:*
> - ❏ What the general properties of perception and sensation are
> - ❏ Which structures are associated with perception and sensation
> - ❏ Which processes are associated with perception and sensation
> - ❏ How perception, sensation and attention are related
> - ❏ How forms of perception and sensation differ

Assessment advice

Essay questions in this area will usually ask you to compare, contrast or evaluate two forms of perception, sensation or attention. For example, you may be asked to compare the biological contributions towards visual and auditory perception and attention. Alternatively, you may be asked to compare and contrast biological and non-biological factors which influence human perception and attention. For these types of questions you will need to adopt a critical and evidence-based approach which considers the various influences on perception and attention. It is also vital to discuss the strengths, limitations, supporting evidence and contrary evidence for each of the approaches or types of perception and attention you include and clearly define all technical terms or processes. You should also remember to link back regularly to the essay question to ensure you do not lose your chain of thought and the marker can follow your argument. This will allow you to gradually build on your response to the question if you incorporate critical analyses of theories and evidence. You should also remember that your conclusion should be based on the strength of the evidence and the topics you have discussed. Most importantly, you must make sure that you answer the question and do not go off topic or lose your marker in the narrative.

Sample question

Could you answer this question? Below is a typical essay question that could arise on this topic.

 Sample question   *Essay*

Compare, contrast and evaluate the traditional and contemporary biological theories concerning the nature and organisation of perception and attention with reference to the primary, secondary and associational cortices.

Guidelines on answering this question are included at the end of this chapter, whilst further guidance on tackling other exam questions can be found on the companion website at: **www.pearsoned.co.uk/psychologyexpress**.

General properties of perception, sensation and attention

The key terms box below presents definitions of attention, perception and sensation. You should be able to clearly identify how these processes are related but at the same time function independently. There are five exteroceptive sensory systems which rely on these processes. These are vision, audition (hearing), touch (somatosensation), smell (olfaction) and taste (gustation). Each of these systems receives sensory information originally derived from external sources, pressures upon the body and internal cues. This can either direct or be informed by attention and perception (Broerse, 2001; Carlson, 2004; Pinel, 2003). Indeed, an interesting case study of how these processes can be dissociated is also presented below.

Key terms

Attention: The allocation of cognitive resources to stimuli.

Exteroceptive sensory systems: The systems responsible for the senses of touch, smell, taste, hearing and vision.

Perception: Higher-order processes of integrating, reorganising and interpreting a complete pattern of sensation.

Sensation: The process of detecting a stimulus.

Visual agnosia: A neuropsychological condition characterised by deficits in perception.

KEY STUDY

Sacks (1985), *The man who mistook his wife for a hat*

An interesting insight into the differentiation of sensation and perception and the nature of *visual agnosia* was provided by the case study of Dr. P. which was presented by Sacks in 1985. Dr. P. is famous for making numerous perceptual errors such as mistaking inanimate objects for people and mistaking body parts for clothing, including believing that his foot was in fact his shoe and that his wife's head was actually a hat. This pattern of impairment suggests that while the patient appeared to have unimpaired sensation because he was able to experience the stimuli, his perception of these stimuli was severely impaired.

Some of the details surrounding the complex transmission of messages along the sensory systems were covered in more detail in Chapter 2. However, it is especially important that you can understand what happens when these signals reach the brain. Each of these exteroceptive sensory systems feed into their own respective primary sensory cortex via the thalamic relay nuclei for that system (Broerse, 2001; Carlson, 2004; Goldstein, 2009; Pinel, 2003). This signal then transmits to a secondary sensory cortex facilitating the further processing of stimuli. You should remember that multiple regions will receive information from a sensory system and that these structures are each referred to as an association cortex (Pinel, 2003). These cerebral structures are organised hierarchically in that each additional system receives input from the previous levels and provides another level of processing (Goldstein, 2009). This means that while destruction of the initial receptor cells will abolish sensory information for the corresponding stimuli, damage to the secondary and association cortices will result in more specific patterns of impairment (Carlson, 2004; Goldstein, 2009; Pinel, 2003).

However, there has been considerable theoretical and experimental development concerning the organisation and function of these systems which you will need to understand in your assessments. For example, the early perspective was that the cerebral structures which receive information from the sensory systems are organised hierarchically and that processing is homogeneous (uniform across structures) and serial in nature (Broerse, 2001; Carlson, 2004; Goldstein, 2009; Pinel, 2003). According to this perspective, processing could only proceed in one direction and was identical in nature across each cerebral structure. You should remember that this perspective was based on early experimental methods which lacked the advanced technology which is available today (Pinel, 2003; Rayner, 2009). It cannot fully explain the complex nature of human perception, sensation and attention and it fails to consider how an early process may be impaired while later processes remain intact (Carlson, 2004; Pinel, 2003). In contrast, the current perspective is that while the structures are indeed organised hierarchically, they are functionally segregated and rely on parallel processing (Broerse, 2001; Carlson, 2004; Goldstein, 2009; Grossman et al., 2000; Kourtzi & Kanwisher, 2000; Pinel, 2003). This means that there is a division of labour, with cerebral structures serving qualitatively and quantitatively different functions with multiple levels of processing. These functions are performed simultaneously, and while most pathways carry information from lower to higher systems this is not universal because there is feedback between the cerebral structures (Carlson, 2004; Pinel, 2003; Shaw, Lien, Ruthruff & Allen, 2011). Jeannerod, Arbib, Rizzolatti and Sakarta (1995) also argued that there are two distinct parallel streams of information in the sensory systems in which one influences behaviour without conscious awareness (for example, in the case of reflexes) and another which influences behaviour by engaging our conscious awareness and attention (such as in intentional touch). You should remember from earlier chapters that neuropsychological patients do appear to have specific deficits while other abilities remain intact, processing does appear to be parallel in nature and action and awareness can indeed be dissociated (such as in the cases of blind-sight and split-brain studies). The following sections will also refresh your memory of these organisational properties with specific reference to each of the sensory systems.

? Sample question — Essay

To what extent do cerebral structures regulate and facilitate human perception, sensation and attention?

Further reading The general biological properties of perception and attention

Topic	Key reading
Sensation and perception	Goldstein, B. E. (2009). *Sensation and perception* (8th ed.). Belmont, CA: Wadsworth.
Perception and language	Pulvermüller, F., & Fadiga, L. (2010). Active perception: Sensorimotor circuits as a cortical basis for language. *Nature Reviews Neuroscience, 11*(5), 351–360.
Dissociated perception and attention	Shaw, K., Lien, M., Ruthruff, E., & Allen, P.A. (2011). Electrophysiological evidence of emotion perception without central attention. *Journal of Cognitive Psychology, 23*(6), 695–708.

Test your knowledge

5.1 How did early theories describe the cerebral structures and processes of perception and attention?

5.2 How do current theories describe the cerebral structures and processes of perception and attention?

5.3 What are the five exteroceptive sensory systems?

Answers to these questions can be found on the companion website at:
www.pearsoned.co.uk/psychologyexpress

Visual perception and attention

Vision allows us to quickly perceive our environment and it is an exceptionally complex process (Carlson, 2004; Goldstein, 2009; Pinel, 2003). While it is not vital for successful functioning, life can be considerably more difficult when this sensory system is not fully functional. This section is primarily concerned with how the brain facilitates vision. To enhance your revision of the initial micro-processes of vision I direct your attention to introductory texts such as Goldstein (2009) and articles such as Hubel and Wiesel (1977).

You should remember that images detected in the left visual field are transmitted to the right hemisphere and images which are detected in the right visual field are transmitted to the left hemisphere (Carlson, 2004; Goldstein, 2009; Pinel, 2003). Vision is governed by the retina, the entire occipital cortex of the brain (also known as the striate cortex), large areas of the temporal cortex and parts of the parietal cortex. In the case of vision, the striate cortex is the primary cortex and from here signals are transmitted to the secondary visual cortex which consists of the prestriate cortex and inferotemporal cortex. The association cortex for vision consists of numerous regions throughout the brain but the largest area is located in the posterior parietal cortex (Carlson, 2004; Pinel, 2003). Based on the principles of the current perspective of vision as a hierarchical, functionally segregated system which relies on parallel processing, minor damage to the system should result in specific deficits although other higher-order structures should be able to compensate for these deficits (Carlson, 2004; Huberle, Driver & Karnath, 2010; Pinel, 2003). You will see from the Critical focus box below that this is probably a correct assumption.

CRITICAL FOCUS

Scotoma – completion of scenes, blind-sight and dissociation between sensation and perception

Damage to the primary visual cortex results in areas of blindness in the corresponding areas of the contralateral visual field of both eyes. This area of blindness is known as a scotoma and research with patients suffering from this condition has provided several interesting insights into the nature of human vision (Carlson, 2004). The range of the scotoma can be assessed using a perimetry task in which dots are presented in all areas of the visual field and the individual indicates when a dot has been seen. If a dot is presented in the same location of a scotoma the individual claims that nothing has been presented, indicating an area of blindness (Pinel, 2003). However, despite these areas of blindness, individuals with scotomas tend to report scene completion in which other aspects of the scene and their expectations allows them to see an intact image. Individuals with scotomas also display blind-sight in that they are still able to reach for and grasp items which are presented in the area of blindness despite lacking conscious perception of the object. These findings suggest that vision is organised hierarchically with functionally segregated systems or structures and that it relies on parallel processing. It is also consistent with Jeannerod et al.'s (1995) perspectives that perception and sensation can be with or without conscious experience. However, it remains unclear whether this pattern of visual perception is due to top-down cognitive processes, functions of areas of the striate cortex which have remained intact or whether there are pathways leading to the secondary visual cortex which bypass the primary visual cortex (Carlson, 2004; Pinel, 2003). It may also be unwise to conclude that this is how normal vision functions because neuropsychological patients' performance may reflect the reorganisation of the system.

However, you will also probably be aware that visual perception and reality are not always synonymous in the visual system. Indeed, visual illusions can confuse this system into perceiving items which are not actually present. This suggests that the processes seen in patients with scotomas are present in unimpaired individuals (Carlson, 2004; Pinel, 2003). Researchers have also identified over a dozen separate, functional areas of the visual cortex using fMRI and PET scans suggesting that the visual system is functionally segregated (Grossman et al., 2000; Kourtzi & Kanwisher, 2000).

Key terms

Scotoma: An area of blindness produced through damage to the primary visual cortex.

Perimetry task: A task which identifies the location and scope of a scotoma by asking participants to identify when they are able to see a series of dots presented in the visual field.

In regards to parallel processing, there appear to be two streams of information in the visual system (Goldstein, 2009; Goodale & Milner, 2006; Pinel, 2003). The dorsal stream flows from the primary visual cortex to the dorsal and posterior prestriate cortex and the inferotemporal cortex. In contrast, the ventral stream flows from the primary cortex to the ventral prestriate cortex and inferotemporal cortex (Pinel, 2003). The traditional distinction between these two systems is that the dorsal stream processes information relating to where stimuli are, while the ventral stream processes information relating to what things are (Carlson, 2004; Milner & Goodale, 1993). However, this view has been widely replaced with the distinction that the dorsal stream directs behavioural interaction with objects while the ventral stream mediates conscious perception of objects (Goodale & Milner, 2006; Milner & Goodale, 1993). You should be aware that damage to the ventral stream does impair conscious perception, while damage to the dorsal stream impairs perceptually mediated action such as grasping unfamiliar perceived objects (Pinel, 2003). For example, prosopagnosia (the inability to recognise faces) can be produced through bilateral lesions to the ventral stream (Carlson, 2004; Pinel, 2003).

Key term

Prosopagnosia: A neuropsychological condition in which people are unable to recognise faces.

? Sample question   Essay

To what extent has neuropsychology contributed towards our understanding of normal visual attention and perception?

Further reading Visual perception and attention

Topic	Key reading
Selective colour vision	Anderson, S. K., Müller, M. M., & Hillyard, S. A. (2009). Color-selective attention need not be mediated by spatial attention. *Journal of Vision, 9*(6), 1–7.
Audiovisual perception	Anderson, T. S., Tiippana, K., Laarni, J., & Sams, M. (2009). The role of visual spatial attention in audiovisual speech perception. *Speech Communication, 51*(2), 184–193.
Selective visual perception	Correa, A., Sanabria, D., Spence, C., Tudela, P., & Lupiáñez, J. (2006). Selective temporal attention enhances the temporal resolution of visual perception: Evidence from a temporal order judgement task. *Brain Research, 1070*(1), 202–205.

Transcranial stimulation and visual perception	Grosbras, M., & Paus, T. (2002). Transcranial magnetic stimulation of the human frontal eye field: Effects on visual perception and attention. *Journal of Cognitive Neuroscience, 14*(7), 1109–1120.
Neuropsychology and visual perception	Huberle, E., Driver, J., & Karnath, H. (2010). Retinal versus physical stimulus size as determinants of visual perception in simultanagnosia. *Neuropsychologia, 48*(6), 1677–1682.
Visual perception and attention	Palermo, R., & Rhodes, G. (2007). Are you always on my mind? A review of how face perception and attention interact. *Neuropsychologia, 45*(1), 75–92.

Test your knowledge

5.4 Vision is governed by which structures in the brain?

5.5 What are the primary differences between the dorsal and ventral streams?

5.6 What is prosopagnosia?

5.7 Does visual perception always reflect reality?

Answers to these questions can be found on the companion website at: www.pearsoned.co.uk/psychologyexpress

Auditory perception and attention

Audition (hearing) is based on molecule vibrations for which humans are able to hear between 20–20,200 hertz (Goldstein, 2009; Pinel, 2003). Sounds are made up of physical dimensions with corresponding physical stimuli and perceptual dimensions. These properties are presented in Table 5.1. The physical dimensions reflect the sensation of the stimuli and the perceptual dimensions reflect what is perceived. However, it is important to remember that the physical dimensions are on a scale rather than dichotomised at two extremes and pure tones only exist in laboratories and recording studios (Carlson, 2004; Pinel, 2003).

Table 5.1 Properties of sounds

Physical stimuli	Physical dimensions	Perceptual dimensions
Amplitude	Loud–soft	Loudness
Frequency	Low–high	Pitch
Complexity	Pure–rich	Timbre

The process of audition is complex and involves a range of structures which are summarised below to refresh your memory (Carlson, 2004; Pinel, 2003; Shamma & Micheyl, 2010):

- Sound waves travel down the auditory canal causing the tympanic membrane (eardrum) to vibrate.
- These vibrations are transferred to the three ossicles (bones of the middle ear) consisting of the malleus (hammer), incus (anvil) and the stapes (stirrup).
- This results in vibrations of the oval window and cochlear internal membrane which acts as a receptor for the organ of Corti.
- The organ of Corti consists of two membranes called the basilar and tectorial membranes. The hair cells on the basilar membrane act as receptor cells while the tectorial membrane rests on top of the hair cells. These structures are responsible for triggering action potentials in the axons of the auditory nerves, beginning the transmission of the signal from the ear to the brain.
- The vestibular system of the ear also carries information about the direction and intensity of head movements, making it vital for balance.
- From the ear, the action potentials are carried along the auditory nerves to the primary auditory cortex. However, unlike the visual system there is no major pathway. The auditory system is more like a network of pathways (Carlson, 2004; Pinel, 2003).
- The axons of each auditory nerve synapse in the ipsilateral cochlear nuclei leading to the superior olives, lateral lemniscus, inferior colliculi and medial geniculate nuclei.

? Sample question   Essay

To what extent is auditory attention and perception dependent on biological factors?

Hence, the auditory system is organised hierarchically. You should remember from your studies that the primary auditory cortex is located in the lateral fissure and is surrounded by the secondary auditory cortex. This structure is also organised in functional segregated columns consistent with the current perspective concerning the organisation of perceptual systems (Carlson, 2004; Goldstein, 2009; Pinel, 2003). Furthermore, the perception of sound location is controlled by the medial and lateral superior olives (Carlson, 2004; Pinel, 2003). For example, the medial olive is sensitive to the time delay between the two ears as they receive vibrations from different angles. In contrast, the lateral olive is sensitive to differences in amplitude which also arise because it receives vibrations from different angles. However, the nature, structure and physiology of the secondary auditory cortex are difficult to assess because the neurons respond weakly and inconsistently to even pure tones, reflecting the distributed nature of the auditory system (Carlson, 2004; Pinel, 2003; Stevens, Fanning, Coch, Sanders & Neville, 2008). It is also difficult to track and isolate the effects of brain damage since the location of the auditory cortex makes it virtually impossible to damage without also destroying other structures.

> **? Sample question** Essay
>
> To what extent is neuropsychological research limited due to the location of the auditory cortex? Discuss with reference to the strengths and limitation of neuropsychology.

Further reading Auditory perception and attention

Topic	Key reading
Auditory attention	Bee, M. A., & Micheyl, C. (2008). The 'Cocktail party problem': What is it? How can it be solved? And why should animal behaviourists study it? *Journal of Comparative Psychology, 122*(3), 235–251.
Tone deafness	Loui, P., Guenther, F. H., Mathys, C., & Schlaug, G. (2008). Action–perception mismatch in tone-deafness. *Current Biology, 18*(8), 331–332.
Auditory perception	Shamma, S. A., & Micheyl, C. (2010). Behind the scenes of auditory perception. *Current Opinions in Neurobiology, 20*(3), 361–366.
Auditory perception and action planning	Zmigrod, S., & Hommel, B. (2009). Auditory event files: Integrating auditory perception and action planning. *Attention, Perception and Psychophysics, 71*(2), 352–362.

Test your knowledge

5.8 What are the physical dimensions of audition?

5.9 What are the perceptual dimensions of audition?

5.10 Where is the primary auditory cortex located?

Answers to these questions can be found on the companion website at: www.pearsoned.co.uk/psychologyexpress

Somatosensation

Somatosensation refers to bodily sensations and comprises three interacting systems, which are the exteroceptive system (see previous section on the general properties of perception, sensation and attention), proprioceptive system and interoceptive system.

Key terms

Proprioceptive system: The structures and processes responsible for processing information concerning the position of the body.

Interoceptive system: The structures and processes responsible for processing information concerning conditions within the body.

There are four types of cutaneous receptors found in both hairy and hairless skin which facilitate somatosensation (Lumpkin & Caterina, 2007; Pinel, 2003). The free nerve endings are sensitive to temperature changes and pain. Secondly, the Pacinian corpuscles adapt rapidly and respond to the displacement of skin. Finally, the Merkel's disks and Ruffini endings both adapt slowly and respond to skin indentation and stretching. Nerve fibres carrying information from these cutaneous receptors gather together into dorsal roots which feed into the spine. However, consistent with the current perceptive on the organisation of the perceptual system you should also remember that the somatosensory system has two main, parallel routes to the cortex through either the dorsal column-medial lemniscus route or the anterolateral system.

- **Dorsal column-medial lemniscus:** This pathway carries information relating to light touch, vibration, pressure and the position of the body. The nerves enter the spinal cord via a dorsal root ascending ipsilaterally in the dorsal columns and synapse in the dorsal column nuclei of the medulla. Here they cross over and ascend to the medial lemniscus to the ventral posterior nucleus of the thalamus.

- **Anterolateral system:** This pathway carries information relating to pain and temperature and consists of three separate tracts. These are the spinothalamic, spinoreticular and spinotectal tracts. Firstly, the spinothalamic tract culminates in the thalamus and is important for the localisation of painful and thermal stimuli. Secondly, the spinoreticular tract culminates in the reticular formation and is responsible for facilitating alertness and physiological arousal in response to pain. Finally, the spinotectal tract culminates in the tectum and directs attention toward the stimuli.

? Sample question   Essay

To what extent has biological psychology contributed towards the contemporary understanding of somatosensation?

You will need to be able to discuss and differentiate these somatosensory pathways in your assessments. As the above description demonstrates, these systems are also organised hierarchically with functionally segregated systems and parallel processing (Carlson, 2004; Goldstein, 2009; Jeannerod, et al., 1995; Pinel, 2003). However, further insights have been provided by neuropsychology (Carlson, 2004; Goldstein, 2009; Pinel, 2003). For example, lesions to the ventral posterior nuclei reduce sensitivity to touch, changes in temperature and sharp pain while lesions to the parafascicular and intralaminar nuclei reduce deep chronic pain while leaving other sensations intact. In contrast, damage to the somatosensory cortex results in specific impairments dependent upon the location and severity of the injury. This is consistent with the characteristics of the somatosensory pathways and principles of parallel processing and segregation of function.

There is a notable issue when arguing that cerebral regions are responsible for pain perception in that there are significant individual differences in sensitivity to somatosensory information. This may be due to different functioning of anatomy, physiology, cognitive processing or other individual differences. Other paradoxes of pain include:

- While it feels like a negative experience, it is vital for survival as a form of information concerning danger and bodily harm.
- Pain can be controlled through cognitive, emotional and pharmacological means.
- There is a lack of cortical representation of pain although the anterior cingulate cortex has been associated levels and patterns of activation are variable.

In an attempt to explain individual differences in pain perception, Melzack and Wall (1965, 1982/2008) devised the gate-theory of pain and argued that cognition can indeed mediate and block pain signals from the somatosensory system. In this model, signals descending in the centrifugal pathway can activate neural gating circuits in the spinal cord and block incoming pain signals. This is supported by evidence that electrical stimulation of the periaqueductal grey matter has an effect synonymous with anaesthesia (Carlson, 2004; Goldstein, 2009; Pinel, 2003). This model remains influential today and has revolutionised how some medical practitioners treat pain by encouraging patients to change their attitude toward the experience thereby reducing their levels of discomfort (Fitzgerald, 2010). Therefore, it is important for you to understand that while bottom-up processes can result in somatosensation, top-down processes may control the extent to which perception results in the experience of pain.

Further reading Somatosensation

Topic	Key reading
Pain	Fitzgerald, M. (2010). The lost domain of pain. *Brain*, *133*(6), 1850–1854.
Social perception	Keyers, C., Kaas, J. H., & Gazzola, V. (2010). Somatosensation in social perception. *Nature Reviews Neuroscience*, *11*(6), 417–428.
Age differences	Low Choy, N., Brauer, S. G., & Nitz, J. C. (2007). Age-related changes in strength and somatosensation during midlife. *Annals of the New York Academy of Science, 1114*, 180–193.
Sensory transduction	Lumpkin, E. A., & Caterina, M. J. (2007). Mechanisms of the sensory transduction in the skin. *Nature, 445*(7130), 858–865.
Gate control theory of pain	Melzack, R., & Wall, P.D. (2008). *The challenges of pain* (2nd ed.). London: Penguin Books. (Original work published 1982.)

Test your knowledge

5.11 Somatosensation consists of which three interacting systems?

5.12 What do Merkel's disks and Ruffini endings respond to?

5.13 Through which two main pathways does somatosensory information reach the cortex?

5.14 What are the paradoxes of pain?

Answers to these questions can be found on the companion website at: www.pearsoned.co.uk/psychologyexpress

---

Chemical senses

The chemical senses are those which provide information concerning the chemical content of the environment (Anderson et al., 2003; Gibson & Garbers, 2000; Goldstein, 2009; Pinel, 2003). These include olfaction (smell) and gustation (taste), although you should remember that these senses are intrinsically linked. These systems are also organised hierarchically according to functionally segregated structures and incorporate parallel processing. Gibson and Garbers (2000) have argued that there are over 1000 olfactory receptors in the nose which each respond to different types of odour. These receptors are located in a layer of mucus-covered tissue called the olfactory mucosa. The axons of these receptors pass through the cribriform plate of the skull into the olfactory bulbs where they synapse on the neurons of mitral cells, which project via the olfactory tracts to several structures in the medial temporal lobes including the amygdala and piriform cortex (Carlson, 2004; Pinel, 2003). You should be aware that the correct term for an inability to detect odours is anosmia which can be caused through damage to this system.

Sample question Essay

Compare and contrast the biological structures and processes underlying chemical and somatosensory perception and attention.

In contrast, the receptors for taste are located on the tongue and are often found around small protuberances called papillae. Conventionally, there are five different tastes, which are sweet, salty, sour, bitter and unami (savoury or meaty) although it is notable that many flavours cannot be experienced by combining these tastes, suggesting that this list is incomplete (Carlson, 2004; Pinel, 2003). Unlike olfaction receptors, these taste buds do not have their own axons but rather cluster together. These afferents leave the mouth as part of the facial, glossopharyngeal and vagus cranial nerves and terminate in the solitary nucleus of the medulla. Here they synapse on neurons which project to the ventral posterior nucleus of the thalamus and subsequently to the primary and secondary gustatory cortex. The correct term for an inability to taste is called ageasia which can be caused through damage to this system.

Further reading Chemical senses

Topic	Key reading
Gustation	Chaudhari, N., & Roper, S. D. (2010). The cell biology of taste. *Journal of Current Biology, 190*(3), 285–296.
Receptor cells	Damann, N., Voets, T., & Nilius, B. (2008). TRPs in our senses. *Current Biology, 18*(18), 880–889.
Gustation	Singh, P. B., Iannilli, E., & Hummel, T. (2011). Segregation of gustatory cortex in response to salt and umami taste studied through event-related potentials. *Neuroreport, 22*(6), 299–303.

Test your knowledge

5.15 What are the chemical senses?

5.16 What is olfaction?

5.17 What is gustation?

5.18 How many tastes are there and what are they called?

Answers to these questions can be found on the companion website at: www.pearsoned.co.uk/psychologyexpress

Chapter summary – pulling it all together

→ Can you tick all the points from the revision checklist at the beginning of this chapter?

→ Attempt the sample question from the beginning of this chapter using the answer guidelines below.

→ Go to the companion website at www.pearsoned.co.uk/psychologyexpress to access more revision support online, including interactive quizzes, flashcards, You be the marker exercises as well as answer guidance for the Test your knowledge and Sample questions from this chapter.

Answer guidelines

 Sample question   *Essay*

Compare, contrast and evaluate the traditional and contemporary biological theories concerning the nature and organisation of perception and attention with reference to the primary, secondary and associational cortices.

Approaching the question

This question is asking you to compare, contrast and evaluate the older view that the cerebral structures responsible for perception and attention are hierarchical, serial and homogeneous processes and the contemporary view that these structures and processes are hierarchical, functionally segregated and parallel.

Important points to include

Your essay should begin with a brief introduction which summarises the topic and outlines the structure and content of your response. This will ideally include the identification and differentiation of the older and contemporary perspectives. The main body of your essay will describe, evaluate and compare these theories, drawing heavily on examples from the literature. Your report should identify their commonalities, differences and the extent to which each perspective is supported by the literature surrounding perception and attention. You should make specific reference to whether the contemporary view has completely replaced the older perspective or if elements of this account are still dominant. For example, while both perspectives see these processes as hierarchical they differ in their account of the interaction between the primary, secondary and associational cortices. It may also be useful to discuss how applicable these views are to two forms of perception (such as vision and olfaction for example). Your response should finally include a concise, coherent and evidence-based conclusion which summarises your response to the question.

Make your answer stand out

To make an answer stand out on this topic you will need to demonstrate abilities to synthesise and critically evaluate a variety of evidence and directly relate this to the perspectives. The best essays will be well structured, demonstrate a balance between description and evaluation, give examples of academic debate and provide clear evidence-based and persuasive conclusions.

Explore the accompanying website at www.pearsoned.co.uk/psychologyexpress

→ Prepare more effectively for exams and assignments using the answer guidelines for questions from this chapter.
→ Test your knowledge using multiple choice questions and flashcards.
→ Improve your essay skills by exploring the You be the marker exercises.

Notes

Notes

6

Biological mechanisms of sleep and dreaming

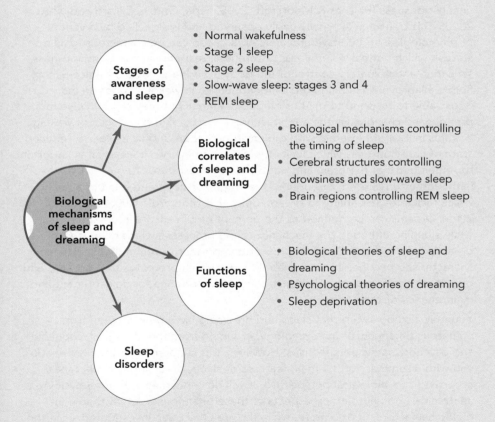

Stages of awareness and sleep
- Normal wakefulness
- Stage 1 sleep
- Stage 2 sleep
- Slow-wave sleep: stages 3 and 4
- REM sleep

Biological mechanisms of sleep and dreaming

Biological correlates of sleep and dreaming
- Biological mechanisms controlling the timing of sleep
- Cerebral structures controlling drowsiness and slow-wave sleep
- Brain regions controlling REM sleep

Functions of sleep
- Biological theories of sleep and dreaming
- Psychological theories of dreaming
- Sleep deprivation

Sleep disorders

A printable version of this topic map is available from
www.pearsoned.co.uk/psychologyexpress

Introduction

The topics of sleep, dreaming and levels of awareness have been prominent areas of research and theorisation in philosophy and science for centuries. Indeed, these areas form significant components of research investigating the nature and scope of consciousness and have generated considerable research and debate (Belcher & Moorcroft, 2005; Carlson, 2004; Pinel, 2003). Sleep can be defined as a natural and potentially vital state which inevitably follows a period of wakefulness in healthy mammals, birds, reptiles, fish and amphibians. Sleep can also be defined as a series of transient states, meaning that the individual can rapidly switch from various stages of sleep to normal wakefulness unlike in other states of altered consciousness such as coma and unconsciousness (Belcher & Moorcroft, 2005; Espa, Ondze, Billiard & Bessett, 2000). This transition is usually easily observed and is signalled by a variety of physiological and behavioural indicators. Sleep can be characterised as a state in which normal wakefulness, awareness, responsiveness, consciousness, sensation and voluntary control of the body is no longer evident (Pace-Schott, Solms, Blagrove & Harnald 2003). Indeed, unlike in wakeful states an individual is less able to respond to mild or moderate stimuli but may still perceive more pronounced changes via the somatosensory system if in the stages of waking. It is this inability to interact with the environment around us while in a reduced state of consciousness which limits the chance of injury. However, it is important to remember that the brain and our physiology responses remain active (although often altered) throughout the stages of sleep and it is this activity which facilitates the ability to dream (Belcher & Moorcroft, 2005; Stickgold, 2005). Dreams can be defined as the perception of sensory information while sleeping although the mechanisms and processes which give rise to dreaming are still unascertained. It is also important to remember that sleep is characterised by a heightened anabolic state which promotes the recovery and growth of bodily systems, demonstrating its importance for development and maintenance of the body.

You may also be aware that sleep and dreaming have been studied from numerous perspectives in psychology, including from the biological, cognitive and psychodynamic perspectives. However, this chapter will primarily provide you with a summary of the main features of sleep, dreaming and awareness according to a biological perspective. It will be concerned with the physiological, anatomical and neurological aspects of these phenomena rather than non-biological factors. Furthermore, while the area has been investigated since the early days of psychology, this chapter will provide you with a contemporary summary of sleep and dreaming, not an historical overview. While early studies tended to investigate the effects of brain lesions on sleep and dreaming in laboratory animals, this technique is mostly redundant due to the more advanced techniques and measures used in human sleep laboratories and will not be discussed in detail (Pace-Schott et al., 2003). You should also remember that it would be impossible to incorporate all of the information on sleep and dreaming in one revision chapter and that the area is constantly evolving as new research and theories are established. As such, you should remember to direct your further reading to maintain a contemporary understanding.

> **→ Revision checklist**
>
> *Essential things to revise are:*
> - ❑ What the normal stages of sleep are
> - ❑ How several theories explain the functions and nature of sleep
> - ❑ What the biological correlates of sleep and wakefulness are
> - ❑ How abnormal sleep patterns or the presence of sleep disorders can influence an individual's ability to function

Assessment advice

Essay questions in the area of sleep and dreaming will typically ask you to discuss the validity and reliability of certain theories or methodologies, evaluate the insights into normal sleep and dreaming based on the study of sleep disorders, or critically evaluate the extent to which research in this area can contribute towards understanding consciousness. For essays like this you will need to demonstrate a broad understanding of the theories, techniques, research findings, strengths and limitations of this field of study. This will mean clearly defining all of the technical terms and theories that you mention in your essay, supporting all of your claims with evidence and critically evaluating the theories and research you incorporate. However, you should also remember that it has generated considerable amounts of literature and while your initial understanding may be based on older research you should make sure that you have an understanding of recent theoretical and methodological developments. Important points to remember include:

- Conduct a detailed literature review which is relevant to the question.
- Make sure you understand the literature and how it applies to the issues you are discussing. An essay plan will help you to organise your ideas.
- Take an evidence-based approach. This means supporting all of your claims and points with appropriate citations in text.
- Take a critical approach. This means that you must evaluate all of the theories and evidence and frame your argument accordingly. For example, does a certain study support your argument while most of the others refute it?
- Stay on topic. It is easy to get lost in your own narrative but you need to state explicitly how each section has answered the question.

- Stick to the conventions of your institution. Assignment time is not the time to try out new (and often incorrect) styles, formats or referencing.
- Draw conclusions. The ability to draw conclusions based on the evidence is often part of the marking critera.
- Proof-read your essay. Carelessness, errors and omissions will be detected by your marker and, depending upon your institution's guidelines, could reduce your mark. This is also a good practice to get into if you ever intend to submit work for publication.

Sample question

Could you answer this question? Below is a typical essay question that could arise on this topic.

 Sample question   *Essay*

To what extent can research and theorisation in biological psychology contribute towards our understanding of sleep and dreaming?

Guidelines on answering this question are included at the end of this chapter, whilst further guidance on tackling other exam questions can be found on the companion website at: **www.pearsoned.co.uk/psychologyexpress**.

Stages of awareness and sleep

In contemporary psychology the stages and nature of sleep are typically monitored, measured and manipulated using a combination of polysomnography (sleep recording) and observation within tightly controlled sleep laboratories. The measures taken include electroencephalogram (EEG) to monitor brain waves, electrooculogram (EOG) to assess eye movements and electromyogram (EMG) to monitor skeletal muscles. These measures allow us to identify, monitor and record the physiological correlates of sleep and have provided valuable insights concerning the nature and time-course of the sleep cycle. For example, sleep studies have informed us that there are variable levels of physiological activity which can differentiate several stages of sleep, each lasting around 90–110 minutes, and potentially serve different functions. There is a gradual decrease in muscle tone and heart rate as the stages of sleep progress, demonstrating that the individual becomes more relaxed the longer the transition continues. Furthermore, growth hormones are secreted during the first few hours of sleep, suggesting that there is recuperation and repair during sleep. If stages are skipped an individual can feel as though they have not slept. These stages will now be discussed in more detail to refresh your memory. They consist of:

- normal wakefulness
- non-REM sleep (stages 1–4 which includes slow-wave sleep)
- REM sleep (stage 5).

Key terms

Non-REM sleep: Constituting stages 1–4 of normal sleep which is not characterised by rapid eye movements.

Normal wakefulness: Full consciousness and engagement with the environment.

Polysomnography: The measurement of physiological activity during sleep.

REM sleep: Stage 5 of sleep characterised by rapid eye movement.

Normal wakefulness

Normal wakefulness refers to the conscious state we are in most of the time. In this state we can think, perceive, move, vocalise, problem solve and reason by conscious thought. It is characterised by two forms of EEG. These are called beta activity and alpha activity. The following sections and key terms box should refresh your understanding of these patterns of activity.

Stage 1 sleep

This is the initial stage observed as individuals begin to fall asleep. EEG indicates that brain activity gradually slows to a frequency of 3–7.5 Hz. This level of activation is referred to as theta waves. It is occasionally also called somnolence or drowsy sleep.

Stage 2 sleep

Stage 2 sleep is characterised by waves of activity at the same frequency as that observed during stage 1 sleep, but also features small bursts of faster activity and large spikes of activity. These are referred to as sleep spindles and K complexes respectively. There is a notable decrease in muscle activity and conscious experience of external stimuli. However, individuals are unlikely to realise that they have been asleep if they are disturbed during the first two stages of sleep.

Slow-wave sleep: stages 3 and 4

Stage 3 of sleep typically begins after 30 minutes of undisturbed sleep. This stage of sleep is characterised by fewer sleep spindles and K complexes and brain activity which is even slower. This can be less than 3 Hz and is termed delta activity. It typically has higher amplitude than the earlier stages of sleep.

However, stage 4 of sleep is difficult to differentiate from stage 3. The only notable change is that delta activity increases in amplitude. Both stages 3 and 4 can be combined under the term of slow-wave sleep. This stage typically lasts 30 minutes in the first cycle. Stage 4 sleep is typically only observed during the first few cycles of sleep.

It is important to remember that it is during slow-wave sleep that phenomena such as night terrors, sleep walking, somniloquy (sleep talking) and nocturnal enuresis (bed wetting) tend to occur if the transition to REM sleep is disturbed or the sleep pattern is unusual (Espa et al., 2000).

REM sleep

After stage 4 the sleep cycle returns to stage 1. However, at this point the muscles are relaxed to a much greater degree, preventing any voluntary movement. At the same time, heart rate, breathing and the activity of sympathetic nervous system all increase to the level usually observed during physical exertion. At this stage beta activity is also observed (Pinel, 2003), demonstrating that the brain appears to be actively processing information. This stage of sleep gains its name from the observable phenomenon of rapid eye movements in which the eyeball can be seen to move quickly despite eyes being closed. REM sleep is also distinct from the other stages of sleep in that it is the stage in which dreams are experienced. Indeed, EEG has revealed that the hippocampus which is involved in memory processes produces a theta of 4–7 Hz during REM sleep, suggesting that some form of memory retrieval or consolidation may occur during this stage of sleep (Belcher & Moorcroft, 2005; Stickgold, 2005). While individuals in REM sleep are often difficult to waken and will appear more disoriented than if woken from earlier stages of sleep, they remain receptive to personally salient information.

 Sample question   *Essay*

To what extent can biological activity differentiate between the various stages of sleep?

Key terms

Alpha activity: This is the pattern of brain activity observed when an individual is in a state of relaxation. It is observed while the eyes are closed, implying that the individual is also in a state of relative inactivity. This activity is considerably slower at 8–12 Hz and the levels of activity observed in the various areas of the brain is relatively synchronised.

Beta activity: A pattern of activity observed when actively engaging in mental activity characterised by 13–30 Hz. Activity is desynchronised in that areas of the brain vary in their levels and pattern of activity.

Delta activity: This is brain activity at less than 3 Hz but with higher amplitude than the earlier stages of sleep. Observed during stages 3 and 4 of sleep.

K complexes: Large spikes of activity initially observed during stage 2 sleep and declining in stage 3.

Sleep spindles: Bursts of faster activity initially observed during stage 2 sleep and declining in stage 3.

Slow-wave sleep: The combined stages 3 and 4 in which brain activity is less than 3 Hz.

Theta activity: This is brain activity observed during stage 1 sleep and is characterised by a frequency of 3–7.5 Hz.

Further reading	The stages of sleep
Topic	Key reading
General physiology	Belcher, P., & Moorcroft, W. H. (2005). *Understanding sleep and dreaming*. New York: Kluwer Academic/Plenum Publishers.
Advances	Pace-Schott, E., Solms, M., Blagrove, M., & Harnad, S. (Eds.) (2003). *Sleep and dreaming: Scientific advances and reconsiderations*. Cambridge: Cambridge University Press.
Sleep and memory	Stickgold, R. (2005). Sleep-dependent memory consolidation. *Nature, 437*, 1272–1278.

Test your knowledge

6.1 In which states are beta waves observed?

6.2 What type of activity is observed during states of relaxation when the eyes are closed?

6.3 What are the main characteristics of slow-wave sleep?

6.4 How is REM sleep different from slow-wave sleep?

6.5 When are sleep spindles and K complexes observed?

Answers to these questions can be found on the companion website at: www.pearsoned.co.uk/psychologyexpress

Biological correlates of sleep and dreaming

You will need to understand and be able to discuss some of the biological factors which may control or regulate sleep and dreaming. The following sections and 'Test your knowledge' questions should refresh your memory on these topics.

Biological mechanisms controlling the timing of sleep

The timing of sleep is controlled by an internal hypothetical mechanism known as the circadian clock, which regulates sleep–wake homeostasis, and zeitgebers, which reset this clock. This mechanism works in conjunction with the neurotransmitter adenosine, the hormone melatonin and temperature fluctuations to stimulate the feeling of tiredness and determine the ideal time for sleep. However, it is important to remember that in humans the amount and timing of sleep can also be controlled by the individual to some extent and it is subject to significant individual and group differences. For example, newborns tend to sleep the most while adults sleep the least.

Research has suggested that the regulation of circadian rhythms, including the sleep–wake cycle, may be mediated by the suprachiasmatic nucleus (SCN), raphe nucleus, pons and the locus coeruleus area of the reticular formation in the brain stem. This suggests that these regions may correspond with the location of the circadian clock. Indeed, Aston-Jones and Bloom (1981) observed increased activity of noradrenergic neurons in this region three seconds before animals awoke. However, you should also remember that the hypothalamus has been associated with regulating sleep–wake cycles (e.g. Saper, Scammell & Lu, 2005).

Key terms

Circadian clock: A hypothetical biological mechanism which is theorised to control sleep–waking patterns and the other biological prerequisites for sleep (such as temperature change, the release of growth hormones and the secretion of neurotransmitters).

Circadian rhythm: A behavioural or physiological process which changes daily according to a set pattern, such as the sleep–wake cycle.

Zeitgebers: Stimuli which can reset the circadian clock and circadian rhythms. These usually come in the form of changing light.

KEY STUDY

The suprachiasmatic nucleus and circadian rhythms

Silver, LeSauter, Tresco and Lehman (1996) identified that surgical removal of the SCN of hamsters eradicated their circadian rhythms, suggesting that this structure may be the locus of the circadian clock. Furthermore, when SCN tissue was transplanted into the hamsters' third ventricles using small semi-permeable capsules, the circadian rhythms recommenced. However, the notable issue with this finding is that while chemicals and nutrients could pass through the capsule to replenish the SCN tissue, the tissue itself was not able to establish synaptic connections to the surrounding tissue due to the nature of the capsules. This suggests that the SCN may control circadian rhythms through chemicals rather than electrical signals although the nature of these chemicals is yet to be determined.

Cerebral structures controlling drowsiness and slow-wave sleep

There are two main regions in the brain which appear to control slow-wave sleep. These are the basal forebrain and the nucleus of the solitary tract (Carlson, 2004). Researchers have known for a considerable amount of time that destroying the basal forebrain region produces insomnia, while electrical stimulation of this area promotes synchronisation of brain waves and drowsiness (Carlson, 2004; Pinel, 2003). As you will remember from the earlier sections, the synchronisation of brain waves across regions of the brain is an indication of relaxation. In contrast, stimulation of the nucleus of the solitary tract can also produce synchronised brain activity and observable sleepiness (Carlson, 2004; Pinel 2003). However, there are several limitations to this evidence:

- The majority of research in this area is outdated and the more advanced techniques we have today may present a different picture.
- The majority of the evidence concerning regions controlling sleepiness was conducted using laboratory animals, making it difficult to generalise findings to humans who appear to have a greater role in determining when they sleep.
- The evidence presented in support of biological mechanisms controlling slow-wave sleep actually examines drowsiness and tiredness rather than slow-wave sleep itself.

Brain regions controlling REM sleep

Research has demonstrated that the following regions may all play an active role in controlling REM sleep:

- **The locus coeruleus:** Exerts an inhibitory influence on REM sleep.
- **Raphe nucleus:** Exerts an inhibitory influence on REM sleep.
- **Pedunculopontine tegmental nucleus (PPT) of the pons:** Promotes REM sleep.
- **Laterodorsal tegmental nucleus (LDT) of the pons:** Promotes REM sleep.

However, it is important to remember that these influences are likely to be dependent upon the neurotransmitters released by these structures and research has demonstrated that acetylcholine and catecholamine neurotransmitters do indeed play a significant role in controlling REM sleep. For example, REM sleep and the phasic transitions appear to reflect the activity of these regions and the balance between these respective neurotransmitters (Aston-Jones & Bloom, 1981; Gottesmann, 2008; Shouse & Siegel, 1992; Silver et al., 1996). Medications which act as antagonists or agonists of these chemicals also produce the following effects. The following chemicals are secreted in these regions and significantly influence REM sleep:

- **Acetylcholine:** Released from the pons and stimulates REM sleep and brain synchronisation.
- **Serotonin:** Released from the raphe nucleus and inhibits REM sleep.
- **Nonepinephrine:** Released from the locus coeruleus and inhibits REM sleep.

The start of REM sleep is characterised by a decrease in serotonin and norepinephrine but also by an increase in acetylcholine.

 Sample question *Essay*

Critically discuss the evidence surrounding the biological correlates of sleep and dreaming.

Further reading The biological aspects of sleep

Topic	Key reading
Neurotransmitters	Gottesmann, C. (2008). Noradrenaline involvement in basic and higher integrated REM sleep processes. *Progress in Neurobiology*, *85*(3), 237–272.
Regulation	Moore, R. Y. (1997). Circadian rhythms: Basic neurobiology and clinical applications. *Annual Review of Medicine*, *48*, 253–266.
Hypothalamic control	Saper, C. B., Scammell, T., & Lu, J. (2005). Hypothalamic regulation of sleep and circadian rhythms. *Nature*, *437*, 1257–1263.

Test your knowledge

6.6 What are the main functions of the circadian clock?

6.7 Which regions of the brain may control drowsiness?

6.8 Which regions of the brain may control REM sleep?

6.9 What are the primary roles of neurotransmitters during sleep?

Answers to these questions can be found on the companion website at: www.pearsoned.co.uk/psychologyexpress

---

Functions of sleep

Several theories have been proposed to explain the functions of sleep and dreaming. To help you establish academic debates in your assignments and exams, those discussed in this text will enable you to revise the biological and psychological theories of sleep and dreaming.

Biological theories of sleep and dreaming

There are several theories concerning why living creatures need sleep and what functions it may serve (Carlson, 2004; Pinel, 2003). Indeed, as you should be aware, if sleep were not required for survival, researchers would have observed animals which do not require sleep or benefit from it, or suffer consequences when deprived of sleep. This is not the case, suggesting that sleep is of vital importance for wellbeing and survival of all animal species. Table 6.1 shows the main theories concerning the functions of sleep.

Table 6.1 **Biological theories concerning the functions of sleep**

Theory	Description
Evolutionary adaptation	The evolutionary or adaptive theories state that sleeping at night maximises the chance of survival due to incapacitating individuals during the darkest and most dangerous times of day when normal activities would be inhibited (Carlson, 2004; Pinel, 2003). The main limitations with this perspective include the redundancy of this in modern society where technology means we can be active during darker hours, and despite the drive to sleep, individuals are not passive in this process and can control when they sleep.
Restorative and reparative functions	The restorative theories of sleep state that sleep is needed to enable the repair of bodily structures, systems and functions. This includes the endocrine, central and peripheral nervous systems. For example, Zager, Anderson, Ruiz, Antunes and Tufik (2007) observed that sleep-deprived rats had 20 per cent fewer white blood cells than rats which had slept. This demonstrated a significant difference in the immune system but may have arisen due to stress rather than sleep deprivation per se. Growth hormones are released during sleep, promoting the restoration of bodily structures and functions. Neurotransmitters may also be replenished during REM sleep which is discussed in more detail in the final chapter. However, Horne (1978) reviewed over 50 sleep deprivation studies and observed that it does not appear to impair the ability to perform physical activities and does not produce a stress response. This is significant evidence against the restorative theories of sleep and dreaming.
Neurobiological functions	These theories state that sleep and dreaming serve the function of promoting and restoring cognitive functions such as the storage, integration, organisation and processing of information. For example, the reverse learning theory proposed that dreams function as a means of sorting the information encountered during the day and filtering out any information which is no longer needed. This would conserve storage (Crick & Mitchison, 1983). However, it is important to remember that dreams can be incoherent and meaningless. Another possibility is that sleep has a beneficial effect on working memory. For example, Turner, Drummond, Salamat and Brown (2007) also observed that performance on working memory tests showed a 38 per cent decline in individuals who were deprived of sleep compared to control subjects. However, you should remember that these effects may result from general tiredness rather than processes which occur during sleep.

However, it is important to remember that other theories have been presented concerning the functions of sleep and dreaming which you will need to consider in any essay on this topic. This is especially the case for the psychological theories of why we sleep and dream.

KEY STUDY

A sleep deprivation meta-analysis

Horne (1978) reviewed over 50 studies of sleep deprivation and observed that deprivation does not impair an individual's ability to perform physical exercise and it does not result in a stress response. This is counterintuitive to the restorative theories of sleep. However, Horne (1978) did identify a trend for sleep-deprived individuals to display impaired cognitive functions (such as perception and attention) and also hallucinations. This may suggest that sleep serves the function of allowing the brain to rest, recuperate and facilitate the processing of information.

 Sample question   *Essay*

Critically evaluate the evolutionary perspective of sleep and dreaming

Psychological theories of dreaming

Several attempts have been made to explain the functions of dreaming, although most are considerably dated (Carlson, 2004; Crick & Mitchison, 1983; Freud, 1953; Pinel, 2003; Webb & Cartwright, 1978). These have primarily been proposed in psychodynamic and cognitive schools of thought and will provide useful comparisons to those presented by biological psychology. You should ensure that you are at least aware of these alternative accounts and remember that the individual does not exist in a vacuum. Hence, there are likely to be both biological and psychological influences on sleep and dreaming.

- **Sigmund Freud's 'Theory of Dreaming':** Freud proposed that dreams reflect the 'wish fulfilment' of repressed thoughts and desires, so were able to give us access to our own unconscious thoughts and feelings (Freud, 1953). For example, you should remember that he differentiated between the manifest content of a dream which is the actual content and a latent content which is the real meaning hidden inside the symbolism the dream. There is very little research which supports this perspective and Freudian theory has been highly criticised for its subjectivity, preoccupation with sexual references and unreliable methodologies. You should also ensure you know the alternative views provided by Jung.

- **The 'Problem Solving Theory of Dreaming':** Webb and Cartwright (1978) suggested that dreaming may serve the function of enabling problem solving through creating unusual situations or analogues in our dreams which allow us to think more flexibly and solve difficult problems. Indeed, they observed that if participants slept undisturbed after they were exposed to a problem, they were significantly better at solving the problem when they woke than those whose sleep was interrupted.

- **Learning theories:** Like the neurobiological theories of sleep and dreaming, these theories also state that dreaming facilitates the functions of the cognitive system. These theories may or may not incorporate biological factors. For example, Winson (2002) argued that new information is cross-referenced with existing information through dreams to improve cognition and survival strategies. The limitations of these perspectives include that you cannot guarantee learning did not occur prior to sleep or that sleep and/or dreaming were the cause for change in ability.

? **Sample question**   *Essay*

Compare and contrast biological and non-biological theories concerning the functions of sleep and dreaming.

Further reading The functions of sleep

Topic	Key reading
Working memory	Turner, T. H., Drummond, S. P. A., Salamat J. S., & Brown G. G. (2007). Effects of 42-hour sleep deprivation on component processes of verbal working memory. *Neuropsychology, 21*, 787–795.
Immune system	Zager, A., Anderson, M. L., Ruiz, F. S., Antunes, I. B., & Tufik, S. (2007). Effects of acute and chronic sleep loss on immune modulation of rats. *Regulatory, Integrative and Comparative Psychology, 293*, 504–509.

Test your knowledge

6.10 According to evolutionary theory, what are the functions of sleep?

6.11 Which theories attempt to clarify the biological functions of sleep?

6.12 How do neurobiological theories explain sleep and dreaming?

6.13 How do restorative theories explain sleep and dreaming?

6.14 How do non-biological theories explain sleep and dreaming?

Answers to these questions can be found on the companion website at: www.pearsoned.co.uk/psychologyexpress

Sleep deprivation

There are several different ways in which an individual may become sleep deprived in the absence of a sleep disorder. These include intentional deprivation in laboratory or similar settings, jet lag and unsociable work patterns (Belcher & Moorcroft, 2005). The effects of sleep deprivation are still open to debate and you should remember that hundreds of studies have been conducted in this area with variable results.

Induced sleep deprivation

Researchers often attempt to study the patterns of sleep and sleep deprivation in controlled laboratory settings where they are able to monitor an individual and intervene if necessary (Gallo & Eastman, 1993; Gulevich, Dement & Johnson, 1966; Horne, 1978; Pilcher & Huffcutt, 1996). These studies can deprive participants of one or all stages of sleep to assess the implications for normal performance. These studies can be with humans or laboratory animals and you should be careful when attempting to generalise the findings of one type of study to other groups. You should also remember that a significant number of these studies are considerably dated so, while their general conclusions may be insightful, the measures obtained may be different with current technologies. As demonstrated in the Key Study box below, several individuals have chosen to deprive themselves of sleep for other reasons and scientific insights occurred serendipitously.

KEY STUDY

Sleep debt

Gulevich et al. (1966) reported a study of a boy who stayed awake for 264 hours to obtain a place in the *Guinness Book of Records*. Despite this significant sleep deprivation, the boy only needed to sleep for almost 15 hours the following night before waking and feeling rested. He slept just over ten hours the subsequent night and nine hours on the third night demonstrating that 67 hours of lost sleep were never recovered. However, what was most interesting about this pattern of sleep was that the percentage of hours recovered was not equal across all of the stages of sleep. There was also evidence for the 'REM rebound' in which more time is spent in REM sleep than earlier stages of sleep after deprivation:

- 7 per cent of stage 1–2 sleep
- 68 per cent of slow-wave sleep
- 53 per cent of REM sleep.

While the boy did not appear to suffer long-term consequences of sleep deprivation, he did experience slurred speech, visual impairment and mild paranoia during his time awake. However, you should remember that there are significant individual differences in how a person responds to sleep deprivation and there have been reported cases in which individuals have experienced delusions, hallucinations, severe cognitive impairment and other psychological difficulties (Belcher & Moorcroft, 2005; Pace-Schott et al., 2003).

In regards to research with laboratory animals, several studies have identified that prolonged sleep deprivation appears to result in sickness, muscle weakness, disinterest, poor co-ordination, inability to regulate body temperature, high metabolism and finally death within 33 days (Rechschaffen & Bergmann, 1995; Rechschaffen, Gilliland, Bergmann & Winter, 1983; Rechschaffen, Bergmann, Everson, Kushida & Gilliland 1989). However, as a psychology student you should also remember that animals are put under high degrees of stress in experiments where they are kept awake indefinitely and this stress may in itself result in illness or death if prolonged. You should also be thinking of the ethical issues which arise when conducting this type of research.

Shift work

Individuals who work shifts may suffer several psychological impairments including in their abilities to concentrate and perform tasks correctly (Gallo & Eastman, 1993; Nicholson & D'Auria, 1999; Sack & Lewy, 1997). In severe cases shift-work sleep disorder can also develop, which is characterised by insomnia and excessive drowsiness if shifts are repeatedly scheduled during normal sleeping times. Even when rotating shifts, altering the circadian rhythm is difficult to do without eliciting consequences on the shift worker's health (Gallo & Eastman, 1993; Nicholson & D'Auria, 1999; Sack & Lewy 1997). You should also remember that the pattern of shift work is important if the timetable rotates. For example, it is easier for the employee to do an early then a late shift than if they do a late shift followed by an early one.

 Sample question　　　　　　*Problem-based learning*

You have been asked to provide advice to a company which is considering changing their employees' working hours to a shift pattern. What advice would you provide to maximise the employees' work output and wellbeing?

Jet lag

Jet lag is a problem which arises when flying long distances into a different time zone which displaces the circadian clock, resulting in tiredness and the drive to sleep at what would be the normal time in the original time zone (Cho, Ennaceur, Cole & Suh, 2000; Reilly, Atkinson & Waterhouse, 1997). The circadian clock normally runs at 25 hours (rather than 24 hours) meaning that it is easier to stay awake past the normal time we sleep than to wake up at what feels like an earlier time. This can result in symptoms of sleep deprivation when travelling long distances in an eastern direction but few detrimental effects when travelling in a western direction. Cho et al. (2000) also observed that chronic jet lag (as experienced by cabin crew) can result in cognitive deficits.

> **? Sample question**   Essay
>
> Critically discuss the claim that sleep deprivation can seriously impair the ability to function normally.

Further reading Sleep deprivation

Topic	Key reading
Shift work	Nicholson, P. J., & D'Auria, D. A. (1999). Shift work, health, the working time regulations and health assessments. *Occupational Medicine, 49*(3), 127–137.
Sleep deprivation meta-analysis	Pilcher, J. J., & Huffcutt, A. I. (1996). Effects of sleep deprivation on performance: A meta-analysis. *Sleep, 19*(4), 318–326.
Jet lag and ability	Reilly, T., Atkinson, G., & Waterhouse, J. (1997). Travel fatigue and jet-lag. *Journal of Sports Sciences, 15*(3), 365–369.
Shift work	Sack, R. L. & Lewy, A. J. (1997). Melatonin as a chronobiotic: Treatment of circadian desynchrony in night workers and the blind. *Journal of Biological Rhythms, 12*(6), 595–603

Sleep disorders

There are numerous forms of sleep disorders and a selection of these is presented in Table 6.2 to direct your revision. It is important to remember that sleep disorders form a broad category which includes all abnormal patterns of sleep-related behaviour. You should be able to clearly differentiate and discuss each of these conditions with reference to examples from the literature. Definitions for these conditions can also be found in the Glossary at the end of this book.

> **? Sample question**   Essay
>
> To what extent does the study of sleep disorders inform the understanding of the normal mechanisms, processes and functions of sleep?

Table 6.2 Common sleep disorders

Condition	Description
Insomnia	This condition is characterised by the difficulty in falling asleep or only sleeping for brief intervals of time. However, you should remember that there are a substantial number of individual differences in regards to the time and quality of sleep experienced by all individuals. Insomnia is typically treated with medication, including valium and librium. Other techniques include relaxation, meditation, diet changes and alterations to the evening routine.
Sleep apnoea	Sleep apnoea refers to the condition in which individuals temporarily cease breathing while asleep. The individual is awoken due to the building levels of carbon dioxide in the bloodstream but quite often will not know this has happened. The condition may be caused by the malfunction of the central nervous system or obstruction of the airways.
Narcolepsy	Narcolepsy refers to the condition in which individuals are unable to control their sleep pattern, suffer from excessive daytime sleepiness (EDS), fall asleep at inappropriate times or in inappropriate places and enter REM sleep after only ten minutes. As such it is a distressing and highly visible condition which can impair normal daily functioning. Individuals with narcolepsy tend to present with other sleep disorders including hypnagogic hallucinations in the transition between sleeping and waking.
Cataplexy	Cataplexy refers to the sudden loss of muscle tone which can be anything from slight paralysis of a body part to complete collapse. The cause of this condition is believed to result from highly emotional states and treatment usually takes the form of mood stabilisers.
Parasomnias	Parasomnias include sleep walking, night terrors and bruxism (each of which are discussed in more detail below).
Somnambulism (sleep walking)	Sleep walking is a common phenomenon in which individuals are able to unconsciously interact with their environment for a short interval of time while sleeping. The activity tends to reflect tasks which would be performed while awake but episodes manifest during slow-wave sleep so does not reflect dream states.
Pavor nocturnus (night terrors)	Night terrors refer to another condition which arises during slow-wave sleep and is characterised by extreme fear, gasping and often screaming. It is also important to remember that when an individual experiencing a night terror wakes they are rarely in a fully conscious state and can become physically aggressive towards the imagined object of their fear. Sometimes the individual automatically goes back to sleep without any conscious recollection of the experience. The causes of this condition are still open to debate although possible causes include malfunction of the sleep–wake cycle regulatory mechanisms, genetic predisposition, emotional distress, tiredness or impaired cognition.
Bruxism	Bruxism is a condition in which individuals grind their teeth and clench their jaw while asleep, potentially resulting in a sore jaw, damaged teeth and headaches.

Sleep paralysis	Sleep paralysis is the condition in which the muscle atonia which normally occurs during REM sleep actually occurs when going to sleep (hypnagogic) or waking up (hypnopompic). It can cause states of extreme panic, and in severe cases it can occur in conjunction with terrifying hallucinations. However, while it is important to remember that most individuals will experience this at some point in their lives, others experience it much more frequently.
Nocturia	Nocturia refers to frequent waking due to the need to urinate, which can result in sleep deprivation. This condition is caused by drinking too much or due to certain medical conditions.
Enuresis	Enuresis refers to persistent bedwetting. However, it does not refer to childhood bedwetting which is often the result of inexperience in interpreting physiological cues or inability to wake at appropriate times. In primary enuresis, bedwetting has not stopped since childhood, while in secondary enuresis the condition arises after a long period of dryness. Possible causes of secondary enuresis include emotional distress, while primary enuresis may arise due to a lack of nocturnal anti-diuretic hormone or bladder problems.

Further reading Sleep disorders

Topic	Key reading
Sleep walking	Harris, M., & Grunstein, R. R. (2009). Treatments for somnambulism in adults: Assessing the evidence. *Sleep Medicine Reviews*, *13*(4), 295–297.
Narcolepsy	Kanbayashi, T., Nakamura, M., Shimizu, T., & Nishino, S. (2010). Symptomatic narcolepsy or hypersomnia, with or without hypocretin (Orexin) deficiency. *Narcolepsy*, *2*, 135–165.
Pavor nocturnus	Nguyen, B. H., Pérusse, D., Paquet, J., Petit, D., Boivin, M., Tremblay, R. E., & Montplaisir, J. (2008). Sleep terrors in children: A prospective study of twins. *Pediatrics*, *122*(6), 1164–1167.
Sleep disorders in childhood	Petit, D., Touchette, E., Tremblay R. E., Boivin, M., & Montplaisir, J. (2007). Dyssomnias and parasomnias in early childhood. *Pediatrics*, *119*(5), 1016–1025.

Chapter summary – pulling it all together

→ Can you tick all the points from the revision checklist at the beginning of this chapter?

→ Attempt the sample question from the beginning of this chapter using the answer guidelines below.

→ Go to the companion website at www.pearsoned.co.uk/psychologyexpress to access more revision support online, including interactive quizzes, flashcards, You be the marker exercises as well as answer guidance for the Test your knowledge and Sample questions from this chapter.

Answer guidelines

 Sample question   *Essay*

To what extent can research and theorisation in biological psychology contribute towards our understanding of sleep and dreaming?

Approaching the question

This question is asking you to evaluate the extent to which biological theories and research techniques have informed our understanding of sleep and dreaming. As such, it will require that you discuss and critique the theories concerning biological factors which determine, regulate or arise due to sleep and dreaming. It will also require that you evaluate the evidence presented in support and opposition of these theories.

Important points to include

Your essay should begin by summarising the main features of sleep and dreaming including the respective stages and how these are assessed. It should also briefly outline the course of your argument including which theories and evidence you are going to evaluate. You should subsequently describe and evaluate the theories concerning the biological aspects of sleep and dreaming, drawing on a range of suitable evidence and critical evaluation. It is important to remember that the question asks 'to what extent', meaning that you can establish an academic debate by highlighting evidence which has contributed towards our understanding while also stating when studies have confused the understanding of sleep and dreaming. Your essay should finally draw conclusions which are directly related to the question.

Make your answer stand out

To make an essay stand out in the topic of the biological aspects of sleep and dreaming you need to demonstrate that you have considered a range of biological and non-biological perspectives. This will demonstrate to your marker that you have considered the evidence with reference to the broader literature and that you understand the multiple factors which may influence sleep and dreaming.

Explore the accompanying website at www.pearsoned.co.uk/psychologyexpress
→ Prepare more effectively for exams and assignments using the answer guidelines for questions from this chapter.
→ Test your knowledge using multiple choice questions and flashcards.
→ Improve your essay skills by exploring the You be the marker exercises.

Notes

7

Biological aspects of emotion

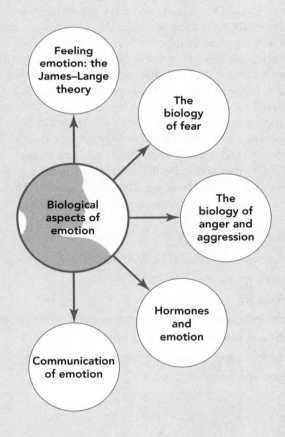

A printable version of this topic map is available from
www.pearsoned.co.uk/psychologyexpress

Introduction

This chapter will aid your revision of the biological factors associated with emotional experiences and expressions. You should already remember that emotion can be defined as a positive or negative feeling in response to an internal or external stimulus which is characterised by physiological changes and species-typical behaviour (Carlson, 2004; Pinel, 2003). There are also three distinct and interacting components of emotion which will be discussed in this chapter. These are the behavioural, autonomic and hormonal aspects of emotional states. In particular, this chapter focuses on the biological factors associated with states such as fear and anger. These are the most studied emotional states in biological psychology because they can be clearly differentiated from baseline measures and have the clearest evolutionary origins (Carlson, 2004; Pinel, 2003). In contrast, positive emotions are considerably harder to define and measure as they are less pronounced, and these states tend to be studied in other areas such as social psychology. This chapter also reviews the biological factors associated with the expression of emotions and revisits the theme of hormonal influences on behaviour which were previously covered in Chapter 3. You should also remember that the content of Chapters 1–3 is also relevant to this topic because emotion relies heavily on the CNS, PNS, endocrine system and approaches in biological psychology. More extreme, maladaptive states are considered in Chapter 9. However, again you should remember that cognition, social influences and individual differences exert significant influences on the experience and expression of emotion and you should read around the topic to acquire a comprehensive understanding of emotion.

> ### → *Revision checklist*
>
> *Essential points to revise are:*
> - ❏ What emotions are
> - ❏ What the physiological processes associated with emotion are
> - ❏ Which cerebral structures facilitate or respond to emotion
> - ❏ How emotion has been assessed in biological psychology
> - ❏ How emotions are communicated

Key terms

Emotion: A positive or negative feeling in response to an internal or external stimulus which is characterised by physiological changes and species-typical behaviour.

Assessment advice

Essay questions on the topic of emotion will usually ask you to compare, contrast and evaluate two different approaches to studying emotion or to evaluate theoretical perspectives. This may include discussions of neuropsychology, physiological psychology, cognitive neuroscience, pharmacology, cognitive psychology, social psychology and the James–Lange theory. This means that you will need to acquire a broad understanding of the topic. Most essays will also expect you to discuss how these approaches or theories explain two or more emotional states using examples from the literature. For example, you would need to discuss whether one approach explains more about an emotional state than others, whether each approach provides a complementary level of analysis or contradicts another and whether there are significant methodological issues with any of the approaches. It is also vital that you adopt a critical and evidence-based view which reviews all of the approaches and evidence included in your response. Remember that your essays should also have an 'hour-glassed' structure. This means that the essay should start as a broad introduction which narrows down to the specific issues and points in the middle of the essay and then builds on your argument until you reach your conclusion.

Sample question

Could you answer this question? Below is a typical essay question that could arise on this topic.

 Sample question   **Essay**

Compare and contrast two biological approaches to studying human emotion.

Guidelines on answering this question are included at the end of this chapter, whilst further guidance on tackling other exam questions can be found on the companion website at: www.pearsoned.co.uk/psychologyexpress

Feeling emotion: the James–Lange theory

Proponents of the widely endorsed James–Lange theory of emotion argue that emotional behaviour and physiological responses are directly elicited by situations and that 'feelings' are the result of feedback from these behavioural and physiological responses (Carlson, 2004; D'Hondt et al., 2010; Mauss & Robinson, 2009; Oatley, Keltner & Jenkins, 2006; Russell, 2003). This means that according to this theory, individuals are self-observers who base their emotional states on behavioural and physiological cues rather than the alternative view that emotional states cause behavioural and physiological changes (Carlson, 2004; Oatley et al., 2006). This may be difficult to understand, but if you consider the number of times you have found yourself to be happy, sad, angry, stressed or anxious without knowing the cause you may be able to appreciate this perspective. You may have also found yourself crying in a situation where you cannot understand why you have been affected although your mood may have consequently changed (Carlson, 2004). Interestingly, the physiological feedback from facial expressions does appear to alter the activity of the autonomic nervous system (Carlson, 2004; Oatley et al., 2006). The following Key Study will help you to understand this phenomenon.

KEY STUDY

Physiological responses to behavioural cues

You will probably be aware that Levenson, Ekman and Friesen (1990) provided participants with step-by-step instructions on how to perform a facial expression without informing them of the expression they would eventually be expressing. They discovered that these artificial expressions produced the expected activity in the autonomic nervous system even though mood was not altered. This means that despite participants not being in states such as anxiety, happiness, fear or sadness, unknowingly displaying the facial expression appeared to produce physiological responses associated with the emotional state (Carlson, 2004; D'Hondt et al., 2010; Lewis, 2011; Russell, 2003).

Therefore, based on these findings and consistent with the James–Lange theory, physiological feedback from the behavioural components of emotion did appear to inform emotional states. However, it is vital that you consider both sides of this argument and it is equally possible that causation works in the opposite direction or that both are possible (Carlson, 2004; Oatley et al., 2006; Pinel, 2003). For example, the participants may have guessed which expression they were meant to portray and induced a suitable, temporary mood-state to help them to express this emotion. They may have already been in the mood-state and there is nothing to say that the components of emotion have causal rather than correlational effects (Oatley et al., 2006; Mauss & Robinson, 2009; Russell, 2003). It is also significant that this is based on anecdotal evidence and artificial laboratory experiments. Performance may be different in more naturalistic settings.

Key term

James–Lange theory: A theory in which emotional behaviour and physiological responses are directly elicited by situations and that 'feelings' are the result of feedback from these behavioural and physiological responses.

Sample question Essay

To what extent is the James–Lange theory supported by research in biological psychology?

Further reading Feeling emotion

Topic	Key reading
Psychophysiology of emotion	Critchley, H. D. (2009). Psychophysiology of neural, cognitive and affective integration: fMRI and autonomic indicants. *International Journal of Psychophysiology, 73*(2), 88–94.
Mind–body links in emotion	D'Hondt, F., Lassonde, M., Collignon, O., Dubarry, A., Robert, M., Rigoulot, S., Honoré, J., Lepore, F., & Sequeira, H. (2010). Early brain–body impact of emotional arousal. *Human Neuroscience, 4,* 1–10.
Introduction to emotion	Oatley, K., Keltner, D. and Jenkins, J. M. (2006). *Understanding emotions* (2nd ed.). Malden, MA: Blackwell.

Test your knowledge

7.1 What are the three components of emotion?

7.2 Which components produce feedback according to the James–Lange theory?

7.3 What produces emotions according to the James–Lange theory?

7.4 How do artificial facial expressions of emotion influence the ANS?

Answers to these questions can be found on the companion website at: www.pearsoned.co.uk/psychologyexpress

---

The biology of fear

Fear is experienced in response to threatening and dangerous situations and stimuli in which the stress response of 'fight-or-flight' (discussed previously) would usually be beneficial for survival (Carlson, 2004; Pinel, 2003). It is characterised by action readiness, increased heart rate, palpitations, fast breathing and hypervigilance among other experiences. This should also remind you that the negative emotions of fear, anxiety, stress and anger are closely linked and often co-occur making these processes transferable (Oatley et al., 2006; Pinel, 2003). However, several physiological responses associated with fear were covered in more detail in the discussion of the sympathetic and parasympathetic divisions of the peripheral nervous system in Chapter 2. To refresh your memory of the complete system and these physiological responses, consult Figure 2.3 in Chapter 2. This section will primarily discuss the cerebral structures associated with the fear response to expand your revision of this topic.

You will probably already be aware that the amygdala is one of the most significant cerebral structures in the fear response and shows significantly increased levels of activation in response to threat (Carlson, 2004; Phelps et al., 2001). This structure has also been associated with the perception of pain and the processing of potentially harmful stimuli, demonstrating its importance for fight-or-flight and survival (Carlson, 2004; Phelps et al., 2001; Pinel, 2003). However, the amygdala can be divided into several regions which serve different functions and pathways during the fear response (Carlson, 2004; Pinel, 2003). Firstly, the medial nucleus receives sensory information and relays these signals to the medial basal forebrain and the hypothalamus. Secondly, the lateral nucleus receives sensory information from the neocortex, thalamus and hippocampus and projects these signals to the basal, accessory basal and central nucleus regions. Finally, the central nucleus receives information from various regions and transmits these signals to numerous cerebral regions including the hypothalamus, midbrain, pons and medulla. The central nucleus and associated structures are vital for the expression of all three components of emotion (behavioural, autonomic and hormonal). If the central nucleus is damaged, animals (including humans) are no longer able to show the fear or startle responses, they tend to behave tamely and in the case of humans do not show the usual effects of emotion on memory such as the formation of emotionally driven flashbulb memories and mood-state dependent memory (Carlson, 2004). However, while they show lower levels of stress they are also more likely to be harmed by their environment through lack of fear (Carlson, 2004; Pinel, 2003). In contrast, if the central nucleus is electrically stimulated, animals show fear, aggression, arousal and agitation, making them more confrontational and more likely to both harm and be harmed by others in the environment (Carlson, 2004). This demonstrates the importance of the balance in this structure for facilitating survival.

However, you should remember that the amygdala transmits signals to several other regions of the brain which are also associated with the fear response. These include:

- **Lateral hypothalamus:** Involved in the activation of the sympathetic nervous system. Increases heart rate, blood pressure and paleness.

- **Dorsal motor nucleus of the vagus:** Involved in the activation of the parasympathetic nervous system. Associated with the formation of ulcers, urination and defecations.

- **Parabrachial nucleus:** Increases respiration.

- **Ventral tegmental area:** Involved in the regulation and release of dopamine and promotes behavioural arousal.

- **Locus coeruleus:** Involved in regulation and release of norepinephrine and promotes vigilance.

- **Dorsal lateral tegmental nucleus:** Involved in the regulation and release of acetylcholine and cortical activation.
- **Nucleus reticular ponis caudalis:** Involved in the augmented startle response.
- **Periaqueductal grey matter:** Involved in behavioural arrest (freezing).
- **Trigeminal facial motor nucleus:** Involved in the facial expression of fear.
- **Paraventricular nucleus:** Involved in the regulation and release of ACTH and glucocorticoid.
- **Nucleus basalis:** Involved in cortical activation.

This should remind you that the fear response is a complex emotion which relies heavily on the central and peripheral nervous system in addition to a range of neurotransmitters (Chan et al., 2011; Phelps et al., 2001; Sotres-Bayon & Quirk, 2011). The amygdala also has an unusually high concentration of benzodiazepine receptors and the central nucleus in particular has a high concentration of opiate receptors (Carlson, 2004; Pinel, 2003). This suggests that anti-anxiety medications exert their influence here by blocking these receptors and preventing the initiation of the fear response (Carlson, 2004).

 Sample question   *Essay*

Critically discuss the insights into fear which have been provided by biological psychology.

Further reading The biology of fear

Topic	Key reading
Prefrontal cortex mediation	Chan, T., Kyere, K., Davis, B. R., Shemyakin, A., Kabitzke, P. A., Shair, H. N., Barr, G. A., & Wiedenmayer, C. P. (2011). The role of the medial prefrontal cortex in innate fear regulation in infants, juveniles and adolescents. *The Journal of Neuroscience, 31*(13), 4991–4999.
Behaviourism approach	Kindt, M., Soeter, M., & Vervliet, B. (2009). Beyond extinction: Erasing human fear responses and preventing the return of fear. *Nature Neuroscience, 12*(3), 256–258.
Prefrontal cortex mediation	Sotres-Bayon, F. & Quirk, G. (2011). Prefrontal control of fear: More than just extinction. *Current Opinions in Neurobiology, 20*(2), 231–235.

Test your knowledge

7.5 Which area of the amygdala relays signals to the basal medial forebrain?

7.6 Which area of the amygdala relays signals to the thalamus and hippocampus?

7.7 What functions are served by the lateral hypothalamus in the fear response?

7.8 Which types of receptors have unusually high concentrations in the amygdala?

Answers to these questions can be found on the companion website at:
www.pearsoned.co.uk/psychologyexpress

The biology of anger and aggression

Anger and aggression are observed in nearly every animal species and appear to have neural, physiological and genetic mediators (Carver & Harmon-Jones, 2009; Huer & Kravitz, 2010; Potegal, Stemmler & Spielberger, 2010). Anger can also occur in conjunction with fear and anxiety but exists as an emotional state in its own right (Carver & Harmon-Jones, 2009). However, the expression of anger and aggression is species-typical and may consist of threat behaviours, defensive behaviours and submissive behaviours (Carlson, 2004). Typically, threatening displays outweigh actual attacks and some form of agreement is reached prior to physical violence. Some species also show predation in which stalking and aggression are exhibited towards members of another species. However, this is the means of acquiring food and is usually a product of necessity rather than a display of anger (Carlson, 2004; Potegal et al., 2010).

You should remember that the physical expression of anger and aggression appears to be restricted by the biological constraints of the species, their neural circuits, the hypothalamus, amygdala and by the overall limbic system which receives sensory information (Huer & Kravitz, 2010; Potegal et al., 2010). For example, predatory and defensive behaviours can be induced through the stimulation of the periaqueductal grey matter, amygdala and hypothalamus (Carlson, 2004; Pinel, 2003). It is also significant that increasing the activity of serotonergic synapses of rats inhibits anger and aggression, while damaging the serotonergic axons in their brains elicits anger and aggression (Carlson, 2004; Vergnes, Depaulis, Boehrer & Kempf 1988). Similar effects of serotonin have also been observed in species, even to the extent of predicting their survival (Bouwknecht et al., 2001; Carlson, 2004).

For example, animals with high levels of serotonin tend to be less aggressive and less confrontational meaning that they are more likely to survive (Carlson, 2004; Pinel, 2003). However, you should already be thinking critically and be considering whether these findings can be generalised to humans who live in potentially more constrained societies. Interestingly, this is a false assumption and serotonin does appear to mediate human anger and aggression in a similar way to that of other animals (Bouwknecht et al., 2001; Carlson, 2004; Carver & Harmon-Jones, 2009; Huber & Kravitz, 2010; Pinel, 2003; Potegal et al., 2010). You will already know that increasing serotonin levels through the use of agonists such as Prozac reduces irritability, aggression, impulsive behaviours, anxiety and depression (Carlson, 2004; Oatley et al., 2006; Pinel, 2003). This suggests that serotonin serves a significant inhibitory effect for anger and aggression in most species.

However, most of us are able to control how we express anger in most situations because we are also guided by social norms, morality, cognition, reason and signals from other cerebral structures. Most importantly, the recognition of the emotional significance of situations, regulation of emotional expression, rationality and control of arousal are some of the main functions of the prefrontal cortex (Anderson, Bechara, Damasio, Tranel & Damasio, 1999; Carlson, 2004; Pinel, 2003; Potegal et al., 2010). The orbitofrontal cortex in particular receives information from the dorsal medial thalamus, temporal cortex, ventral tegmental area and amygdala. This structure acts as an interface between automatic emotional responses and the control of more complex behaviours so is able to regulate emotional expression (Carlson, 2004; Huber & Kravitz, 2010; Pinel, 2003; Potegal et al., 2010). In addition, lesions or deficits in the prefrontal cortex can result in poor moral judgement, insensitivity to consequences of one's own actions, anti-social behaviour and aggression (Anderson et al., 1999; Carlson, 2004; Pinel, 2003; Raine et al., 2002).

 Sample question   *Essay*

To what extent are the experience and expression of anger dependent upon biological factors?

Further reading The biology of anger and aggression

Topic	Key reading
Anger, anxiety and fear	Carver, C. S. & Harmon-Jones, E. (2009). Anger is an approach-related affect: Evidence and implications. *Psychological Bulletin, 135*(2), 183–204.
Aggression	Huber, R. & Kravitz, E. A. (2010). Aggression: Towards an integration of gene, brain and behaviour. In T. Székely, A. J Moore, and J. Komdeur (eds.). *Social Behaviour: Genes, Ecology and Evolution* (pp.165–180). New York: Cambridge University Press.
Anger	Potegal, M., Stemmler, G., & Spielberger, C. (Eds.) (2010). *International handbook of anger: Constituent and concomitant biological, psychological and social processes.* New York: Springer.
Prefrontal cortex	Raine, A., Meloy, J. R., Bihrle, S., Stoddard, J., LeCasse, L., & Colletti, P. (2002). Reduced prefrontal gray matter volume and reduced autonomic activity in antisocial personality disorder. *Archives in General Psychiatry, 57*(2), 119–127.

Test your knowledge

7.9 How does serotonin relate to the level of anger and aggression?

7.10 What is the role of the prefrontal cortex in anger and aggression?

7.11 What are species-typical behaviours?

7.12 What would a low level of serotonin produce?

7.13 What can lesions to the prefrontal cortex produce?

Answers to these questions can be found on the companion website at: www.pearsoned.co.uk/psychologyexpress

Hormones and emotion

The effects of hormones on behaviour were discussed in more detail in Chapter 3 and you can refresh your memory of this topic by re-reading this chapter. Most importantly, you should remember that there are few established arguments for causal effects of hormones in human emotional behaviour and experience (Carlson, 2004; Oatley et al., 2006). In addition, you should remember that most of the research surrounding hormonal influences on behaviour and experience has been conducted with non-human animals and has been primarily concerned with aggression and physiological stress (covered in Chapter 9) in laboratory conditions, making it difficult to generalise these results to humans. Nevertheless, you should remember that fear, stress and anxiety are often experienced at the same time and stress hormones are able to alter neural structures which are associated with emotion (Rodrigues, LeDoux & Sapolsky,

2009). This can make people more susceptible to these emotions as the neural circuits become sensitive to lower thresholds through repeated activation (Carlson, 2004; Pinel, 2003).

In regards to anger and aggression, it is interesting that androgens are released prenatally but then decline until puberty when the levels of these hormones significantly increase. It is also in this period that increased irritability, anger, sadness, anxiety and aggression are often observed in most species including humans (Carlson, 2004; Oatley et al., 2006; Pinel, 2003). Early exposure to androgens also has a lasting effect in that it configures neural pathways to be more responsive to testosterone which facilitates aggression in most species (Carlson, 2004; Pinel, 2003). In regards to humans, you will already be aware that boys tend to be more assertive and aggressive than girls. As aggression in every other species is mediated by androgens it would be parsimonious to assume that hormones also influence human anger and aggression (Carlson, 2004; Oatley et al., 2006; Pinel, 2003; Potegal et al., 2010).

However, you should keep in mind that socialisation and the adoption of gender roles is likely to play a large role in determining the expression of emotion in humans (Carlson, 2004; Pinel, 2003; Potegal et al., 2010). It is also difficult to assess the effects of hormones on human emotional experience and expression because it would be unethical to alter levels of hormones for any significant amount of time and studies would not be able to isolate the effects of hormones from those of other factors, meaning that cause and effect could not be inferred.

? Sample question   *Essay*

Using your broader understanding of biological psychology, critically discuss the claim that hormones do not predispose the experience and expression of emotion in humans.

Further reading The effects of hormones on behaviour and experience

Topic	Key reading
Hormones in interactions	Adkins-Regan, E. (2009). Under the influence of hormones. *Science*, 324(5931), 1145–1146.
Stress	Ranabir, S. & Reetu, K. (2011). Stress and hormones. *Indian Journal of Endocrinology and Metabolism, 15*(1), 18–22.
Stress, fear and hormones	Rodrigues, S. M., LeDoux, J. E., & Sapolsky, R. M. (2009). The influence of stress hormones on fear circuitry. *Annual Review of Neuroscience, 32*(1), 289–313.
Stress	Yehuda, R. (2001). Biology of posttraumatic stress disorder. *Journal of Clinical Psychiatry, 62*(17), 41–46.

7.14 What role do androgens serve in emotion in non-human animals?

7.15 How do androgens alter neural pathways?

7.16 Why is it difficult to assess the effects of hormones on human emotional experience?

7.17 Can an individual experience several emotions at the same time?

Answers to these questions can be found on the companion website at: www.pearsoned.co.uk/psychologyexpress

Communication of emotion

The expression of emotion is one of the most common human behaviours and, although it is often unconscious and unintentional, some aspects of emotional expression can be produced voluntarily. For examples, humans express emotion through facial expressions, touch, gestures and language (Carlson, 2004; Hertenstein, Holmes, McCullough & Keltner, 2009; Lewis, 2011). Other animals are also able to communicate their emotions using pheromones, which were discussed previously. You may already know that the expression of emotion may have served evolutionary functions of promoting closeness through love, affection and happiness and promoting survival through anger, aggression and fear (Carlson, 2004; Pinel, 2003). Several findings appear to support this claim:

- Infants actively seek, observe and imitate emotional expressions of those around them from very shortly after birth (Carlson, 2004; Pinel, 2003).
- Matsumoto and Willingham (2009) have observed spontaneous emotional facial expression in blind individuals despite the lack of visual cues for the behaviours (Carlson, 2004; Oatley et al., 2006).
- The communication and recognition of core emotional expressions appears to be consistent across cultures despite different cultural exposure, although there are variations in the display rules for which emotions are socially acceptable in a culture (Carlson, 2004; Oatley et al., 2006).

This suggests that the motivation to seek, learn and communicate emotion may be pre-programmed into the human genome and supports Darwin's theory that emotional expressions are innate, evolved, unlearnt and complex gestures (Carlson, 2004; Oatley et al., 2006; Pinel, 2003). However, it also demonstrates how these predispositions can be mediated by cognitive and social motivations (Oatley et al., 2006).

In biological terms, the right hemisphere is more dominant in the expression and recognition of emotions and this includes both visual and auditory cues (Carlson, 2004). For example, Blonder, Bowers and Heilman (1991) observed that lesions to the right hemisphere impair the recognition of emotional expressions and gestures but do not impair emotional decisions. However, the correct functioning of the somatosensory cortex is also required for the recognition and identification of facial expressions, while the amygdala is involved in the recognition of threatening and fearful expressions (Carlson, 2004; N'Diaye, Sander & Vuilleumier, 2009; Oatley et al., 2006; Pinel, 2003). This demonstrates how several regions of the brain mediate our ability to identify and understand facial expressions and emotional gestures.

It may help you to understand the biological prerequisites of emotional expression if you remember that it is exceptionally difficult to fake emotions in a manner which appears to be genuine (Carlson, 2004; Pinel, 2003). For example, a genuine smile which arises due to happiness also includes the muscles around the eyes, while an artificial smile cannot recreate this (Carlson, 2004; Oatley et al., 2006). Interestingly, volitional facial paralysis is a medical condition which arises due to damage to the facial region of the primary motor cortex or associated nerve fibres. Individuals with this condition are unable to voluntarily move their facial muscles to express an emotion but they are able to express genuine facial expressions (Carlson, 2004; Pinel, 2003). In contrast, damage to the insular region of the prefrontal cortex, white matter of the frontal lobe or parts of the thalamus can impair the ability to express genuine emotions while patients remain able to voluntarily move their facial muscles to form artificial expressions (Carlson, 2004; Pinel, 2003). This demonstrates how different genuine and artificial expressions are and how important the central and peripheral nervous systems are in our ability to express emotions.

? Sample question   Essay

Critically discuss the claim that the communication of emotion is innate and relies purely on biological factors.

Further reading The communication of emotion

Topic	Key reading
Touch	Hertenstein, M. J., Holmes, R., McCullough, M., & Keltner, D. (2009). The communication of emotion via touch. *Emotion*, 9(4), 566–573.
States and expressions	Lewis, M. (2011). Inside and outside: The relation between emotional states and expressions. *Emotion Review*, 3(2), 189–196.
Facial expressions	Matsumoto, D. & Willingham, B. (2009). Spontaneous facial expressions of emotion of congenitally and noncongenitally blind individuals. *Journal of Personality and Social Psychology*, 96(1), 1–10.
The amygdala	N'Diaye, K., Sander, D., & Vuilleumier, P. (2009). Self-relevance processing in the human amygdala: Gaze direction, facial expression, and emotional intensity. *Emotion*, 9(6), 798–806.

Test your knowledge

7.18 How can emotions be communicated?

7.19 How did Darwin believe emotional expressions originated?

7.20 What insights into the communication of emotion have been provided by cross-cultural studies?

7.21 Which hemisphere is more influential in the recognition of emotion?

Answers to these questions can be found on the companion website at:
www.pearsoned.co.uk/psychologyexpress

Chapter summary – pulling it all together

→ Can you tick all the points from the revision checklist at the beginning of this chapter?

→ Attempt the sample question from the beginning of this chapter using the answer guidelines below.

→ Go to the companion website at www.pearsoned.co.uk/psychologyexpress to access more revision support online, including interactive quizzes, flashcards, You be the marker exercises as well as answer guidance for the Test your knowledge and Sample questions from this chapter.

Answer guidelines

 Sample question   *Essay*

Compare and contrast two biological approaches to studying human emotion.

Approaching the question

This question is asking you to apply your understanding of human emotion and two different approaches in biological psychology to discuss how these approaches present similar or different interpretations. This can include any of the approaches described in Chapter 1 and any emotional state. You will also need to critically evaluate these perspectives.

Important points to include

Your response to the question should begin with a brief introduction which informs the marker of the emotional states and approaches you will discuss, compare, contrast and evaluate in your essay. You will also need to define these and provide an indication of how you will answer the question. The main section of your essay should apply the two approaches you have chosen to discuss the emotional states, drawing heavily on examples and insights provided by these perspectives in the literature. You should also remember to establish a balance between description and evaluation. For example, you cannot only describe the approaches and their techniques; you must also compare, contrast and evaluate them. This may mean identifying where one approach provides a better insight, if there are methodological limitations and whether the two approaches can be combined to enhance the understanding of human emotion. Your essay should end with a clear, coherent and evidence-based conclusion which summarises your response to the question and highlights your main points.

Make your answer stand out

To make an answer stand out on this topic you need to demonstrate that you have a broad understanding of approaches and research in psychology and that you are able to synthesise this information into a coherent academic debate. This means that you will need to incorporate a wide variety of evidence from appropriate sources and critically evaluate the information, approaches, techniques and theories you include in your response.

Explore the accompanying website at www.pearsoned.co.uk/psychologyexpress
→ Prepare more effectively for exams and assignments using the answer guidelines for questions from this chapter.
→ Test your knowledge using multiple choice questions and flashcards.
→ Improve your essay skills by exploring the You be the marker exercises.

Notes

Notes

The biology of learning and memory

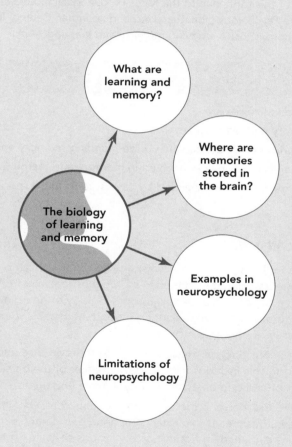

- What are learning and memory?
- Where are memories stored in the brain?
- The biology of learning and memory
- Examples in neuropsychology
- Limitations of neuropsychology

A printable version of this topic map is available from
www.pearsoned.co.uk/psychologyexpress

Introduction

This chapter will aid your revision of the theories and biological aspects of learning and memory. It will discuss some of the insights which have been gained from approaches such as neuropsychology, neuroscience and physiological psychology. You should already have a good understanding of these approaches from previous chapters. More specifically, it will allow you to revise some of the biological structures and mechanisms which facilitate, contribute towards or arise during normal and impaired learning and memory processes. However, as you will already be aware, there are strong interdisciplinary links with topics such as cognitive psychology. This chapter is directed towards providing a review of the more applied aspects of this topic due to the focus on biological factors and you should consult *Cognitive Psychology* (Jonathan Ling and Jonathan Catling) in this series for alternative approaches to studying memory and learning.

→ *Revision checklist*

Essential points to revise are:
❑ What memory and learning are
❑ Which theories contribute towards understanding memory and learning
❑ Which biological factors are involved in memory and learning
❑ What insights have been provided by case studies and experiments

Assessment advice

Essay questions in this area will usually ask you to discuss which biological factors have been associated with human memory or to evaluate the contributions of an approach such as neuropsychology or neuroimaging towards an understanding of memory and learning. Important aspects to remember when writing essays in this area include:

● Provide a clear introduction which summarises the evidence and arguments you will discuss. This includes informing the marker of the perspective you intend to adopt and demonstrating that you have understood the question.

● Summarise the theories and the evidence in a coherent, well-informed and critical manner. This means explicitly comparing and contrasting perspectives and alternative evidence and drawing conclusions concerning the validity and reliability of these factors.

● Your essay should demonstrate a balance between description and evaluation. It is not enough to only include descriptions of research and theories while not evaluating these influences. At the same time, it is not enough to write critically while neglecting the details of the research and theories.

- Your essays should be evidence-based and directed towards individuals with no knowledge of the subject. You will need to define any technical terms, techniques, equipment or structures you discuss in your essays.

- Draw conclusions based on your review of the evidence. Conclusions should follow the argument you have adopted in your essay and should never stand alone from or contradict the rest of the essay.

Sample question

Could you answer this question? Below is a typical essay question that could arise on this topic.

 Sample question   *Essay*

To what extent have case studies in neuropsychology contributed towards the understanding of human learning and memory?

Guidelines on answering this question are included at the end of this chapter, whilst further guidance on tackling other exam questions can be found on the companion website at: www.pearsoned.co.uk/psychologyexpress

What are learning and memory?

You should already know that learning refers to how experiences of the world change the structure and activity of neural networks within the brain (Carlson, 2004). In contrast, memory refers to how these changes are stored and how the information is subsequently reactivated during the retrieval of memories (Henke, 2010). However, it is important for you to know that memory can also be subdivided in several different ways. These terms are defined in the Glossary and include:

- **Short-term memory:** Information which is held in consciousness for a brief amount of time, usually through immediate and continuous rehearsal (Baddeley, Eysenck & Anderson, 2009). This includes iconic memory and echoic memory.

- **Long-term memory:** Information which is stored in the brain for a long period of time and retrieved at a later date despite lacking continuing rehearsal in the interval between encoding, storage and retrieval (Baddeley et al., 2009). These memories can be elaborated over time as new information is encountered and processed.

- **Implicit/procedural memory:** Knowledge which is not easily vocalised; this includes procedural knowledge such as how to ride a bike and most information which is not declarative (Henke, 2010; Voss & Paller, 2008).

- **Explicit/declarative memory:** Knowledge which is easily vocalised, including knowledge about oneself and the world. Includes semantic, autobiographical and episodic memory (Henke, 2010; Voss & Paller, 2008).
- **Semantic memory:** Knowledge about categories, objects, concepts and meanings (Baddeley et al., 2009).
- **Autobiographical memory:** Memory for events, experiences and personal information from one's own life (Carlson, 2004).
- **Episodic memory:** Memory for specific events, including times, places and emotions experienced during the event.
- **Prospective memory:** Remembering to perform a planned action at the intended time (Einstein & McDaniels, 2005).
- **Working memory:** Manipulation and use of information in short-term memory (Baddeley, 2007; Smith, 2000).

Key terms

Echoic memory: Short-term memory for information in the auditory field.

Iconic memory: Short-term memory for information in the visual field.

Learning: Learning is concerned with the process in which our experiences of the environment change the pattern and structure of activation in brain.

Memory: How the changes in the brain experienced during learning are stored and subsequently reactivated during the retrieval of information. Memory has been subdivided into various forms including autobiographical, semantic, episodic, implicit, explicit and prospective memory.

 Sample question   *Essay*

To what extent is procedural knowledge different from declarative knowledge?

The processes involved in memory are encoding, storage, retrieval, rehearsal, long-term potentiation and consolidation (Baddeley et al., 2009).

- **Encoding:** How information is converted into physiological signals which change the connections and pattern of activation in the brain.
- **Storage:** How information is stored in the brain as connections between neural networks and their respective patterns of activation.
- **Retrieval:** The reactivation of neural networks and the information contained within them.
- **Rehearsal:** A process which can result in the transition of a memory from a short-term to a long-term memory. Maintenance rehearsal is when individuals rehearse the original information and elaborative rehearsal is when the individual adds to the existing memory.

- **Long-term potentiation:** When pre- and post-synaptic neurons are activated simultaneously upon exposure to a stimulus (Carlson, 2004; Wixted, 2004). This enhances the transmission of both action potentials and neurotransmitters, facilitating learning by altering the connections between neurons and lowering their activation thresholds.

- **Consolidation:** The physiological process by which a memory becomes gradually more resilient to forgetting and interference with time, repeated activation of neurons, rehearsal and entrenchment in the brain (Wixted, 2004).

Further reading The distinctions of memory

Topic	Key reading
Working memory	Baddeley, A. D. (2007). *Working memory, thought and action.* Oxford: Oxford University Press.
Memory	Baddeley, A. D., Eysenck, M., & Anderson, M. C. (2009). *Memory.* Hove: Psychology Press.
Hippocampus and associative learning	Henke, K. (2010). A model for memory systems based on processing modes rather than consciousness. *Nature Reviews Neuroscience, 11,* 523–532.
Implicit and explicit memory	Voss, J. L., & Paller, K. A. (2008). Brain substrates of implicit and explicit memory: The importance of concurrently acquired neural signals of both memory types. *Neuropsychologia, 46*(13), 3021–3029.

Test your knowledge

8.1 Which type of memory is concerned with categories and meanings?

8.2 What types of knowledge are included in explicit memory?

8.3 How do semantic and episodic memories differ?

8.4 What are consolidation and rehearsal?

Answers to these questions can be found on the companion website at: www.pearsoned.co.uk/psychologyexpress

Where are memories stored in the brain?

It is generally agreed in biological psychology that memories are stored diffusely in the cerebral structures which were involved in their acquisition (Baddeley et al., 2009; Carlson, 2004; Pinel, 2003). You should remember from the earlier chapters that different areas of the brain are believed to specialise in the processing of different types of information. Therefore, it stands to reason that different types of memories would be stored in the neural pathways of different areas of the brain. However, you should always remember that this doesn't discount the possibility that other areas of the brain are also involved in these forms of processing (Cohen, Johnstone & Plunkett, 2002). The following bullet points should refresh your memory concerning some of the areas which have been associated with certain forms of memory:

- **Hippocampus:** Associative memory and knowledge concerning the relationship between objects and places (Henke, 2010).
- **Rhinal cortex:** Object recognition memory (Carlson, 2004; Pinel, 2003).
- **Inferotemporal cortex:** The secondary sensory cortex located in this area has been associated with the storage and processing of sensory memories, while the broader inferotemporal cortex is associated with visual perception of objects and the storage of visual patterns (Naya, Yoshida & Miyashita, 2001).
- **Amygdala:** Associated with the encoding and storage of emotional memories and startle responses (Carlson, 2004).
- **Prefrontal cortex:** Associated with procedural knowledge, working memory and remembering the sequences of events (Smith, 2000).
- **Cerebellum:** Associated with the processing and storage of implicit memories and sensorimotor skills (Salmon & Butters, 1995).
- **Striatum:** Associated with habit learning and the processing and storage of memories concerning the relationship between stimuli and responses (Carlson, 2004; Pinel, 2003; Salmon & Butters, 1995).

However, it is also important for you to understand how memories are stored in these areas. The simple answer is through the processes which have already been discussed. Long-term potentiation results in lasting changes to the efficacy of synaptic transmission, facilitating memory formation and changing the neural pathways of the structures involved in their acquisition (Carlson, 2004; Pinel, 2003; Salmon & Butters, 1995; Smith, 2000). This means that memories would not be stored as unified, abstract packages of information; instead they are the product of various neurons firing at the same time and are stored diffusely in these connections (Baddeley et al., 2009; Carlson, 2004; Pinel, 2003). It is also important to remember that the neurotransmitter glutamate and the corresponding N-methyl-D-aspartate (NMDA) receptors significantly contribute towards learning and memory (Carlson, 2004; Pinel, 2003). This is the main excitatory system in the brain and the NMDA receptors respond maximally when these two events occur simultaneously. Two events form the basis of learning and typically require high-frequency and high-intensity stimulation as observed during intentional learning:

- Glutamate binds to the NMDA receptors.
- The postsynaptic neuron is already partially depolarised (activated) triggering action potentials and calcium ions which are required for long-term potentiation.

Sample question *Essay*

Critically evaluate the claim that memories are stored diffusely in the cerebral structures which were involved in their acquisition.

Further reading The physical location of memories

Topic	Key reading
Inferotemporal cortex	Naya, Y., Yoshida, M., and Miyashita, Y. (2001). Backward spreading of memory-retrieval signals in the primate temporal cortex. *Science*, 291(5504), 661–664.
Working memory	Smith, E. E. (2000). Neural basis of human working memory. *Current Directions in Psychological Science*, 9(1), 45–49.

Test your knowledge

8.5 Which types of memories are associated with the amygdala?

8.6 Which types of memories are associated with the prefrontal cortex?

8.7 What types of information may be stored in the inferotemporal cortex?

8.8 How might the hippocampus be involved in the storage of memories?

8.9 What are the differences between the information stored in the cerebellum and striatum?

Answers to these questions can be found on the companion website at: www.pearsoned.co.uk/psychologyexpress

Examples in neuropsychology

Some of the most prominent and far-reaching contributions towards understanding the biological basis of learning and memory have been provided by studies of anterograde and retrograde amnesia in neuropsychology (Carlson, 2004; Cohen et al., 2002; Pinel, 2003). Anterograde amnesia refers to the inability to learn and remember information encountered after brain damage, while retrograde amnesia refers to the inability to retrieve memories which were acquired before brain damage. This section will refresh your memory concerning some of the case studies and examples of memory deficits and will provide an overview of some of the limitations of this approach.

Key terms

Anterograde amnesia: Inability to learn and remember information encountered after brain damage.

Retrograde amnesia: Inability to retrieve memories which were acquired before brain damage.

Patient H.M.

You will probably already know that the multitudes of studies which have assessed patient H.M. have arguably provided the most extensive insights into the biological basis of memory and learning (Baddeley et al., 2009; Pinel, 2003). H.M. was an intelligent adult who suffered from severe epilepsy with seizures originating from both temporal lobes. As a result, doctors performed a bilateral medial temporal lobotomy in which most of the hippocampus, amygdala and adjacent cortex were removed to reduce the number and severity of seizures. He initially adjusted well after the surgery, with his intelligence quotient increasing from 104 to 118, presumably due to the reduction of seizures. H.M.'s memory for events prior to his surgery was relatively intact but he suffered severe anterograde amnesia. For example, if he met someone who subsequently left the room, he could not remember this person when they returned and would not be able to remember what they had been doing. More specifically, H.M. was unable to form explicit long-term memories, demonstrating deficits in the ability to consolidate information. Table 8.1 summarises H.M.'s performance on several tasks and demonstrates that while he was able to hold a small amount of information in short-term memory, any distraction, longer interval of time or exposure to larger amount of information resulted in H.M. being unable to recall the information.

Table 8.1 H.M.'s impairments according to experimental task

Task	Performance
Digit span +1	This tests short-term memory and requires that participants recite a gradually increasing list of digits. While most people's performance improves, H.M. was unable to recall eight digits even after 25 trials. This suggests that H.M. was unable to hold information in short-term memory or that he was unable to consolidate the information to form long-term memories.
Block tapping	This tests memory span and requires participants to copy the experimenter who indicates a sequence of blocks. H.M. was able to learn the sequence of five blocks but was unable to learn the sequence of six, even after 12 attempts. This suggests that H.M. was unable to hold information in short-term memory or that he was unable to consolidate the information to form long-term memories.

Mirror drawing	This is a test of implicit knowledge and requires that participants learn how to trace an image over the course of several days. H.M.'s performance improved despite the fact that he couldn't remember ever doing the task before, suggesting that sensorimotor skills were intact despite a lack of declarative knowledge.
Rotary pursuit	This is also a test of implicit memory in which participants must learn to maintain contact between a stylus and a moving target. H.M.'s performance improved, despite the fact that he couldn't remember ever doing the task before, suggesting that sensorimotor skills were intact despite a lack of declarative knowledge.
Incomplete picture	In this task participants must complete a drawing in which contours have been removed. Again, H.M.'s performance improved even though he wasn't aware that he had seen the task before.
Conditioned fear response	H.M. was able to learn a conditioned blink response, which is another form of implicit knowledge. However, this response took longer to learn than it does with healthy control subjects.

Clive Wearing

Clive Wearing experienced total amnesia after contracting Herpes Simplex Encephalitis. Clive suffered both severe anterograde amnesia and severe retrograde amnesia, which significantly impaired his ability to function (Campbell & Conway, 1995). While he experienced islands of memories, these tended to lack detail and were often incomplete, although his procedural knowledge was relatively intact. As such, he was only able to process information in his immediate consciousness and kept a minute-to-minute diary. He also suffered mood swings due to the emotional turmoil and confusion caused by the amnesia. Several documentaries have been made about Clive Wearing and these are freely available on websites such as YouTube if you wish to see the extent of his amnesia.

Patient A.C.

Patient A.C. experienced a series of strokes which resulted in severely impaired perceptual object knowledge while non-perceptual knowledge remained relatively intact (Coltheart, 2001; Coltheart et al., 1998). For example, A.C. was able to describe any attribute of a stimuli except its visual properties. This demonstrates how selective memory impairment can actually be.

Patient K.F.

Patient K.F. suffered damage to his left parieto-occipital region in a motorcycle accident. While K.F.'s short-term memory was severely impaired, his long-term memory remained largely unaffected. More specifically, his impairments were primarily to his auditory–verbal short-term memory in that he was unable to repeat sequences of digits read to him by experimenters (Shallice & Warrington, 1970).

Sample question Essay

How have studies of patients such as H.M. contributed towards understanding human memory?

Korsakoff's patients

Patients with Korsakoff's syndrome demonstrate sensory deficits, motor problems, confusion, amnesia, personality changes and have an increased risk of death from liver, gastrointestinal or heart disease due to alcoholism (Carlson, 2004; Pinel, 2003). Post-mortems reveal lesions to the medial diencephalon (medial thalamus and medial hypothalamus), neocortex, mammalian bodies and cerebellum. While amnesia is initially anterograde, as the condition progresses patients also develop retrograde amnesia.

 Sample question *Problem-based learning*

You have been asked to present a summary of the risks of alcoholism on memory. What type of information would you include in your report and how would you present this information in a suitable format? Prepare a short summary of your report including some of the evidence you would include.

Alzheimer's disease

Alzheimer's disease is initially characterised by a mild deterioration of memory but progresses to dementia where all cognitive functions are impaired and quality of life is significantly diminished. There are extensive changes in the brain including the development of amyloid plaques and neurofibrillary tangles (Haass, 1999). There is also evidence of atrophy in which the brain significantly reduces in size and mass (Haass, 1999).

Key terms

Alzheimer's disease: A medical condition which is associated with amyloid plaques and neurofibrillary tangles in the brain. It is initially characterised by a mild deterioration of memory but progresses to dementia where all cognitive functions are impaired and quality of life is significantly diminished.

Korsakoff's syndrome: A medical condition produced through alcoholism in which patients demonstrate sensory deficits, motor problems, confusion, amnesia and personality changes. Patients also have an increased risk of death from liver, gastrointestinal or heart disease.

Concussion

Following a blunt force trauma to the head, individuals sometimes experience retrograde amnesia for events just before the incident and anterograde amnesia for a period afterwards (Carlson, 2004; Pinel, 2003). However, the duration and extent of these deficits are dependent upon the extent of the injury. While most cases of retrograde amnesia are resolved with time, people rarely recover memories for things which occurred just before the trauma.

Electroconvulsive shock

Patients who undergo electroconvulsive shock (ECS) for conditions such as obsessive compulsive disorder and major depression experience a degree of retrograde amnesia and a period of confusion following the treatment. Most interestingly, ECS appears to be a useful technique for investigating the time required for memory consolidation in that longer gradients of retrograde amnesia would suggest that memory consolidation is a longitudinal process. This appears to be the case, suggesting that memories become gradually more resilient to damage and interference (Nadel & Moscovitch, 1997; Pinel, 2003).

Medial temporal amnesia

As you will remember from the discussion of patient H.M., damage to the medial temporal area can result in severe anterograde amnesia, but this pattern of impairment is not all-encompassing and there are types of knowledge which can still be acquired. Several studies with laboratory animals have demonstrated that bilateral surgical removal of the hippocampus and rhinal cortex can severely impair object recognition memory. For example, rats demonstrate severe deficits on the delayed non-matching-to-sample task (see Critical Focus box below) after damage to the hippocampus which has been linked to memory for relationships between objects (Mumby, Pinel & Wood, 1989).

CRITICAL FOCUS

The Mumby box

The Mumby box was developed by Mumby et al., (1989) in an attempt to test rats' ability to perform a delayed non-matching-to-sample task after lesions to the hippocampus. Rats were used because the location of their hippocampus means that only a small section of the parietal neocortex would also be damaged during the aspiration (suction) of this area, whereas in other animals the rhinal cortex would also be damaged.

During the experiment, a rat is placed in the middle of a box partitioned into three sections. One of the sliding doors is lifted to reveal a sample object which hides a food source. A trained, intact rat will run to the object and push it aside to obtain the food. The rat returns to the middle section while the first door is closed and the second door is lifted. The rat finds an object identical to the sample and a new object at the end of this section. However, the rat must learn to differentiate these objects and go to the new object to find the food.

Rats which have damage to the hippocampus are unable to learn the relationship between the sample, new object and food source. However, you should remember that human brain damage is rarely as isolated as this and generalisation is difficult across species.

Spatial memory

You should already know that lesions to the hippocampus have a detrimental effect on memory for spatial locations and that there are specialised 'place cells' in the hippocampus which are only activated when in certain locations (Carlson, 2004; Wilson & McNaughton, 1993). This suggests that this structure may mediate spatial memory. Indeed, Maguire, Frith, Burgess, Donnett & O'Keefe (1998) identified that activation of the right hippocampal region was associated with knowing where places were and navigating towards them. Furthermore, Maguire et al. (2000) identified that after 20 years' service, London taxi drivers had significantly more posterior hippocampal grey matter than usual. However, it is important to remember that these changes may give rise to better spatial memory or result from these differences in memory, making it difficult to draw conclusive arguments concerning the role of the hippocampus in spatial memory. The current general consensus is that the rhinal cortex is associated with object recognition while the hippocampus is associated with memories concerning the spatial relationship between them (Henke, 2010).

 Sample question Essay

Critically evaluate two or more theories concerning the role of the hippocampus in memory for spatial locations.

Further reading Neuropsychology and memory deficits

Topic	Key reading
Benzodiazepines and amnesia	Baracochea, D. (2006). Anterograde and retrograde effects of benzodiazepines on memory. *The Scientific World Journal*, 6, 1460–1465.
Case studies	Campbell, R., & Conway, M. (Eds.). (1995). *Broken memories: Case studies in memory impairment*. Oxford: Blackwell.
Alzheimer's disease	Haass, C. (1999). Biology of Alzheimer's disease. *European Archives of Psychiatry and Clinical Neuroscience, 249*(6), 265.
Spatial memory	Maguire, E. A., Burgess, N., Donnett, J. G., Frackowiak, R. S. J., Frith, C. D., & O'Keefe, L. (2000). Knowing where and getting there: A human navigation network. *Science, 280*, 291–924.
Memory consolidation	Nadel, L., Moscovitch, M. (1997). Memory consolidation, retrograde amnesia and the hippocampal complex. *Current Opinions in Neurobiology, 7*, 217–227.

Test your knowledge

8.10 H.M.'s performance may have been intact for which tasks?

8.11 What tests can be used in neuropsychology to assess specific impairments?

8.12 Medial temporal lobectomy impairs performance on what task?

8.13 What are the limitations of case studies in neuropsychology?

8.14 Which substance is in short supply in the brains of patients with Alzheimer's?

Answers to these questions can be found on the companion website at:
www.pearsoned.co.uk/psychologyexpress

Limitations of neuropsychology

While there are numerous significant insights provided by neuropsychology into meaning and memory, you should also be aware of the challenges and limitations encountered with this approach:

- It is difficult to generalise findings which were gained from individual case studies to other populations and situations (Bear, Connors & Paradiso, 2007; Cohen et al., 2002; Crawford & Garthwaite, 2002; Gazzaniga, 2003). Neuropsychology attempts to identify how systems would normally operate by studying what happens when they are impaired.

- Baseline measures are not obtained prior to brain damage. It is impossible to say whether the pattern of impairment is due to brain damage, normal idiosyncratic behaviours or new compensating strategies (Cohen et al., 2002).

- Neuropsychology assumes that the brain can be organised into isolated modules which function independently. However, the brain is highly interconnected and deficits seen in one area may not be restricted to this region and may not have even originated in that location (Carlson, 2004). Deficits may be due to the severing of a pathway rather than damage to a specific region.

- Brain damage is rarely restricted to one location; the damage is usually widespread, making it difficult to link impairments with a specific region (Cohen et al., 2002).

- One of the main assumptions of neuropsychology is that certain regions serve specific functions; however this ignores the issues of plasticity in that neural functions and pathways can be altered to negotiate deficits in one region. You should be aware that performance may reflect attempts to reorganise systems and functions rather than the actual brain damage per se (Cohen et al., 2002; Holdstock et al., 2008).

● Neuropsychology also marginalises the role of individual differences in determining the degree of impairment and recovery (Holdstock et al., 2008). Indeed, how the individual responds to the trauma plays a significant role in determining their subsequent behaviour and their motivation to recover.

Further reading Spatial memory	
Topic	Key reading
Neuropsychology	Cohen, G., Johnstone, R. A., & Plunkett, K. (Eds.) (2002). *Exploring cognition: Damaged brains and neural networks – Readings in cognitive neuropsychology and connectionist modelling.* Hove: Psychology Press.
Case studies	Crawford, J. R., & Garthwaite, P. H. (2002). Investigation of the single case in neuropsychology: Confidence limits on the abnormality of test scores and test score differences. *Neuropsychology, 40*(8), 1196–1208.
Differential effects of lesions	Holdstock, J. S., Parslow, D. M., Morris, R. G., Fleminger, S., Abrahams, S., Denby, C., Montaldi, D., & Mayes, A. R. (2008). Two case studies illustrating how relatively selective hippocampal lesions in humans can have quite different effects on memory. *Hippocampus, 18*, 679–691.

Chapter summary – pulling it all together

→ Can you tick all the points from the revision checklist at the beginning of this chapter?

→ Attempt the sample question from the beginning of this chapter using the answer guidelines below.

→ Go to the companion website at www.pearsoned.co.uk/psychologyexpress to access more revision support online, including interactive quizzes, flashcards, You be the marker exercises as well as answer guidance for the Test your knowledge and Sample questions from this chapter.

Answer guidelines

 Sample question   *Essay*

To what extent have case studies in neuropsychology contributed towards the understanding of human learning and memory?

Approaching the question

This question is asking you to evaluate the methodologies, insights, strengths and limitations of evidence provided by studies of individuals with brain damage or other cognitive impairments.

Important points to include

Your essay should begin with a clear and concise summary of the arguments, evidence and interpretations you will discuss in your response to the question. Important things to consider include:

- A description of what neuropsychology is, including its assumptions, methodologies and participants. This should especially highlight the use of multiple methods in case studies, including experiments, observations, interviews and neuroimaging.
- Insights provided by specific case studies such as patient H.M. These should evaluate the extent to which the findings from these studies have expanded the understanding of memory processes and structures.
- Whether valuable insights have been provided by other biological or non-biological approaches to studying learning and memory.
- The strengths of neuropsychology, including that it takes an indepth look at rare cases, employs a variety of methods, provides valuable insights and has an applied focus on understanding and rehabilitation.
- The weaknesses of neuropsychology, including issues surrounding generalisability, modularity, reductionism, specialism of function, the lack of baseline measures, plasticity and reorganisation of function, problems with interpretation and ethics.
- Your conclusions concerning the validity and reliability of the evidence provided by neuropsychology.

Make your answer stand out

To make an answer stand out in this area you need to demonstrate that you have an understanding of the broader aspects of learning and memory which span across both biological and non-biological approaches and also across clinical and non-clinical samples. This will mean that you will need to be able to synthesise and critically evaluate a range of evidence while explicitly linking this to the essay question. For example, how can research with neurologically damaged patients correspond to research with healthy control subjects? You will also need to demonstrate that you are aware of (and understand) the theoretical and practical challenges directed towards neuropsychology.

Explore the accompanying website at www.pearsoned.co.uk/psychologyexpress

→ Prepare more effectively for exams and assignments using the answer guidelines for questions from this chapter.
→ Test your knowledge using multiple choice questions and flashcards.
→ Improve your essay skills by exploring the You be the marker exercises.

Notes

9

Biological basis of psychological abnormality

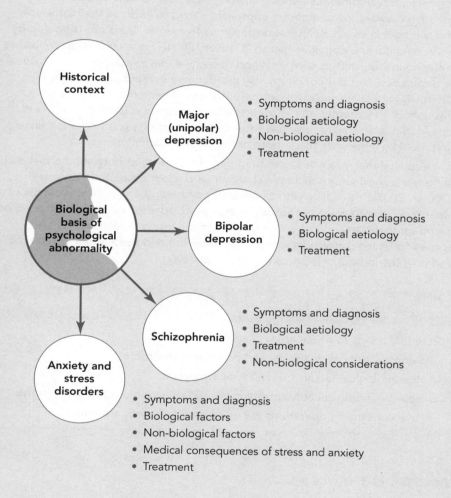

- **Historical context**

- **Major (unipolar) depression**
  - Symptoms and diagnosis
  - Biological aetiology
  - Non-biological aetiology
  - Treatment

- **Biological basis of psychological abnormality**

- **Bipolar depression**
  - Symptoms and diagnosis
  - Biological aetiology
  - Treatment

- **Schizophrenia**
  - Symptoms and diagnosis
  - Biological aetiology
  - Treatment
  - Non-biological considerations

- **Anxiety and stress disorders**
  - Symptoms and diagnosis
  - Biological factors
  - Non-biological factors
  - Medical consequences of stress and anxiety
  - Treatment

A printable version of this topic map is available from
www.pearsoned.co.uk/psychologyexpress

Introduction

Abnormality is one of the most studied areas in psychology and attracts many students to the specialism of clinical and counselling psychology. This is partially due to the fact that everyone encounters some form of psychological distress during their lifetime, whether this is through personal experience or through the experiences of someone who is close to us (Carlson, 2004; Carr & McNulty, 2006; Comer, 2007). You should appreciate that abnormal behaviour is not just studied from a biological perspective but also features prominently in cognitive, developmental, humanistic and social psychology. Indeed, as you may already be aware, contemporary approaches tend to endorse the diathesis–stress model in which biological dispositions to mental illness are triggered by environmental and cognitive factors (Carlson, 2004). For example, an imbalance in the neurotransmitters serotonin and dopamine may predispose an individual to depression, but this condition may not become evident until a major life event triggers an episode. It is important that you remember this principle throughout this chapter as any reports or assignments you write in this field should demonstrate that you can write critically and that you fully appreciate that multiple influences shape both normal and abnormal behaviour.

It is also vital that you can understand that the distinction between normal and abnormal behaviour is constantly changing and is not absolute or universal (Comer, 2007). Indeed, as with all areas of psychology, theoretical accounts of abnormal behaviour are proposed, investigated, adapted or potentially rejected based on theoretical shifts, social norms and emerging evidence. This also applies to issues concerning which treatments are endorsed at any given time and how the individual is perceived and treated.

→ *Revision checklist*

Essential things to revise are:
❏ Symptoms of psychological and psychiatric disorders
❏ How biological factors can produce symptoms
❏ How psychological abnormality is treated using a biological perspective
❏ How converging operations are often used in holistic treatment

Assessment advice

The following points provide guidance concerning essay writing in abnormal psychology. These points will help you to organise your responses to essay questions and to develop an appropriate writing style:

- Read around the topic throughout your module.

- Make sure you understand everything that the question requires. It might help to break the question down into the different topics.

- Make an essay plan or concept map to guide your literature search.

- Ensure your literature search is designed to answer the question.

- Stick to the format suggested by your institution. This includes the style for references both in the text and in the reference section.

- Adopt an evidence-based approach. This means you need to provide examples from the literature which support each of your main points.

- Define all technical terms and explain the principles of all theories and methodologies you discuss. Remember you should assume that your readers have no previous experience in the area and demonstrate that you understand the concepts.

- Establish a debate. For example, compare and contrast competing theories and critically evaluate any evidence you present. It is not enough to just describe studies.

- Always link back to the essay question throughout your report. This means explicitly explaining to your reader how the evidence you have just discussed contributes towards answering the question.

- Don't be afraid to draw conclusions; this is expected and often required! You should decide which theories the majority of the evidence supports and draw your conclusions accordingly.

Sample question

Could you answer this question? Below is a typical essay question that could arise on this topic.

 Sample question   *Essay*

Evaluate the extent to which the distinctions between normal and abnormal behaviour are universally accepted rather than culturally specific.

Guidelines on answering this question are included at the end of this chapter, whilst further guidance on tackling other exam questions can be found on the companion website at: www.pearsoned.co.uk/psychologyexpress

Historical context

It was not that long ago that individuals suffering from psychological illnesses were persecuted and hidden away in mental asylums where they were often subjected to treatments which would be seen as inhumane, brutal and reprehensible today (Comer, 2007; Pinel, 2003). Today, several psychological organisations across the world have developed codes for ethical conduct in both research and practice and the public's interest also safeguards against such maltreatment (Carr & McNulty, 2006; Comer, 2007). While sufferers often report still feeling isolated, it is significant that mental illness is now discussed more openly. Although the representation is occasionally inaccurate, mental illness often features in popular media. In addition, treatment (such as through psychopharmacology) is often community-based, especially in the case of minor disorders (Carr & McNulty, 2006; McWilliams & O'Callaghan, 2006). This should suggest to you that there have been significant developments in promoting positive attitudes and aims to provide support for individuals who are experiencing psychological turmoil. However, while mental illness is significantly less stigmatised than it used to be, prejudice and discrimination often resurface. Indeed, the view that homosexuality was dysfunctional and should be treated as a psychological abnormality has only recently been rejected by mainstream Western psychology. While discrimination has been reduced, it has not yet been fully eradicated and other cultures often hold different perspectives (Carlson, 2004; Comer, 2007; Pinel, 2003). It is not within the scope of this chapter or the job of a psychologist to say any cultural perspective is better than another; you just need to be aware of these cross-cultural differences. Hence, it is important that you remember that other generations and cultures often define mental illness differently from that which is adopted in contemporary Western psychology and that the findings from psychology can be used to both inform and misinform public opinion. Indeed, Comer (2007) defined psychological abnormality by the following aspects:

● deviance from one's cultural norms and concept of suitable functioning
● distress experienced as a result of behaviour, emotions or experiences
● dysfunction characterised by interference to normal life
● danger to oneself or others.

While you will need to maintain a contemporary understanding of the discipline, you are also required to understand how this came about and how it varies from other perspectives. At the same time, you need to be aware of how your own experiences, attitudes and beliefs will shape your interpretation of the literature and how you perceive individuals who have psychological problems. Your reports will require that you write objectively and as such you need to support any claims with evidence and where possible avoid value judgements. These factors may form a significant aspect of your critical evaluation of the literature.

This chapter will provide an overview of the biological factors associated with several forms of psychological dysfunction which are experienced in adulthood. The topics covered are not exhaustive and suggested reading is provided at the end of each section to guide the expansion of your literature search. For issues concerning psychological dysfunction in children I recommend Comer (2007) and Carr (2006). As such, by the end of this chapter you should be able to understand how biological factors may predispose adults to mental illness or contribute towards the manifestation or treatment of the disorders. You will also be reminded of several other influences on human behaviour which may interact with biological factors.

Further reading General abnormal psychology	
Topic	Key reading
DSM-IV-TR symptoms and diagnoses	APA (2000). *Diagnostic and statistical manual for mental disorders* (4th ed. – text revision) (DSM-IV-TR). Washington, DC: American Psychiatric Association.
Symptoms and diagnoses	Carr, A., & McNulty, M. (Eds.) (2006). *The handbook of adult clinical psychology: An evidence-based approach*. Hove: Routledge.
Child clinical psychology	Carr. A. (2006). *The handbook of child and adolescent clinical psychology: A contextual approach*. Hove: Routledge.
General	Comer, R. J. (2007). *Abnormal psychology* (6th ed.). New York: Worth Publishers.
Biomedical approach	McWilliams, S., & O'Callaghan, E. (2006). Biomedical approaches and the use of drugs to treat adult mental health problems. In Carr, A. and McNulty, M. (Eds.), *The handbook of adult clinical psychology: An evidence-based approach* (pp. 220–252). Hove: Routledge.

Major (unipolar) depression

It is important to remember that 10–25 per cent of women and 5–12 per cent of men will experience major (unipolar) depression during their lifetime (APA, 2000). It can either be reactive, in which it arises in response to major life events, or endogenous if there is not a notable preceding trauma. You should already be aware that major depression can involve either a single incidence or recurrent episodes and as such can significantly reduce an individual's quality of life, making it a prominent area in psychology and psychiatry. As an undergraduate student you should also understand that psychological disorders often co-occur (a phenomenon called comorbidity) and it is the practitioner's responsibility to interpret the diagnostic criteria appropriately to differentiate these conditions. For example, patients with major depression often also present with personality disorders, substance dependence and eating disorders. The following sections will provide you with an overview of the symptoms and aetiology of this condition. You should also consider issues concerning the validity and reliability of the diagnostic manuals.

Key terms

Major (unipolar) depression: A psychological condition characterised by low mood, negative thoughts, extreme negativism, reduced interest, lack of pleasure, changes in appetite and sleep patterns and difficulty concentrating. In extreme cases sufferers can also experience hallucinations and delusions.
Comorbidity: The presence of more than one condition at a given time.

Symptoms and diagnosis

The diagnosis of a major depressive episode requires the presence of at least one of the first two items listed below and at least five of the following symptoms in total for a minimum of two weeks. Remember that the patient would need to demonstrate significant distress and impaired functioning. You need to be aware that major depression can take many forms and can also include psychotic or catatonic features. However, it will not include periods of mania and will not reflect a personality disorder.

- depressed mood including feelings of sadness, hopelessness and emptiness
- reduced interest or pleasure in activities which were previously enjoyed (anhedonia)
- changes in appetite and/or weight
- sleep disturbances including either sleeping too much (hypersomnia) or inability to sleep (insomnia)
- fatigue or loss of energy
- slow and often hesitant movement (psychomotor retardation or agitation)
- difficulties in concentrating, including during conversations, decision making or tasks requiring attention
- excessive or inappropriate guilt
- extreme negativism
- suicidal thoughts, intentions or attempts to commit suicide
- delusions
- hallucinations
- catatonic state.

Biological aetiology

There are numerous biological influences which may predispose individuals to unipolar depression and you should be able to discuss these in detail for any report or essay in the area. These include genetics, physiology, neurology and circadian rhythms. Table 9.1 presents a summary of some of the factors you will need to understand.

Table 9.1 Biological factors associated with the development of unipolar depression

Factor	Description
Genetics	A genetic disposition for unipolar depression may be inherited. Indeed, a monozygotic twin has a 46 per cent chance of developing depression if their sibling was diagnosed. In contrast, dizygotic twins have a 20 per cent chance of developing the condition if their sibling was diagnosed (Comer, 2007).
Physiology: neurotransmitters	Imbalances of serotonin, Substance P, norepinephrine, acetylcholine and dopamine have all been associated with unipolar depression. Decreased levels of 5-HIAA (a metabolite of serotonin) are also associated with suicidal impulses.
Physiology: hormones	The endocrine system has been found to release abnormal levels of hormones during major depressive episodes. This is especially the case for the stress hormone cortisol and the chemical melatonin.
Neurology	Unipolar depression has been associated with decreased activity of monoaminergic neurons which transmit chemicals such as serotonin and norepinephrine. Drevets (2001) also provided evidence that the amygdala and prefrontal cortex both exhibit a 50–75 per cent increase in blood flow and metabolism in patients with unipolar depression. These regions are associated with modulating emotion and the expression of negative emotion respectively. Öngür, Drevets and Price (1998) also identified a 24 per cent decrease in glial cells in the subgenual prefrontal cortex amongst deceased patients with major depression. Silent cerebral infarctions (strokes) can also result in late onset depression.
Circadian rhythms and zeitgebers	Sleep patterns of depressed individuals tend to be shallow and fragmented with decreased slow-wave delta sleep and increased stage 1 sleep. Rapid eye-movement (REM) tends to occur earlier and more frequently. There are also significant seasonal influences (for example, seasonal affective disorder).

KEY STUDY

Depression and genetics

Harrington et al. (1993) investigated whether there was a genetic predisposition for unipolar depression. This was accomplished through a family pedigree study in which people with unipolar depression were recruited as a proband before the other family members were evaluated for indications of depression. This was subsequently compared to the prevalence of depression within the general population. Harrington et al. (1993) observed that 20 per cent of proband relatives exhibited indications of depression, compared to just 10 per cent in the general population. This suggests that there is indeed a genetic predisposition for unipolar depression. However, it must not be forgotten that relatives tend to share similar environments, upbringing, life events and attitudes and these factors may also contribute towards the aetiology of depression.

Sample question *Essay*

To what extent is unipolar depression purely the exaggeration of normal emotion? Consider with reference to evolutionary theory, physiology and neurology.

Non-biological aetiology

Some of the non-biological factors which you will need to consider when revising unipolar depression include traumatic life events, personality traits, worry, negative thoughts and observational learning (Carlson, 2004; Carr & McNulty, 2006; Comer, 2007; Pinel, 2003). It is important you remember that individuals do not exist in a vacuum consisting only of biological factors. Including these factors in your reports can demonstrate that you are able to synthesise evidence and write critically if you do it correctly. For example, you may like to compare the role of biological and environmental factors in endogenous and reactive depression. Also, how are cause and effect established? Do biological factors predispose individuals to depression or are they in response to environmental stressors? Just because an environmental influence cannot be identified does this mean that one did not occur? It is these types of questions which allow you to establish a well-rounded and critical account of the literature.

 Sample question *Problem-based learning*

You want to investigate whether imbalances in monoamines determine whether an individual develops unipolar depression or not. How would you control for the non-biological influences during your investigation and which variables could confound your results?

Treatment

There are several biomedical treatments used to reduce the symptoms of unipolar depression. Table 9.2 summarises some of the biological treatments that you will need to know, although this list is not exhaustive and you should direct your further reading appropriately. You should also remember that pharmacological substances are often addictive and are likely result in withdrawal symptoms if terminated too quickly.

 Sample question *Essay*

Critically discuss the biomedical approach to diagnosing and treating depression with reference to both biological and non-biological factors.

Table 9.2 Biological treatments for unipolar depression

Treatment	Description
SSRIs	Selective serotonin reuptake inhibitors (SSRIs) prevent reuptake of serotonin at the terminal buttons thereby increasing the amount of serotonin in the synapse which can bind with the receptors. These medications come in several classes but brand names which you are probably aware of include Prozac, Paxil, Seroxat and Serlain. You should remember that these drugs can have serious side-effects and can be fatal if combined with other substances including alcohol, beta blockers, tricyclic antidepressants, benzodiazepines and MAOIs.
TCAs	Tricyclics inhibit the reuptake of both serotonin and norepinephrine so increase the levels and transmission of both of these neurotransmitters. Tricyclics include Clomipramine, Desipramine and Trimipramine. However, side-effects can include cognitive impairment, drowsiness, nausea, hypotension, tachycardia and irregular heart rhythms. The toxic dose is also significantly lower than SSRIs.
MAOIs	Monoamine oxidase inhibitors prevent the breakdown of monoamine neurotransmitters, increasing the level of these substances in the synaptic gaps and at neuron receptors. MAO-As act primarily on serotonin, epinephrine and norepinephrine and require a strict diet, whereas MAO-Bs act on dopamine and phenethylamine and do not require dietary restrictions.
Sleep deprivation	REM sleep deprivation over several weeks or short-term total sleep deprivation often reduces the symptoms of unipolar depression. It is still uncertain how this occurs although there has been speculation that a substance is produced during sleep which has a depressogenic effect.
ECT	Electroconvulsive therapy is used in extreme cases of depression to shock the brain and induce controlled seizures while the patient is temporarily sedated and paralysed. This has been shown to reduce the symptoms of major depression. Prolonged use can result in brain damage and cognitive impairment.

You should always remember that there are many possible sides to an academic debate and avenues for critical thinking when you are constructing your assignments and revision plan. For example, there have been several well-publicised incidences of which you may already be aware where SSRIs such as Seroxat have been linked to higher suicide rates in adolescents (Wooltorton, 2003). However, while you should understand the evidence which supports this view you must also consider the alternative perspective. Indeed, the validity of these reports is still to be determined and other prominent studies have suggested that this is not the case (Simon, Savarino, Operskalski & Wang, 2006). Indeed, there is a fine line between childhood and adolescence, and many changes occur during this period which may explain varying degrees of suicidal impulses. A question you must consider is whether the benefits of treatment outweigh the potential harm?

If studies are undertaken or funded by pharmacology companies do they have a vested interest in finding results which suggest their products are useful?

Further reading Unipolar depression	
Topic	Key reading
Symptoms and diagnosis	Carr, A., & McNulty, M. (2006). Depression. In A. Carr and M. McNulty (Eds.), The handbook of adult clinical psychology: An evidence-based approach (pp. 291–345). Hove: Routledge.
Neuroscience	Davidson, R. J., Pizzagalli, D., Nitschke, J. B., & Putnam, K. (2002). Depression: Perspectives from affective neuroscience. Annual Review of Psychology, 53(1), 545–574.
Neurology	Drevets, W. C., Videen, T. O; Price, J. L., Preskorn, S. H., Carmichael, S. T., & Raichle, M. E. (1992). A functional anatomical study of unipolar depression. The Journal of Neuroscience, 12(9), 3628–3641.
Monoamine hypothesis	Hindmarch, I. (2001). Expanding the horizons of depression: Beyond the monoamine hypothesis. Human Psychopharmacology, 16(3), 203–218.
SSRIs and suicide	Simon, G. E., Savarino, J., Operskalski, B., & Wang, P. S. (2006). Suicide risk during antidepressant treatment. American Journal of Psychiatry, 163(1), 41–47.
SSRIs and suicide	Wooltorton, E. (2003). Paroxetine (Paxil, Seroxat): Increased risk of suicide in pediatric patients. Canadian Medical Association Journal, 169(5), 446.

Test your knowledge

9.1 Which natural chemicals have been associated with major depression?

9.2 What pharmacological treatments can treat major depression?

9.3 How might circadian rhythms influence mood?

9.4 Which non-biological factors are associated with major depression?

Answers to these questions can be found on the companion website at: www.pearsoned.co.uk/psychologyexpress

Bipolar depression

It is vital that you can differentiate unipolar and bipolar depression regardless of whether you are required to answer an essay question, exam question or analyse a case study (Carr & McNulty, 2006; Comer, 2007). You will also need to appreciate that bipolar disorder can also take several forms. Indeed bipolar disorder is characterised by two subtypes. Bipolar I is characterised by manic episodes, major depressive episodes and often mixed episodes in which both states occur. In contrast, bipolar II is characterised by hypomania (rapid cycle but short-lived mania) and major depressive episodes, but no manic or mixed episodes. Patients with bipolar disorders often present with personality disorders, self-harm, substance dependence and anxiety or panic disorders. The following sections will remind you of the symptoms, diagnoses and treatments for bipolar disorder.

> **Key terms**
>
> **Bipolar disorder**: A psychological condition characterised not only with periods of depression but also by periods of mania.
>
> **Bipolar I**: Bipolar disorder characterised by manic episodes, major depressive episodes and often mixed episodes in which both states occur.
>
> **Bipolar II**: Bipolar disorder characterised by hypomania (rapid cycle but short-lived mania), major depressive episodes but no manic or mixed episodes.
>
> **Hypomania**: Rapid cycle but shorted-lived episodes of mania.

Symptoms and diagnosis

The criteria for bipolar depression are the same as those described for major (unipolar depression). However, the current diagnostic manual (the DSM-IV-TR) also provides guidance on the diagnosis of mania (APA, 2000). These must include the first bullet point in the following list and at least three of the other criteria (or four if the state is only irritable):

- abnormally elevated, expansive or irritable mood lasting at least a week (or any duration if hospitalisation is required)
- inflated self-esteem or grandiosity
- decreased need for sleep
- more talkative than normal or unable to stop talking/moving
- flights of ideas in which the chain of thought constantly jumps
- Distractibility
- Increased goal-directed behaviour (e.g. socially or sexually)
- Excessive involvement in potentially harmful activities
- Marked impairment in functioning.

Biological aetiology

The biological factors associated with depressive episodes in bipolar disorder are discussed in Table 9.3. You will need to be able to both differentiate the symptoms of unipolar and bipolar disorder and also identify their biological commonalities. However, the same non-biological factors discussed under major depression can also interact with bipolar condition.

Table 9.3 Biological factors associated with the development of bipolar depression

Factor	Description
Genetics	A genetic disposition may be inherited from parents and this appears to be significantly more pronounced for bipolar disorder than unipolar depression. Studies have suggested that there may be a dominant gene for bipolar depression on chromosomes 4, 5, 18, 21 or X (Carlson, 2004).
Physiology: neurotransmitters	Imbalances of the neurotransmitters discussed in Table 9.1 are also influential in the development of bipolar disorder.
Neurology	Patients with bipolar disorder tend to present with an increased volume of the lateral ventricles and globus pallidus. Impairment of the sodium pump resulting in cyclical periods of impaired neural activity and hypersensitivity may also explain depression and mania respectively. There are often abnormalities in the hypothalamic–pituitary–adrenal axis which may arise due to stress.

Treatment

The biological treatments for the depressive episodes are similar to those used for major depression, although other treatments which reduce the symptoms of mania are described in Table 9.4. It is important that you remember that the nature of bipolar disorder makes it far more likely that patients will forget doses or choose not to take their medication because they miss the elevated state. Pharmacological substances are also addictive and are likely result in withdrawal symptoms if terminated too quickly.

Table 9.4 Biological treatments for bipolar depression

Treatment	Description
Lithium	Lithium carbonate acts as a mood stabiliser but is more reliable at treating mania than depression. However, once the cycle is broken, depression tends to dissipate also. Side-effects and toxic doses have been associated with significant weight gain, increased thirst, hypothyroidism, motor unco-ordination, confusion and, in the case of overdose, medical coma.
Carbamazepine	Carbamazepine acts as a mood stabiliser which reduces the excitability of neurons and as such can reduce both mania and depression in some cases. However, it can also compete with other chemicals and may also cause anaemia.
Antidepressants	The antidepressants detailed in Table 9.2 can also be used to treat the depressive symptoms of bipolar disorder.

Sample question   *Essay*

Compare and contrast the diagnoses and treatment of unipolar and bipolar depression.

Further reading Bipolar depression

Topic	Key reading
Symptoms and diagnosis	Lam, D. & Jones, S. (2006) Bipolar disorder. In A. Carr & M. McNulty (Eds.), *The handbook of adult clinical psychology: An evidence-based approach* (pp. 346–382). Hove: Routledge.
Lithium and neurology	Sassi, R. B., Nicoletti, M., Brambilla, P., Mallinger, A. G., Frank, E., Kupfer, D. J., Keshavan, M. S., & Soares, J. C. (2002). Increased gray matter volume in lithium-treated bipolar disorder patients. *Neuroscience Letters, 329*(2), 243–245.

Test your knowledge

9.5 What treatments are available in cases of bipolar depression?

9.6 What are the differences between bipolar I and bipolar II?

9.7 How is bipolar disorder diagnosed?

9.8 What are the commonalities between unipolar and bipolar disorders?

Answers to these questions can be found on the companion website at: www.pearsoned.co.uk/psychologyexpress

---

Schizophrenia

Schizophrenia is a debilitating condition which affects one per cent of the general population and typically arises in late adolescence or early adulthood (Carlson, 2004; Carr & McNulty, 2006; Comer, 2007). While it shares some of the symptoms observed in unipolar and bipolar depression, the symptoms are often more pronounced, more evident to anyone who encounters an individual with the condition and it severely impairs normal functioning. It is also associated with self-harm and suicide due to the typically violent and distressing nature of the hallucinations and delusions. As such it is likely to result in at least one incidence of hospitalisation under the Mental Health Act, but this may be longitudinal or repeated if the severity of the symptoms does not reduce. There have been several incidences of individuals with schizophrenia posing a danger to others, although this is actually a rarity and the majority of the danger is to themselves. You may already be aware that once an individual is diagnosed with schizophrenia it is unlikely that they will ever make a full recovery due to the cerebral factors associated with the condition, although the symptoms are significantly less pronounced with the correct treatment and during remission. However, the diagnostic criteria have been highly criticised for lacking validity and reliability, meaning that several practitioners view schizophrenia as a 'failed category' in which many individuals can be placed without successful differentiation (Carr & McNulty, 2006; Comer, 2007; Kuipers, Peters & Bebbington, 2006) and you should be aware of this debate.

 Sample question   *Essay*

Evaluate the DSM-IV-TR criteria for the diagnosis of schizophrenia.

Symptoms and diagnosis

The features of schizophrenia are typically divided into positive and negative symptoms which you should be able to identify and clearly differentiate. A full description is provided below, but it would be useful to test your understanding of these symptoms before progressing to later sections. The positive symptoms can be identified merely by their presence and include hallucination, thought disorders and delusions. The negative symptoms can be identified by the absence of normal functioning and include flattened emotional responses, poverty of speech (alogia), lack of initiative or persistence, inability to experience pleasure (anhedonia) and social withdrawal. You should remember that an individual needs to present with two of the following symptoms and demonstrate dysfunction in social or occupational situations for a month prior to diagnosis, and disturbance should be evident for at least six months:

- delusions which may manifest as beliefs that they are being persecuted or that they are grandiose (for example that they are a martyr or a celebrity)
- hallucinations which tend to be of a violent or distressing nature
- disorganised speech including incoherence, frequent derailment, echolalia (repetition of another's utterances) or 'word salad' in which random words are strung together without meaning
- disorganised or catatonic behaviour
- negative symptoms which can anhedonia (inability to feel pleasure), alogia (impoverished speech) or *avolition* (lack of desire or motivation).

Key terms

Alogia: Impoverished speech observed in cases of schizophrenia.

Anhedonia: An inability to feel pleasure.

Avolition: A lack of desire or motivation.

Echolalia: Involuntary repetition of other peoples utterances.

> **Schizophrenia**: A severe condition in which sufferers experience hallucinations, delusions, speech impairment, irrationality, unusual motor activity and impairment in most aspects of their lives.

Biological aetiology

Several biological factors appear to predispose individuals to schizophrenia or manifest as a result of the condition (see Table 9.5). While earlier psychologies believed that schizophrenia resulted from environmental factors such as cold parenting, this view has been replaced with the diathesis–stress and biomedical approaches. However, you need to remember you are studying psychology and not psychiatry and so you should always consider all possible influences on the individual from each of the main perspectives.

Table 9.5 Biological factors associated with schizophrenia

Factor	Description
Heredity	Schizophrenia has been associated with all chromosomes except 3, 12, 14, 16, 17, 19, 20, 21, and Y. While an unaffected monozygotic twin is slightly more likely to subsequently develop schizophrenia than an unaffected dizygotic twin if their sibling was diagnosed with the condition, this remains below 50 per cent. These findings suggest that while there may be a genetic predisposition, other factors also contribute towards the aetiology.
Physiology: neurotransmitters	The dopamine hypothesis states that schizophrenia may be related to imbalances in dopamine (Kuipers et al., 2006). Indeed, it is significant that dopamine receptor blockers reduce the symptoms of schizophrenia and the antipsychotic medication Clozapine functions by blocking the dopamine receptors in the nucleus accumbens. Levels of dopamine are increased through hypofrontality (discussed below).
Cerebral activity	Patients with schizophrenia tend to display a phenomenon known as hypofrontality in which there is significantly less activity in the prefrontal cortex than in individuals without schizophrenia (Comer, 2007). There may also be increased dopamine metabolism in the nucleus accumbens.
Cerebral structure	CT and MRI scans have identified a general loss of brain grey matter for patients with schizophrenia, which appears to occur suddenly in early adulthood and results in enlarged ventricles due to this atrophy (Wright et al., 2000). However, there also appears to be a loss of volume in the hair-like branching networks of dendrites and axons in the brain (Thompson et al., 2001). Patients with schizophrenia also tend to have a smaller anterior hippocampus and larger lateral and third ventricles (Carlson, 2004; Comer, 2007). Autopsies reveal that schizophrenic patients have a greater number of dopamine receptors in the brain.
Other factors	Parental age has been associated with schizophrenia as the fathers of schizophrenic children tend to be older. There are also seasonal influences with more sufferers being born in late winter or early spring. Schizophrenia is also more likely if the mother of the sufferer was RH-negative and the sufferer is RH-positive, possibly due to the mother's immune system attacking the foetus. Other factors include vitamin D deficiency, prenatal malnutrition, population density, viral epidemics and distance from the equator (Carlson, 2004).

Sample question | Essay

Which factors may contribute towards the development and treatment of schizophrenia?

Treatment

Table 9.6 summarises some of the pharmacological treatments available for use in schizophrenia which you should be familiar with. However, you should remember that long-term use of these substances can result in involuntary movements such as tick-like gestures, rapid movement of arms or legs, grimacing, rapid blinking and tongue protrusion. This condition, known as tardive dyskinesia, is mostly irreversible. These medications can also result in the hypersensitivity of dopamine receptors because long-term blocking causes irreparable neural damage. The substances are also addictive and are likely result in withdrawal symptoms if terminated.

Key term

Tardive dyskinesia: Involuntary movements such as tick-like gestures, rapid movement of arms or legs, grimacing, rapid blinking and tongue protrusion produced through long-term use of anti-psychotic medications.

Table 9.6 Biological treatment for schizophrenia

Treatment	Description
D-Cycloserine	Large doses of the glycine agonist reduce negative symptoms in schizophrenia due to facilitating NMDA activity which is associated with dopamine transmission.
Chlorpromazine	Chlorpromazine reduces the positive symptoms of schizophrenia because it acts as a dopamine receptor blocker, thereby reducing the levels of dopamine absorbed by neuron receptors.
Clozapine	Clozapine is an atypical antipsychotic which blocks dopamine receptors in the nucleus accumbens.

KEY STUDY

Atrophy of grey matter in schizophrenia

Thompson et al. (2001) conducted a longitudinal investigation assessing the magnitude and rate for the loss of cortical grey matter in patients with early-onset schizophrenia and healthy control subjects. MRI scans were undertaken in two-year intervals and the proportion of grey matter was recorded. While the healthy control subjects lost 0.5–1.0 per cent of grey matter during adolescence (a normal phenomenon), this loss was half that of patients with schizophrenia. This loss of grey matter began in the parietal lobes and proceeded to the temporal lobes, somatosensory and motor cortex and dorsolateral prefrontal cortex. It was also significant that the symptoms presented by the patients with schizophrenia corresponded to both the area in which the atrophy was occurring and the extent to which grey matter was lost. Hence, hallucinations occurred when atrophy began in the temporal lobe and the magnitude of this impairment correlated to the proportion of grey matter which was lost.

Non-biological considerations

You should always remember to demonstrate that you have considered a range of influences and not just those from a biological perspective. You must remember that an individual who suffers from schizophrenia does not exist in a biological vacuum and you can demonstrate critical thinking by expanding your knowledge to include alternative factors. For example:

- Cultural norms concerning acceptable and unacceptable behaviour may determine whether the individual is categorised as psychologically abnormal, eccentric or normal.

- The support network available to an individual with schizophrenia will determine when treatment is sought and also influence their rate of recovery and chances of relapse. Also remember that lack of understanding and media coverage which portrays individuals with schizophrenia as dangerous will also influence how people perceive and treat them. This can exacerbate their symptoms and make them socially isolated.

- Socioeconomic status significantly influences the likelihood that they will be diagnosed and treated appropriately. This is especially relevant if health care is not freely available or the individual is homeless and not amongst people who will notice the changes in their behaviour.

- The patient's cognitive strategies and coping mechanisms may influence how they compensate for their symptoms and how well they recover.

Further reading Schizophrenia

Topic	Key reading
Abnormal psychology	Comer, R. J. (2007). *Abnormal psychology* (6th ed.). New York: Worth Publishers.
Abnormal psychology	Kuipers, E., Peters, E., & Bebbington, P. (2006). Schizophrenia. In A. Carr and M. McNulty, (Eds.). *The handbook of adult clinical psychology: An evidence-based approach* (pp. 843–896). Hove: Routledge.
Neurological	Wright, I. C., Rabe-Hesketh, S., Woodruff, P. W. R., David, A. S., Murray, R. M., & Bullmore, E. T. (2000). Meta-analysis of regional brain volumes in schizophrenia. *American Journal of Psychiatry*, 157(1), 16–25.

Test your knowledge

9.9 What are the positive and negative symptoms of schizophrenia?

9.10 Which biological factors may contribute towards the development of schizophrenia?

9.11 How successful are biomedical treatments for schizophrenia?

9.12 What is the prognosis for an individual diagnosed with schizophrenia?

Answers to these questions can be found on the companion website at: www.pearsoned.co.uk/psychologyexpress

Anxiety and stress disorders

Anxiety disorders are multifaceted and you are likely to study several types during your undergraduate studies (Carr & McNulty, 2006; Comer, 2007). These are likely to include acute stress disorder, agoraphobia (with or without panic disorder, generalised anxiety disorder (GAD), obsessive compulsive disorder (OCD), panic disorder (with or without agoraphobia), phobias and post-traumatic stress disorder (PTSD). However, it is important to remember that stress and anxiety are normal emotional states which are related to several physiological factors and were discussed in earlier chapters. The main debates surrounding anxiety disorders concern determinism (for example, biologically driven reflexes) versus free will (for example, intentionally changing thought patterns), the validity and reliability of the diagnostic manuals to differentiate between conditions and the value of combining treatments to maximise the benefits to the patient. You should be able to discuss these debates at length.

Symptoms and diagnosis

The descriptions for several stress and anxiety disorders are presented in Table 9.7 and in the Glossary at the end of this book. You should be able to differentiate these disorders and identify their commonalities.

Table 9.7 Symptoms of anxiety and stress disorders

Disorder	Description
Acute stress disorder	Arises after the experience of a highly traumatic event which threatened injury or death and created feelings of fear and helplessness. Arises within four weeks of the trauma (Brewin, Andrews, Rose & Kirk, 1999; Bryant & Harvey, 2000). Characterised by anxiety, irritability, poor concentration, insomnia, restlessness and dissociative states including detachment, derealisation or depersonalisation. Patients also re-experience the event in flashbacks, avoid associated places or people.
Agoraphobia	A fear of being in places where escape would be difficult or embarrassing (such as in public) which can develop out of specific phobias or be due to a traumatic event. Often arises due to the fear of having a panic attack in public, hence it is associated with panic disorder (Taylor & Asmundson, 2006). Characterised by extreme anxiety, stress, worry and avoidance of public situations. May arise with or without panic disorder.
Panic disorder	A condition which often arises without a discernible cause but may follow periods of high anxiety or arise due to misinterpretation of bodily responses (Taylor & Asmundson, 2006). Characterised by sudden and acute attacks of fear or anxiety resulting in panic attacks, stress, heart palpitations, rapid breathing or hyperventilating, blurred vision, dizziness and flights of thought.
Obsessive compulsive disorder	An anxiety disorder characterised by excessive worry, persistent obsessive thoughts, irrationality and overriding compulsions to perform actions which reduce the patient's anxiety (Swinson, Antony, Rachman & Richter, 1998). Repetitive actions are intended to neutralise the source of the anxiety. May prevent normal daily functioning
Generalised anxiety disorder	A general state of anxiety which is applied across life in general and may have originated due to the exacerbation of other anxieties or traumatic events (Wells & Carter, 2006). Characterised by anxiety, worry, heart palpitations, dizziness and recurrent stress response across a range of situations.
Post-traumatic stress disorder	Anxiety disorder arising after extreme trauma which caused feelings of intense fear and helplessness which can arise at any point after the trauma including years later (Creamer & Carty, 2006). Characterised by flashbacks, nightmares, obsessive thoughts, avoidance of triggers, heightened anxiety and startle response.
Specific phobias	Anxiety disorders often caused by irrational thoughts or a negative experience with specific stimuli (Bates, 2006). Characterised by anxiety, worry, avoidance of triggers, obsessive thoughts, attentional biases and hypervigilance.

CRITICAL FOCUS

The relative nature of psychological abnormality

It is important to remember that the criteria we use today to categorise behaviour as abnormal are not relevant for all cultures, people or times. Indeed, while the APA (2000) provides a contemporary guide for diagnosing psychological disorders, this manual is constantly evolving and 'disorders' are often removed or combined in later editions. This demonstrates how the classifications of psychological illnesses are constantly evolving. However, it is important to remember that you are studying psychology and not psychiatry and as such you need to understand that there are other non-biological factors which differentiate abnormal and normal behaviour. It is also notable that other cultures understand abnormality differently. For example, in several regions of Africa it is still believed that psychological and medical problems are caused by the disgruntled spirits of ancestors and that treatment must initially appease the spirits. Practitioners of several devout world religions also believe that they can hear the voice of their deity in altered states such as meditation and prayer. While these beliefs may seem strange to some people this does not mean that they can be automatically categorised as psychological abnormalities. Indeed, the classification of these behaviours as normal or abnormal is dependent upon the culture in which they occur and the norms and beliefs of individuals within that society rather than on the universality of biological factors associated with human behaviour.

Biological factors

From your reading of the earlier chapters in this text, you should appreciate that stress and anxiety are intrinsically linked to the functions of the central, peripheral and endocrine systems. Table 9.8 summarises some of the biological factors which may contribute towards the development of anxiety and stress disorders with which you should be familiar.

Table 9.8 Biological factors associated with anxiety and stress disorders

Factor	Description
Heritability	Family pedigree studies have identified that individuals with a family history of generalised anxiety disorder have a 15 per cent chance of developing the condition compared to only 6 per cent of the general population. This suggests that there may be a genetic predisposition to the condition although it is uncertain whether this is due to inheriting a lower anxiety threshold or other biological characteristics (Carlson, 2004; Comer, 2007). It is important to remember that there is constant interaction between biological and environmental factors (discussed in Chapter 1).

Evolutionary factors	According to evolutionary theory, stress and anxiety are normal responses which facilitated the survival of our ancestors and were therefore transmitted genetically to following generations. Anxiety and stress disorders would be exaggerations of these normal behaviours which no longer serve evolutionary functions due to changing environments (Comer, 2007).
Neurology	Functions of the limbic system, basal ganglia, caudate nucleus, orbitofrontal cortex, amygdala, thalamus, ventromedial nucleus of the hypothalamus and locus ceruleus have all been associated with the stress and anxiety disorders discussed in this chapter due to their role in processing and regulating emotion (Bryant & Harvey, 2000; Comer, 2007; Swinson et al., 1998; Wells & Carter, 2006).
Physiology and the endocrine system	Low levels of the neurotransmitter gamma-aminobutyric acid (GABA) can result in increased levels of anxiety due to its role in stabilising the activity of the CNS and terminating the stress response. Changes in the levels of epinephrine and norepinephrine can also result in anxiety, stress and panic (Bates, 2006; Creamer and Carty, 2006; Swinson et al., 1998). The endocrine system was covered in Chapter 3 but is explicitly linked to the development and presentation of stress disorders. The hypothalamic–pituitary–adrenal (HPA) pathway also produces adrenocorticotropic hormone (ACTH) and corticosteroids (including cortisol) which are actively involved in the stress response.

Non-biological factors

Non-biomedical factors which you should research also include irrational or obsessive thoughts, negative experiences, occupational status (if the occupation is particularly stressful), sociocultural factors, personality types such as trait anxiety, observational learning, operant conditioning and classical conditioning. These topics are covered in other texts in this series and in the suggested further reading.

Medical consequences of stress and anxiety

As an undergraduate student you should also understand that stress and anxiety have an effect on an individual's general health and wellbeing, which can be lasting if the state is at a clinical level. The following points will refresh your memory concerning how these prolonged and exaggerated states influence the body:

- Lowering of the immune system makes people with high levels of stress or anxiety more prone to viruses, diseases and infection.
- High and prolonged levels of stress are linked to the development of gastric ulcers due to the functions of the endocrine system.
- Susceptibility to other mood disorders including depression.

Treatment

Table 9.9 summarises some of the biomedical treatments available to reduce anxiety. However, you should remember that all of these treatments, with the exception of biofeedback, only offer temporary relief from the symptoms and will not eradicate the individual's beliefs about and attitude towards the source of their anxiety. For this reason you should also consider cognitive behavioural approaches which could be combined with biomedical treatments to maximise the benefits of the treatment and reduce the chance of using medication long-term. For example, medication can be used to reduce the physiological responses but cognitive-behavioural therapy would challenge and replace unhealthy beliefs (such as obsessions) and behaviours (such as avoidance or compulsions) resulting in lasting effects.

Table 9.9 Biological treatment for anxiety disorders

Treatment	Description
Benzodiazepines	These substances include Valium and Xanax which function as a GABA agonist and therefore binds to GABA receptors reducing the physiological responses associated with anxiety.
SSRIs	The SSRIs discussed in the sections on unipolar depression also reduce levels of anxiety and stress due to their influence on norepinephrine.
Biofeedback	This is a technique in which individuals are trained to control and correctly interpret bodily responses. This means that they are able to employ coping mechanisms upon seeing or feeling themselves becoming anxious which consequently lowers their levels of anxiety and stress.

Further reading Anxiety and stress disorders

Topic	Key reading
Social phobia	Bates, T. (2006). The clinical management of social anxiety disorder. In A. Carr and M. McNulty (Eds.), The handbook of adult clinical psychology: An evidence-based approach (pp. 558–590). Hove: Routledge.
Acute stress and PTSD	Brewin, C. R., Andrews, B., Rose, S., & Kirk, M. (1999). Acute stress disorder and posttraumatic stress disorder in victims of violent crime. American Journal of Psychiatry, 156(3), 360–366.
ASD	Bryant, R. A., & Harvey, A. G. (2000). Acute stress disorder: A handbook of theory, assessment, and treatment. Washington, DC: American Psychological Association.
PTSD	Creamer, M., & Carty, J. (2006). Post-traumatic stress disorder. In A. Carr and M. McNulty, (Eds.), The handbook of adult clinical psychology: An evidence-based approach (pp. 523–557). Hove: Routledge.
OCD	Swinson, R. P., Antony, M. A., Rachman, S., & Richter, M. (1998). Obsessive compulsive disorder: Theory, research and treatment. New York: Guilford Press.

Panic disorder	Taylor, S., & Asmundson, J. G. (2006). Panic disorder and agoraphobia. In A. Carr and M. McNulty (Eds.), *The handbook of adult clinical psychology: An evidence-based approach* (pp. 458–486). Hove: Routledge.
GAD	Wells, A., & Carter, K. (2006). Generalized anxiety disorder. In A. Carr and M. McNulty (Eds.), *The handbook of adult clinical psychology: An evidence-based approach* (pp. 423–457). Hove: Routledge.

Test your knowledge

9.13 What are the differences between acute and post-traumatic stress disorders?

9.14 How would OCD be treated from a biomedical perspective?

9.15 When would generalised anxiety disorder prevent normal functioning?

9.16 Which methodological approaches can be used to investigate the aetiology of psychological conditions?

Answers to these questions can be found on the companion website at: www.pearsoned.co.uk/psychologyexpress

Chapter summary – pulling it all together

→ Can you tick all the points from the revision checklist at the beginning of this chapter?

→ Attempt the sample question from the beginning of this chapter using the answer guidelines below.

→ Go to the companion website at www.pearsoned.co.uk/psychologyexpress to access more revision support online, including interactive quizzes, flashcards, You be the marker exercises as well as answer guidance for the Test your knowledge and Sample questions from this chapter.

Answer guidelines

 Sample question   *Essay*

Evaluate the extent to which the distinctions between normal and abnormal behaviour are universally accepted rather than culturally specific.

Approaching the question

This question is asking you to discuss the extent to which the criteria for (and distinction between) normal and abnormal behaviour are universal or mediated by cultural factors. Therefore, it is asking you to discuss whether psychological abnormality arises solely due to universal biological factors or whether it is a matter of interpretation within a culture.

Important points to include

Your essay should begin with a summary concerning the distinction between normal and abnormal behaviour. This may be easier if you mention the distinctions provided by the psychiatric diagnostic manuals. You should also briefly summarise the perspective you are going to adopt and which psychological disorders you are going to discuss. It would be useful to choose two conditions which are differentially influenced by biological and social factors because this will encourage you to establish a debate in your essay. It would also be useful to select conditions which may be acknowledged in one culture but not in another. Your essay should subsequently discuss these conditions with reference to evidence concerning whether the symptoms, causes and treatments for these conditions are universal. You should also discuss both biological and non-biological factors. Your conclusion should be balanced and supported with evidence.

Make your answer stand out

To make your answer stand out you will need to demonstrate that you have considered biological factors, non-biological factors, arguments that psychological abnormality is universal and arguments that psychological abnormality is defined by cultural norms and expectations. You will need to synthesise a range of evidence while writing clearly and critically. You will also need to support all of your arguments with evidence.

Explore the accompanying website at www.pearsoned.co.uk/psychologyexpress
→ Prepare more effectively for exams and assignments using the answer guidelines for questions from this chapter.
→ Test your knowledge using multiple choice questions and flashcards.
→ Improve your essay skills by exploring the You be the marker exercises.

Notes

Notes

Notes

And finally, before the exam . . .

How to approach revision from here

You should be now at a reasonable stage in your revision process – you should have developed your skills and knowledge base over your course and used this text judiciously over that period. Now, however, you have used the book to reflect, remind and reinforce the material you have researched over the year/ seminar. You will, of course, need to do additional reading and research to that included here (and appropriate directions are provided) but you will be well on your way with the material presented in this book.

It is important that in answering any question in psychology you take a research- and evidence-based approach to your response. For example, do not make generalised or sweeping statements that cannot be substantiated or supported by evidence from the literature. Remember as well that the evidence should not be anecdotal – it is of no use citing your mum, dad, best friend or the latest news from a celebrity website. After all, you are not writing an opinion piece – you are crafting an argument that is based on current scientific knowledge and understanding. You need to be careful about the evidence you present: do review the material and from where it was sourced.

Furthermore, whatever type of assessment you have to undertake, it is important to take an evaluative approach to the evidence. Whether you are writing an essay, sitting an exam or designing a webpage, the key advice is to avoid simply presenting a descriptive answer. Rather, it is necessary to think about the strength of the evidence in each area. One of the key skills for psychology students is critical thinking and for this reason the tasks featured in this series focus upon developing this way of thinking. Thus you are not expected to simply learn a set of facts and figures, but to think about the implications of what we know and how this might be applied in everyday life. The best assessment answers are the ones that take this critical approach.

It is also important to note that psychology is a theoretical subject: when answering any question about psychology, not only refer to the prevailing theories of the field, but also outline the development of them as well. It is also important to evaluate these theories and models either through comparison with other models and theories or through the use of studies that have assessed them and highlighted their strengths and weaknesses. It is essential to read widely – within each section of this book there are directions to interesting and pertinent papers relating to the specific topic area. Find these papers, read these papers and make notes from these papers. But don't stop there. Let them lead you to other sources that may be important to the field. One thing that an examiner hates to see is the same old sources being cited all of the time: be innovative and, as well as reading the seminal works, find the more obscure and interesting sources as well – just make sure they're relevant to your answer!

How not to revise

- **Don't avoid revision.** This is the best tip ever. There is something on the TV, the pub is having a two-for-one offer, the fridge needs cleaning, your budgie looks lonely . . . You have all of these activities to do and they need doing now! Really . . . ? Do some revision!

- **Don't spend too long at each revision session.** Working all day and night is not the answer to revision. You do need to take breaks, so schedule your revision so you are not working from dawn until dusk. A break gives time for the information you have been revising to consolidate.

- **Don't worry.** Worrying will cause you to lose sleep, lose concentration and lose revision time by leaving it late and then later. When the exam comes, you will have no revision completed and will be tired and confused.

- **Don't cram.** This is the worst revision technique in the universe! You will not remember the majority of the information that you try to stuff into your skull, so why bother?

- **Don't read over old notes with no plan.** Your brain will take nothing in. If you wrote your lecture notes in September and the exam is in May is there any point in trying to decipher your scrawly handwriting now?

- **Don't write model answers and learn by rote.** When it comes to the exam you will simply regurgitate the model answer irrespective of the question – not a brilliant way to impress the examiner!

Tips for exam success

What you should do when it comes to revision

Exams are one form of assessment that students often worry about the most. The key to exam success, as with many other types of assessment, lies in good preparation and self-organisation. One of the most important things is knowing what to expect – this does not necessarily mean knowing what the questions will be on the exam paper, but rather what the structure of the paper is, how many questions you are expected to answer, how long the exam will last and so on.

To pass an exam you need a good grasp of the course material and, obvious as it may seem, to turn up for the exam itself. It is important to remember that you aren't expected to know or remember everything in the course, but you should be able to show your understanding of what you have studied. Remember as well that examiners are interested in what you know, not what you don't know. They try to write exam questions that give you a good chance of passing – not ones to catch you out or trick you in any way. You may want to consider some of these top exam tips.

- Start your revision in plenty of time.
- Make a revision timetable and stick to it.
- Practise jotting down answers and making essay plans.
- Practise writing against the clock using past exam papers.
- Check that you have really answered the question and have not strayed off the point.
- Review a recent past paper and check the marking structure.
- Carefully select the topics you are going to revise.
- Use your lecture/study notes and refine them further, if possible, into lists or diagrams and transfer them on to index cards/Post-it notes. Mind maps are a good way of making links between topics and ideas.
- Practise your handwriting – make sure it's neat and legible.

One to two days before the exam
- Recheck times, dates and venue.
- Actively review your notes and key facts.
- Exercise, eat sensibly and get a few good nights' sleep.

On the day
- Get a good night's sleep.
- Have a good meal, two to three hours before the start time.
- Arrive in good time.
- Spend a few minutes calming and focusing.

In the exam room
- Keep calm.
- Take a few minutes to read each question carefully. Don't jump to conclusions – think calmly about what each question means and the area it is focused on.
- Start with the question you feel most confident about. This helps your morale.
- By the same token, don't expend all your efforts on that one question – if you are expected to answer three questions then don't just answer two.
- Keep to time and spread your effort evenly on all opportunities to score marks.

- Once you have chosen a question, jot down any salient facts or key points. Then take five minutes to plan your answer – a spider diagram or a few notes may be enough to focus your ideas. Try to think in terms of 'why and how' not just 'facts'.
- You might find it useful to create a visual plan or map before writing your answer to help you remember to cover everything you need to address.
- Keep reminding yourself of the question and try not to wander off the point.
- Remember that quality of argument is more important than quantity of facts.
- Take 30–60-second breaks whenever you find your focus slipping (typically every 20 minutes).
- Make sure you reference properly – according to your university requirements.
- Watch your spelling and grammar – you could lose marks if you make too many errors.

→ *Final revision checklist*

❏ Have you revised the topics highlighted in the revision checklists?
❏ Have you attended revision classes and taken note of and/or followed up on your lecturers' advice about the exams or assessment process at your university?
❏ Can you answer the questions posed in this text satisfactorily? Don't forget to check sample answers on the website too.
❏ Have you read the additional material to make your answer stand out?
❏ Remember to criticise appropriately – based on evidence.

Test your knowledge by using the material presented in this text or on the website: www.pearsoned.co.uk/psychologyexpress

Glossary

action potential An electrical signal which is transmitted along neurons.

acute stress disorder Arises after the experience of a highly traumatic event which threatened injury or death and created feelings of fear and helplessness. Arises within four weeks of the trauma. Characterised by anxiety, irritability, poor concentration, insomnia, restlessness and dissociative states including detachment, derealisation or depersonalisation. Patients also re-experience the event in flashbacks, avoid associated places or people.

adoption study The comparison of siblings reared together or apart to assess heredity.

agoraphobia A fear of being in places where escape would be difficult or embarrassing (such as in public) which can develop out of specific phobias or be due to a traumatic event. Often arises due to the fear of having a panic attack in public, hence it is associated with panic disorder. Characterised by extreme anxiety, stress, worry and avoidance of public situations. May arise with or without panic disorder.

agrammatism Deficits in understanding or employing grammatical devices.

agraphia An inability to write while still able to read.

alexia An inability to read while still able to write.

alogia Impoverished speech observed in cases of schizophrenia.

alpha activity The pattern of brain activity observed when an individual is in a state of relaxation. It is observed while the eyes are closed, implying that the individual is also in a state of relative inactivity. This activity is considerably slower at 8–12 Hz and the levels of activity observed in the various areas of the brain is relatively synchronised.

Alzheimer's disease A medical condition which is associated with amyloid plaques and neurofibrillary tangles in the brain. It is initially characterised by a mild deterioration of memory but progresses to dementia where all cognitive functions are impaired and quality of life is significantly diminished.

anhedonia An inability to feel pleasure.

anomia Deficits in remembering an appropriate word.

anterograde amnesia Inability to learn and remember information encountered after brain damage.

anxiety disorder A psychological condition characterised by high levels of stress and anxiety, usually elicited by an external stimuli but also influenced by internal processes.

aphagia A condition in which a neurologically damaged individual ceases to eat.

aphasia A deficit in language usually produced through brain damage.

apraxia of speech Deficits in the ability to programme movements of the lips, tongue and throat to produce normal speech sounds.

aromatisation The process by which sex steroids derived from cholesterol are converted into other sex steroids.

atrophy The decay or wasting of a structure, organ or system.

attention The allocation of cognitive resources to stimuli.

autobiographical memory Memory for events, experiences and personal information from one's own life.

autonomic nervous system A division of the peripheral nervous system which is responsible for governing responses which are largely beyond conscious control.

autotopagnosia The inability to name and identify body parts.

avolition A lack of desire or motivation.

behavioural genetics An approach in psychology which attempts to identify what proportion of the variance in a trait or behaviour can be attributed to genetics and to the environment.

behaviourism A school of thought concerned with purely observable and measureable human and animal behaviour.

beta activity A pattern of activity observed when actively engaging in mental activity, characterised by 13–30 Hz (cycles per second). Activity is desynchronised in that areas of the brain vary in their levels and pattern of activity.

bipolar disorder A psychological condition characterised not only with periods of depression but also by periods of mania.

bipolar I Bipolar disorder characterised by manic episodes, major depressive episodes and often mixed episodes in which both states occur.

bipolar II Bipolar disorder characterised by hypomania (rapid cycle but short-lived mania), major depressive episodes but no manic or mixed episodes.

bloodletting An ancient technique of releasing blood from the body in an attempt to restore balance.

Broca's aphasia A deficit in language production caused by damage to Broca's area in the prefrontal cortex. Characterised by anomia, agrammatism and difficulties in articulation. Also known as expressive aphasia.

bruxism A condition in which individuals grind their teeth and clench their jaw while asleep, potentially resulting in a sore jaw, damaged teeth and headaches.

cataplexy The sudden loss of muscle tone which can be anything from slight paralysis of a body part to complete collapse.

central nervous system A complex system which governs all top-down processes and consists of the brain and the spinal cord.

circadian clock A hypothetical biological mechanism which is theorised to control sleep–waking patterns and the other biological prerequisites for sleep (such as temperature change, the release of growth hormones and the secretion of neurotransmitters).

circadian rhythm A behavioural or physiological process which changes daily according to a set pattern, such as the sleep–wake cycle.

clinical trial The procedure by which medications are tested and legalised.

cognitivism A school of thought concerned with human cognition.

comparative psychology An approach in psychology which is concerned with the general biology of behaviour and performs comparisons across species.

conduction aphasia Inability to repeat words which are heard while still being able to speak normally. Caused by damage to the arcuate fasciculus which connects Broca's area and Wernicke's area.

connectionist A computational model used to simulate human performance and neural activity.

consolidation The physiological process by which a memory becomes gradually more resilient to forgetting and interference with time, repeated activation of neurons, rehearsal and entrenchment in the brain.

converging operations Combining two or more different approaches or techniques to study the same phenomenon at different levels of analysis.

comorbidity The presence of more than one condition at a given time.

corpus callosum A bundle of neural fibres connecting the left and right hemispheres of the brain.

cross-cultural study The study and comparison of groups of people from different cultural backgrounds.

declarative memory Knowledge which is easily vocalised, including knowledge about oneself and the world. Includes semantic, autobiographical and episodic memory.

delta activity This is brain activity at less than 3 Hz but with higher amplitude than the earlier stages of sleep. Observed during stages 3 and 4 of sleep.

dextral Right-handed.

diathesis–stress A theoretical model which states that behaviour and experience are produced by both biological and environmental factors.

dichotic listening test A task in which dual messages are presented to the left and right ears and participants must try to recite both messages.

direct dyslexia The ability to read words despite lacking an understanding of them.

dizygotic twins Non-identical twins who only share half of their DNA.

double dissociation Observed when one brain-damaged patient shows one pattern of impairment while another shows a different pattern of impairment. Potentially due to the damage of different specialised cerebral structures.

dualism/dualist A perspective which states the mind and body both exist as separate entities which contribute toward the sense of reality.

echoic memory Short-term memory for information in the auditory field.

echolalia Involuntary repetition of other people's utterances.

emotion A positive or negative feeling in response to an internal or external stimulus which is characterised by physiological changes and species-typical behaviour.

encoding How information is converted into a physiological signal which changes the connections and pattern of activation in the brain.

endocrine glands Glands which secrete hormones directly into the bloodstream having fast-acting and concentrated effects.

endocrine system The network of glands and organs which release and regulate hormones.

enteric nervous system A division of the autonomic nervous system which is responsible for maintaining the gastrointestinal system.

enuresis Persistent bedwetting occurring after a child has been potty trained.

episodic memory Memory for specific events including times, places, emotions experienced during the event.

ethological research A research technique in which animals are studied in their natural environment with little intervention by the researcher.

eugenics A school of thought in which intelligent people are encouraged to reproduce in an attempt to improve the species.

evolutionary theories Theories that behaviour and experience have developed through centuries of genetic mutation, evolution and survival of the fittest.

exocrine glands Glands which secrete substances into ducts, from which they pass from cell to cell through diffusion.

explicit memory Knowledge which is easily vocalised, including knowledge about oneself and the world.

exteroceptive sensory systems The structures and processes responsible for the senses of touch, smell, taste, hearing and vision.

family study A research technique in which the prevalence of a trait or type within a family is assessed in regards to heredity.

functionalism An approach which is concerned with identifying the functions which behaviour and experience serve.

generalised anxiety disorder A general state of anxiety which is applied across life in general and may have originated due to the exacerbation of other anxieties or traumatic events. Characterised by anxiety, worry, heart palpitations, dizziness and recurrent stress response across a range of situations.

genetic engineering The manipulation or cloning of the genome within laboratory settings.

heredity The proportion of variance in a given trait or type which can be accounted for by genetics and the environment.

homeostasis The naturally balanced state of the body. This is the ideal state and the parasympathetic nervous system strives to restore this equilibrium when physiology is imbalanced.

hormones Endogenous substances produced by the glands of the body.

humorism An ancient school of thought concerned with the balance of the body's naturally produced substances: bile, blood and phlegm.

hypomania Rapid-cycle but shorted-lived episodes of mania. Common in bipolar II.

iconic memory Short-term memory for information in the visual field.

idealism A perspective which states that the only reality is that created by the mind.

implicit memory Memory which cannot be easily articulated, such as in the case of procedural knowledge.

insomnia This condition is characterised by the difficulty in falling asleep or only sleeping for brief intervals of time.

interoceptive system The structures and processes responsible for processing information concerning the position of the body.

introspection A technique developed by Wundt (1902) to study the subjective experience of patients based on their description of their thoughts and feelings.

James–Lange theory A theory in which emotional behaviour and physiological responses are directly elicited by situations and that 'feelings' are the result of feedback from these behavioural and physiological responses.

K complexes Large spikes of activity initially observed during stage 2 sleep and declining in stage 3.

Korsakoff's syndrome A medical condition produced through alcoholism in which patients demonstrate sensory deficits, motor problems, confusion, amnesia and personality changes. Patients also have an increased risk of death from liver, gastrointestinal or heart disease.

lateralisation The theory that one hemisphere of the brain is dominant in a given process while the other serves only minor roles.

learning Learning is concerned with the process in which our experiences of the environment change the pattern and structure of activation in brain.

lesions The severing of connections or damage to structures in the brain.

linguistic universals The 13 principles of language which Hockett (1960) argued could be observed across all languages.

localisation The theory that specialised structures of the brain facilitate specific functions.

long-term memory Information which is stored in the brain for a long period of time and retrieved at a later date, despite lacking continuing rehearsal in the interval between encoding, storage and retrieval. These memories can be elaborated over time as new information is encountered and processed.

long-term potentiation When pre- and post-synaptic neurons are activated simultaneously upon exposure to a stimulus. This enhances the transmission of both action potentials and neurotransmitters, facilitating learning by altering the connections between neurons and lowering their activation thresholds.

major (unipolar) depression A psychological condition characterised by low mood, negative thoughts, extreme negativism, reduced interest, lack of pleasure, changes in appetite and sleep patterns and difficulty concentrating. In extreme cases sufferers can also experience hallucinations and delusions.

materialism A perspective which states that the only reality is that experienced by the body.

memory How the changes in the brain experienced during learning are stored and subsequently reactivated during the retrieval of information. Memory has been subdivided into various forms, including autobiographical, semantic, episodic, implicit, explicit and prospective memory.

mind–body problem A philosophical debate concerning the relationship between and dominance of the mind and the body.

monist/monism A perspective which states that either the mind or the body exists independently. There is only one reality and that may be through the mind (idealism) or the body (materialism).

monozygotic twins Identical twins who share the same DNA.

narcolepsy A condition in which individuals are unable to control their sleep patterns, suffer from excessive daytime sleepiness (EDS), fall asleep at inappropriate times or in inappropriate places and enter REM sleep after only ten minutes.

nature–nurture A theoretical debate surrounding the topic of whether an individual's behaviour and experience are determined and inevitable due to biological factors or undetermined and changeable due to environmental factors.

neuroimaging A procedure in which neurological imaging technology is used to visualise and record the activity of the brain.

neuropsychology An approach in psychology which attempts to identify both normal and impaired human function, usually through studying the effects of brain damage.

neuroscience An approach in psychology which attempts to identify the neural correlates of cognition using a combination of physiological, experimental and computational measures.

neurotransmitter A naturally occurring chemical produced in the body at the terminal buttons of neurons which facilitates the transmission of action potentials across synaptic gaps. The activation threshold and compatibility of the post-synaptic receptor cells will determine their efficiency. Neurotransmitters can have excitatory or inhibitory effects.

nocturia Frequency waking due to the need to urinate, which can result in sleep deprivation.

non-REM sleep Constituting stages 1–4 of normal sleep which is not characterised by rapid eye movements.

normal wakefulness Full consciousness and engagement with the environment.

obsessive compulsive disorder An anxiety disorder characterised by excessive worry, persistent obsessive thoughts, irrationality and overriding compulsions to perform actions which reduce the patient's anxiety. Repetitive actions are intended to neutralise the source of the anxiety. May prevent normal daily functioning.

orthographic dysgraphia A writing disorder in which individuals are unable to spell irregularly spelled words while still being able to spell regularly spelled words.

panic disorder A condition which often arises without a discernible cause but may follow periods of high anxiety or arise due to misinterpretation of bodily responses. Characterised by sudden and acute attacks of fear or anxiety resulting in panic attacks, stress, heart palpitations, rapid breathing or hyperventilating, blurred vision, dizziness and flights of thought.

parasomnias Parasomnias include sleep walking, night terrors and bruxism.

pavor nocturnus Night terrors. A condition which arises during slow-wave sleep and is characterised by extreme fear, gasping and often screaming.

parasympathetic nervous system A division of the autonomic nervous system which promotes the conservation of resources.

perception Higher-order processes of integrating, reorganising and interpreting a complete pattern of sensation.

perimetry task A task which identifies the location and scope of a scotoma by asking participants to identify when they are able to see a series of dots presented in the visual field.

peripheral neuropathy A condition in which the nerves that stimulate muscles to move are damaged and can result in muscle atrophy and facial palsy.

peripheral nervous system A complex system which governs all bottom-up processes and consists of all of the nerves, muscles and organs beyond the CNS.

pheromone A chemical substance transmitted from one animal to another via smell or taste, usually to signal receptivity, availability, challenge or threat.

phonological dysgraphia A writing disorder in which individuals are unable to sound out words and write them phonetically.

phonological dyslexia Ability to read familiar words but deficits in the ability to read unfamiliar words and pronounceable non-words.

physiological psychology An approach in psychology which attempts to identify the neural correlates of behaviour and experience, often in laboratory animals.

polysomnography The measurement of physiological activity during sleep.

post-traumatic stress disorder Anxiety disorder arising after extreme trauma which caused feelings of intense fear and helplessness which can arise at any point after the trauma, including years later. Characterised by flashbacks, nightmares, obsessive thoughts, avoidance of triggers, heightened anxiety and startle response.

procedural memory Knowledge including all non-declarative skills and abilities. This is concerned with how to do things.

proprioceptive system The structures and processes responsible for processing information concerning conditions within the body.

prosopagnosia A neuropsychological condition in which people are unable to recognise faces.

prospective memory Remembering to perform a planned action at the intended time.

psychopharmacology An approach in psychology which is concerned with the effects of medication on behaviour and experience.

psychophysiology An approach in psychology which investigates the correspondence between physiological activity, behaviour and experience in human subjects.

pure alexia An inability to read without the loss of the ability to write produced by brain damage.

pure word deafness The ability to speak, hear, write and read without being able to comprehend the meaning of speech. Caused by damage to Wernicke's area and the disruption of auditory input.

reductionist/reductionism Attempting to explain a higher-order function based on lower-order processes.

rehearsal A process which can result in the transition of a memory from the short-term to long-term memory. Rehearsal can be through maintenance, in which individuals rehearse the original information, or elaboration, in which the individual adds to the existing memory.

REM sleep Stage 5 of sleep characterised by rapid eye movement.

retrieval The reactivation of neural networks and the information contained within them.

retrograde amnesia Inability to retrieve memories which were acquired before brain damage.

schizophrenia A severe condition in which sufferers experience hallucinations, delusions, speech impairment, irrationality, unusual motor activity and impairment in most aspects of their lives.

scotoma An area of blindness produced through damage to the primary visual cortex.

semantic memory Knowledge about categories, objects, concepts and meanings.

sensation The process of detecting a stimulus.

serendipitous Findings which were observed but were not originally the subject of the investigation.

short-term memory Information which is held in consciousness for a brief amount of time, usually through immediate and continuous rehearsal. This includes iconic and echoic memory. Also reconceptualised as working memory.

sinestral Left-handed.

sleep apnoea A condition in which individuals temporarily cease breathing while asleep.

sleep paralysis A condition in which the muscle atonia, which normally occurs during REM sleep, actually occurs when going to sleep (hypnagogic) or waking up (hypnopompic). It can cause states of extreme panic and in severe cases it can occur in conjunction with terrifying hallucinations.

sleep spindles Bursts of faster activity initially observed during stage 2 sleep and declining in stage 3.

slow-wave sleep This is the activity observed during stage one sleep and is characterised by a frequency of 3–7.5 Hz.

sodium amytal test A test in which one hemisphere of the brain is anaesthetised to test the performance of the other hemisphere.

somatic nervous system A division of the peripheral nervous system which is responsible for monitoring and interacting with the external world.

somatosensory Information derived from the bodily senses.

somnambulism Sleep walking. A condition in which individuals are able to unconsciously interact with their environment while sleeping for a short interval of time.

specific phobias Anxiety disorders often caused by irrational thoughts or a negative experience with specific stimuli. Characterised by anxiety, worry, avoidance of triggers, obsessive thoughts, attentional biases and hypervigilance.

split-brain study A study which examines the performance of people who have had their hemispheres surgically separated.

storage How information is stored in the brain as connections between neural networks and their respective patterns of activation.

stress response The physiological, cognitive and behavioural response to threat and anxiety characterised by action readiness for 'fight-or-flight'.

structuralism An approach which is concerned with studying how the structure and organisation of the mind influence behaviour and experience.

surface dyslexia Ability to read words phonetically but deficits in the ability to read irregularly spelled words.

sympathetic nervous system A division of the autonomic nervous system which promotes action readiness.

tardive dyskinesia Involuntary movements such as tick-like gestures, rapid movement of arms or legs, grimacing, rapid blinking and tongue protrusion produced through long-term use of anti-psychotic medications.

targeted mutation Intended genetic mutations are produced in a laboratory and injected into laboratory animals to produce the desired mutation.

theta activity This is brain activity observed during stage 1 sleep and is characterised by a frequency of 3–7.5 Hz.

topic The term assigned to hormones which stimulate or inhibit the release of other hormones.

transcortical sensory aphasia Deficits in comprehending and producing meaningful spontaneous speech while being able to repeat speech. Caused by damage to the posterior region of Wernicke's area.

trepanning An ancient technique in which holes are drilled in the skull in an attempt to relieve pressure.

twin study The comparison of siblings on a specific measure to assess heredity.

unipolar depression A psychological condition characterised by unusually low mood, lethargy, negative thoughts and negative emotions.

visual agnosia A neuropsychological condition characterised by deficits in perception.

Wernicke's aphasia Deficits in the ability to comprehend speech and/or the production of fluent but meaningless speech. Produced by damage to Wernicke's area in the auditory association cortex in the left temporal lobe. Also known as receptive aphasia.

word form dyslexia An individual is only able to read words after spelling out the individual letters. Also known as spelling dyslexia.

working memory Manipulation and use of information in short-term memory.

zeitgebers Stimuli which can reset the circadian clock and circadian rhythms. These usually come in the form of changing light.

References

Adkins-Regan, E. (2009). Under the influence of hormones. *Science, 324*(5931), 1145–1146.

Anand, B. K., & Brobeck, J. R. (1951). Hypothalamic control of food intake in rats and cats. *Yale Journal of Biology and Medicine, 24*(1), 123–140.

Anderson, A. K., Christoff, K., Stappen, I., Panitz, D., Ghahremani, D. G., Glover, G., Gabrieli, J. D. E., & Sobel, N. (2003). Dissociated neural representations of intensity and valence in human olfaction. *Nature Neuroscience, 6*(2), 196–202. Available: http://bork.hampshire.edu/~bart/temp/anderson.pdf

Anderson, S. K., Müller, M. M., & Hillyard, S. A. (2009). Color-selective attention need not be mediated by spatial attention. *Journal of Vision, 9*(6), 1–7. Available: http://calendar.arvo.org/9/6/2/article.aspx

Anderson, S. W., Bechara, A., Damasio, H., Tranel, D., & Damasio, A. R. (1999). Impairment of social and moral behavior related to early damage in human prefrontal cortex. *Nature Neuroscience, 2*(11), 1032–1037. Available: www.science.mcmaster.ca/psychology/psych3l03/ReviewPapers/social%20behavior-Demasio(1999).pdf

Anderson, T. S., Tiippana, K., Laarni, J., & Sams, M. (2009). The role of visual spatial attention in audiovisual speech perception. *Speech Communication, 51*(2), 184–193.

APA (2000). *Diagnostic and statistical manual for mental disorders* (4th ed.). Washington, DC: American Psychiatric Association.

Ardila, A. (2010). A review of conduction aphasia. *Current Neurology and Neuroscience Reports, 10*(6), 499–503.

Aston-Jones, G., & Bloom, F. E. (1981). Activity of norepinephrine-containing locus coeruleus neurons in behaving rats anticipates fluctuations in the sleep-waking cycle. *Journal of Neuroscience, 1*(8), 876–886.

Baddeley, A. D. (2007). *Working memory, thought and action*. Oxford: Oxford University Press.

Baddeley, A. D., Eysenck, M., & Anderson, M. C. (2009). *Memory*. Hove: Psychology Press.

Baracochea, D. (2006). Anterograde and retrograde effects of benzodiazepines on memory. *The Scientific World Journal, 6*, 1460–1465. Available: http://neurologiauruguay.org/home/images/publicacion/benzodiazepines%20and%20memory.pdf

Bates, T. (2006). The clinical management of social anxiety disorder. In A. Carr and M. McNulty (Eds.), *The handbook of adult clinical psychology: An evidence-based approach*, (pp. 558–590). Hove: Routledge.

Bavelier, D., Corina, D., Jezzard, P., Padmanabhan, S., Clark, V. P., Karni, A., Prinster, A., Braun, A., Lalwani, A., Rauschecker, J., Turner, R., & Neville, H. (1997). Sentence reading: A functional MRI study at 4 tesla. *Journal of Cognitive Neuroscience, 9*(5), 664–686.

Bear, M. F., Connors, B., & Paradiso, M. (2007). *Neuroscience: Exploring the brain* (3rd ed.). Baltimore, MD: Lippincott Williams, & Watkins.

Bee, M. A., & Micheyl, C. (2008). The 'Cocktail party problem': What is it? How can it be solved? And why should animal behaviourists study it? *Journal of Comparative Psychology, 122*(3), 235–251. Available: www.ncbi.nlm.nih.gov/pmc/articles/PMC2692487/

Belcher, P., & Moorcroft, W. H. (2005). *Understanding sleep and dreaming*. New York: Kluwer Academic/Plenum Publishers.

Belmonte, M. K., Allen, G., Beckler-Mitchener, A., Boulanger, L. M., Carper, R. A., & Webb, S. J. (2004). Autism and abnormal development of brain connectivity. *The Journal of Neuroscience, 24*(42), 9228–9231. Available: www.jneurosci.org/content/24/42/9228.full.pdf+html

Bernal, B., & Ardila, A. (2009). The role of the arcuate fasciculus in conduction aphasia. *Brain, 132*(9), 2309–2316. Available: http://brain.oxfordjournals.org/content/132/9/2309.full

Bi, Y., Wei, T., Wu, C., Han, Z., Jiang, T., & Caramazza, A. (2009). The role of the left anterior temporal lobe in language processing revisited: Evidence from an individual with ATL resection. *Cortex, 47*(5), 575–587.

Blonder, L. X., Bowers, D., & Heilman, K. M. (1991). The role of the right hemisphere in emotional communications. *Brain, 114*(3), 1115–1127.

Bouwknecht, J. A., Hijzen, T. H., Gugten, J. van der, Maes, R. A. A., Hen, R., & Olivier, B. (2001). Absence of 5-HT1B receptors is associated with impaired impulse control in male 5-HT1B knockout mice. *Biological Psychiatry, 49*(7), 557–568.

Brewin, C. R., Andrews, B., Rose, S., & Kirk, M. (1999). Acute stress disorder and posttraumatic stress disorder in victims of violent crime. *American Journal of Psychiatry, 156*(3), 360–366.

Brodal, P. (2010). *The central nervous system: Structure and function* (4th ed.). New York: Oxford University Press.

Broerse, P. J. (2001). Perception and attention. In N. W. Bond and K. M. McConkey (Eds.), *Psychological science: An introduction* (pp. 42–96). Sydney: McGraw-Hill.

Bryant, R. A., & Harvey, A. G. (2000). *Acute stress disorder: A handbook of theory, assessment, and treatment.* Washington, DC: American Psychological Association.

Burton, R. (1989/1994). *The anatomy of melancholy.* Oxford: Oxford University Press.

Cabeza, R., & Nyberg, L. (2000). Imaging cognition II: An empirical review of 275 PET and fMRI studies. *Journal of Cognitive Neuroscience, 21*(1), 1–47.

Campbell, R., & Conway, M. (Eds.) (1995). *Broken memories: Case studies in memory impairment.* Oxford: Blackwell.

Carlson, N. R. (2004). *Physiology of behavior* (8th ed.). New York: Pearson Education Inc.

Carr, A. (2006). *The handbook of child and adolescent clinical psychology: A contextual approach.* Hove: Routledge.

Carr, A., & McNulty, M. (Eds.) (2006). *The handbook of adult clinical psychology: An evidence-based approach.* Hove: Routledge.

Carver, C. S., & Harmon-Jones, E. (2009). Anger is an approach-related affect: Evidence and implications. *Psychological Bulletin, 135*(2), 183–204. Available: www.socialemotiveneuroscience.org/pubs/carver_hj2009psy_bull.pdf

Castrén, E. (2005). Is mood chemistry? *Nature Reviews Neuroscience, 6*, 241–246.

Chan, S., & Kirby, M. D. (2000). Thyroid hormone and central nervous system development. *Journal of Endocrinology, 165*(1), 1–8. Available: http://joe.endocrinology-journals.org/content/165/1/1.full.pdf

Chan, T., Kyere, K., Davis, B. R., Shemyakin, A., Kabitzke, P. A., Shair, H. N., Barr, G. A., & Wiedenmayer, C. P. (2011). The role of the medial prefrontal cortex in innate fear regulation in infants, juveniles and adolescents. *The Journal of Neuroscience, 31*(13), 4991–4999.

Chaudhari, N., & Roper, S. D. (2010). The cell biology of taste. *Journal of Current Biology, 190*(3), 285–296. Available: http://jcb.rupress.org/content/190/3/285.full

Cho, K., Ennaceur, A., Cole, J. C., & Suh, C. K. (2000). Chronic jet lag produces cognitive deficits. *The Journal of Neuroscience, 20*, 1–5. Available: www.jneurosci.org/content/20/6/RC66.short

Cohen, G., Johnstone, R. A., & Plunkett, K. (Eds.) (2002). *Exploring cognition: Damaged brains and neural networks – Readings in cognitive neuropsychology and connectionist modelling.* Hove: Psychology Press

Coltheart, M,. (2001). *Assumptions and methods in cognitive neuropsychology.* Hove: Psychology Press.

Coltheart, M., Ingles, L., Cupples, L., Michie, P., Bates, A., & Budd, B. (1998). A semantic subsystem specific to the storage of information about visual attributes of animate and non-animate objects. *Neurocase, 4*, 353–370.

Comer, R. J. (2007). *Abnormal psychology* (6th ed.). New York: Worth Publishers.

Corkin, S., Sullivan, E. V., Twitchell, T. E., & Grove, E. (1981). The amnesic patient H.M.: Clinical observations and a test performance 28 years after operation. *Society of Neuroscience Abstracts, 7*, 235.

References

Correa, A., Sanabria, D., Spence, C., Tudela, P., & Lupiáñez, J. (2006). Selective temporal attention enhances the temporal resolution of visual perception: Evidence from a temporal order judgement task. *Brain Research, 1070*(1), 202–205.

Coull, J. T. (1998). Neural correlates of attention and arousal: Insights from electrophysiology, functional neuroimaging and psychopharmacology. *Progress in Neurobiology, 55*(4), 343–361. Available: http://dionysus.psych.wisc.edu/Lit/Articles/CoullJ1998a.pdf

Counsell, C. E., & Ruddell, W. S. (1994). Coeliac disease and autoimmune thyroid disease. *Gut, 35*(6), 844–846.

Crawford, J. R., & Garthwaite, P. H. (2002). Investigation of the single case in neuropsychology: Confidence limits on the abnormality of test scores and test score differences. *Neuropsychology, 40*(8), 1196–1208. Available: http://abdn.ac.uk/~psy086/dept/pdfs/Neuropsychologia_2002_conflims_singlecase.pdf

Creamer, M., & Carty, J. (2006). Post-traumatic stress disorder. In A. Carr and M. McNulty (Eds.), *The handbook of adult clinical psychology: An evidence-based approach* (pp. 523–557). Hove: Routledge.

Crick, F., & Mitchison, G. (1983). The functions of dream sleep. *Nature, 304*(5922), 111–114.

Critchley, H. D. (2009). Psychophysiology of neural, cognitive and affective integration: fMRI and autonomic indicants. *International Journal of Psychophysiology, 73*(2), 88–94. Available: www.ncbi.nlm.nih.gov/pmc/articles/PMC2722714/

Damann, N., Voets, T., & Nilius, B. (2008). TRPs in our senses. *Current Biology, 18*(18), 880–889. Available: https://lirias.kuleuven.be/bitstream/123456789/221461/2/TRPs

Damasio, H., Grabowski, T. J., Tranel, D., Hichwa, R. D., & Damasio, A. R. (1996). A neural basis for lexical retrieval. *Nature, 380*, 499–505.

Damasio, H., Tranel, D., Grabowski, T., Adolphs, R., & Damasio, A. (2004). Neural systems behind word and concept retrieval. *Cognition, 92*(1–2), 179–229.

Darwin, C. (1872/1965). *The expression of the emotions in man and animals.* Chicago: University of Chicago Press.

Darwin, C. (1859). *The origin of the species by natural selection, or the preservation of favoured races in the struggle for life.* London: John Murray.

Davidson, R. J. (2003). Affective neuroscience and psychophysiology: Towards a synthesis. *Psychophysiology, 40*, 655–665. Available: http://dionysus.psych.wisc.edu/lit/articles/DavidsonR2003b.pdf

Davidson, R. J., Pizzagalli, D., Nitschke, J. B., & Putnam, K. (2002). Depression: Perspectives from affective neuroscience. *Annual Review of Psychology, 53*(1), 545–574.

Dewsbury, D. A. (1990). *Contemporary issues in comparative psychology.* Sunderland, MA: Sinauer Associates Inc.

D'Hondt, F., Lassonde, M., Collignon, O., Dubarry, A., Robert, M., Rigoulot, S., Honoré, J., Lepore, F., & Sequeira, H. (2010). Early brain–body impact of emotional arousal. *Human Neuroscience, 4*, 1–10. Available: www.ncbi.nlm.nih.gov/pmc/articles/PMC2859881/

Drevets, W. C. (2001). Neuroimaging and neuropathological studies for the cognitive–emotional features of mood disorders. *Current Opinion in Neurobiology, 11*(2), 240–249.

Drevets, W. C., Videen, T. O., Price, J. L., Preskorn, S. H., Carmichael, S. T., & Raichle, M. E. (1992). A functional anatomical study of unipolar depression. *The Journal of Neuroscience, 12*(9), 3628–3641.

Ehlert, U., Gaab, J., & Heinrichs, M. (2001). Psychoneuroendocrinological contributes to the etiology of depression, posttraumatic stress disorder, and stress related bodily disorders: The role of the hypothalamus–pituitary–adrenal axis. *Biological Psychology, 57*, 141–152. Available: www.socialbehavior.uzh.ch/static/home/heinrichs/downloads/BiolPsychol-UE01.pdf

Einstein, G. O., & McDaniels, M. A. (2005). Prospective memory: Multiple retrieval processes. *Current Directions in Psychological Science, 14*(6), 286–290. Available: www2.furman.edu/academics/psychology/facultyandstaff/einstein/documents/2005a.pdf

Escobar, G. M., Obregón, M. J., & Rey, F. E. (2004). Maternal thyroid hormones early in pregnancy and fetal brain development. *Clinical Endocrinology and Metabolism, 18*(2), 225–248.

Espa, F., Ondze, B., Billiard, M., & Besset, A. (2000). Sleep architecture, slow-wave activity, and sleep spindles in adolescent patients with sleepwalking and sleep terrors. *Clinical Neurophysiology, 111*(5), 929–939.

Fitzgerald, M. (2010). The lost domain of pain. *Brain, 133*(6), 1850–1854.

Freud, S. (1953). *The interpretation of dreams* (3rd ed.) (A. A. Brill Trans.). Plain Label Books. (Original work published 1931.) Available: http://koyakin.yolasite.com/resources/Interpretation%20Of%20Dreams%20326%20Pages.pdf

Furness, J. B. (2006). *The enteric nervous system*. Malden, MA: Wiley-Blackwell.

Gallo, L. C., & Eastman, C. I. (1993). Circadian rhythms during gradually delaying and advancing sleep and light schedules. *Physiology and Behavior, 53*(1), 119–126.

Galton, F. (1865). Hereditary talent and character. *Macmillan's Magazine, 12*, 157–166. Available: http://psychclassics.yorku.ca/Galton/talent.htm.

García-Aragón, J., Lobie, P. E., Muscat, G. O., Gobius, K. S., Norstedt, G., & Waters, M. J. (1992). Prenatal expression of the growth hormone (GH) receptor/binding protein in the rat: A role for GH in embryonic and fetal development. *Development, 114*, 869–876.

Gardner, R. A., Gardner, B. T., & Van Cantfort, T. E. (1989). *Teaching sign language to chimpanzees*. Albany, NY: State University of New York Press.

Gaskell, M. G. (Ed.) (2007). *The Oxford handbook of psycholinguistics*. Oxford: Oxford University Press.

Gazzaniga, M. (2003). *Cognitive neuroscience: The biology of the mind* (3rd edn.). New York: W. W. Norton, & Co.

Geschwind, N. (1970). The organization of language and the brain. *Science, 170*(3961), 940–944.

Gibson, A. D., & Garbers, D. L. (2000). Guanylyl cyclases as a family of putative odorant receptors. *Annual Review of Neuroscience, 23*(1), 417–439.

Glaser, R., & Kiecolt-Glaser, J. K. (Eds.) (1994). *Handbook of human stress and Immunity*. San Diego: Academic Press.

Goldstein, B. E. (2009). *Sensation and perception* (8th edn.). Belmont, CA: Wadsworth.

Goodale, M., & Milner, D. (2006). One brain – two visual systems. *The Psychologist, 19*(11), 660–663.

Gottesmann, C. (2008). Noradrenaline involvement in basic and higher integrated REM sleep processes. *Progress in Neurobiology, 85*(3), 237–272.

Grosbras, M., & Paus, T. (2002). Transcranial magnetic stimulation of the human frontal eye field: effects on visual perception and attention. *Journal of Cognitive Neuroscience, 14*(7), 1109–1120.

Grossman, E., Donnelly, M., Price, R., Pickens, D., Morgan, V., Neighbor, G., & Blake, R. (2000). Brain areas involved in perception of biological motion. *Journal of Cognitive Neuroscience, 12*(5), 711–720.

Gulevich, G., Dement, W. C., & Johnson, L. (1966). Psychiatric and EEG observations on a case of prolonged (264 hours) wakefulness. *Archives in General Psychiatry, 15*, 29–35.

Guzick, D. S. (2004). Polycystic ovary syndrome. *Obstetrics and Gynaecology, 103*(1), 181–193. Available: www.utilis.net/Morning%20Topics/Gynecology/PCOS.PDF

Haass, C. (1999). Biology of Alzheimer's disease. *European Archives of Psychiatry and Clinical Neuroscience, 249*(6), 265.

Harris, M., & Grunstein, R. R. (2009). Treatments for somnambulism in adults: Assessing the evidence. *Sleep Medicine Reviews, 13*(4), 295–297.

Handwerger, S., & Freemark, M. (2000). The roles of placental growth hormone and placental lactogen in the regulation of human fetal growth and development. *Journal of Pediatric Endocrinology and Metabolism, 13*, 343–356.

Harley, R. (2007). *The psychology of language: From data to theory* (3rd edn.). Hove: Psychology Press.

Harrington, R. C., Fudge, H., Rutter, M. L., Bredenkamp, D., Groothues, C., & Pridham, J. (1993). Child and adult depression: A test of continuities with data from a family study. *British Journal of Psychiatry, 162*, 627–633.

References

Henke, K. (2010). A model for memory systems based on processing modes rather than consciousness. *Nature Reviews Neuroscience, 11*, 523–532. Available: http://psychology.stanford.edu/~jlm/pdfs/HenkeNRNpaper.pdf

Hergenhahn, B. R. (2009). *An introduction to the history of psychology* (6th ed.). Belmont, CA: Wadsworth.

Herman, L. M., Kuczaj, S. A., & Holder, M. D. (1993). Responses to anomalous gestural sequences by a language-trained dolphin: Evidence for processing of semantic relations and syntactic information. *Journal of Experimental Psychology: General, 122*(2), 184–194.

Hertenstein, M. J., Holmes, R., McCullough, M., & Keltner, D. (2009). The communication of emotion via touch. *Emotion, 9*(4), 566–573.

Hindmarch, I. (2001). Expanding the horizons of depression: Beyond the monoamine hypothesis. *Human Psychopharmacology, 16*(3), 203–218.

Hirschfeld, R. M. A. (2000). History and evolution of the monoamine hypothesis of depression. *Journal of Clinical Psychiatry, 61*(6), 4–6.

Hockett, C. F. (1960). The origins of speech. *Scientific American, 203*, 89–96.

Holdstock, J. S., Parslow, D. M., Morris, R. G., Fleminger, S., Abrahams, S., Denby, C., Montaldi, D., & Mayes, A. R. (2008). Two case studies illustrating how relatively selective hippocampal lesions in humans can have quite different effects on memory. *Hippocampus, 18*, 679–691. Available: www.julietholdstock.com/pdfs/Holdstock%20et%20al%202008.pdf

Horne, J. A. A. (1978). A review of the biological effects of total sleep deprivation in man. *Biological Psychology, 7*, 55–102.

Hubel, D. H., & Wiesel, T. N. (1977). Functional architecture of macaque monkey visual cortex. *Proceedings of the Royal Society of London, 198*, 1–59.

Huber, R., & Kravitz, E. A. (2010). Aggression: Towards an integration of gene, brain and behaviour. In T. Székely, A. J. Moore, & J. Komdeur (Eds.), *Social behaviour: Genes, ecology and evolution* (pp.165–180). New York: Cambridge University Press.

Huberle, E., Driver, J., & Karnath, H. (2010). Retinal versus physical stimulus size as determinants of visual perception in simultanagnosia. *Neuropsychologia, 48*(6), 1677–1682.

Jaffee, S. R., Caspi, A., Moffitt, T. E., Dodge, K. A., Rutter, M., Taylor, A., & Tully, L. A. (2005). Nature x nurture: Genetic vulnerabilities interact with physical maltreatment to promote conduct problems. *Developmental Psychopathology, 17*(1), 67–84. Available: http://www.ncbi.nlm.nih.gov/pmc/articles/PMC2768347/

James, W. (1890). *The principles of psychology* (vol. 1). Available: http://psychclassics.yorku.ca/James/Principles/index.htm

Jeannerod, M., Arbib, M. A., Rizzolatti, G., & Sakata, H. (1995). Grasping objects: The cortical mechanisms of visuomotor transformation. *Trends in Neuroscience, 18*(7), 314–320

Kanbayashi, T., Nakamura, M., Shimizu, T., & Nishino, S. (2010). Symptomatic narcolepsy or hypersomnia, with or without hypocretin (Orexin) deficiency. *Narcolepsy, 2*, 135–165.

Keyers, C., Kaas, J. H., & Gazzola, V. (2010). Somatosensation in social perception. *Nature Reviews Neuroscience, 11*(6), 417–428.

Kindt, M., Soeter, M., & Vervliet, B. (2009). Beyond extinction: Erasing human fear responses and preventing the return of fear. *Nature Neuroscience, 12*(3), 256–258. Available: www.psypoli.nl/webdata/files/kindt%20beyond%20extinsion.pdf

Kirschbaum, C., Kudielka, B. M., Gaab, J., Schommer, N. C., & Hellhammer, D. H. (1999). Impact of gender, menstrual cycle phase, and oral contraceptives on the activity of the hypothalamus–pituitary–adrenal axis. *Psychosomatic Medicine, 61*, 154–162. Available: http://dionysus.psych.wisc.edu/lit/Articles/KirschbaumC1999a.pdf.

Kourtzi, Z., & Kanwisher, N. (2000). Cortical regions involved in processing object shape. *Journal of Neuroscience, 20*(9) 3310–3318.

Kuipers, E., Peters, E., & Bebbington, P. (2006). Schizophrenia. In A. Carr and M. McNulty (Eds.), *The handbook of adult clinical psychology: An evidence-based approach* (pp. 843–896). Hove: Routledge.

Lam, D., & Jones, S. (2006). Bipolar disorder. In A. Carr & M. McNulty (Eds), *The handbook of adult clinical psychology: An evidence-based approach* (pp. 346–382). Hove: Routledge.

Lashley, K. S. (1930). Basic neural mechanisms in behaviour. *Psychological Review, 37*(1), 1–24. Available: http://psychclassics.yorku.ca/Lashley/neural.htm.

LeDoux, J. E. (1995). Emotion: Clues from the brain. *Annual Review of Psychology, 46,* 209–235.

Legro, R. S., Kunselman, A. R., Dodson, W. C., & Dunaif, A. (1999). Prevalence and predictors of risk for type 2 diabetes mellitus and impaired glucose tolerance in polycystic ovary syndrome: a prospective, controlled study in 254 affected women. *The Journal of Endocrinology and Metabolism, 84*(1), 165–169.

Levenson, R. W., Ekman, P., & Friesen, W. V. (1990). Voluntary facial expression generates emotion-specific autonomic nervous system activity. *Psychophysiology, 27,* 363–384.

Lewis, M. P. (Ed.) (2009). *Ethnologue: Languages of the world* (16th ed.). Dallas, TX.: SIL International. Online version: www.ethnologue.com

Lewis, M. (2011). Inside and outside: The relation between emotional states and expressions. *Emotion Review, 3*(2), 189–196. Available: www.depauw.edu/learn/lab/publications/documents/touch/2009_Touch_The_communication_of_emotion_via_touch.pdf

Liddle, P. F., Laurens, K. R., Kiehl, K. A., & Ngan, E. T. (2006). Abnormal function of the brain system supporting motivated attention in medicated patients with schizophrenia: An fMRI study. *Psychological Medicine, 38*(8), 1097–1108.

Loui, P., Guenther, F. H., Mathys, C., & Schlaug, G. (2008). Action–perception mismatch in tone-deafness. *Current Biology, 18*(8), 331–332.

Low Choy, N., Brauer, S. G., & Nitz, J. C. (2007). Age-related changes in strength and somatosensation during midlife. *Annals of the New York Academy of Science, 1114,* 180–193.

Lumpkin, E. A., & Caterina, M. J. (2007). Mechanisms of the sensory transduction in the skin. *Nature, 445*(7130), 858–865.

Madsen, P. L., Holm, S., Vorstrup, S., Friberg, L., Lassen, N. A., & Wildschiodz, G. (1991). Human regional cerebral blood flow during rapid-eye-movement sleep. *Journal of Cerebral Blood Flow and Metabolism, 11,* 502–507.

Maguire, E. A., Burgess, N., Donnett, J. G., Frackowiak, R. S. J., Frith, C. D., & O'Keefe, L. (2000). Knowing where and getting there: A human navigation network. *Science, 280,* 291–924.

Maguire, E. A., Frith, C. D., Burgess, N., Donnett, J. G., & O'Keefe, L. (1998). Knowing where things are: Parahippocampal involvement in encoding objects in virtual large-scale space. *Journal of Cognitive Neuroscience, 19,* 61–76.

Mani, S. K., Allen, J. M. C., Clark, J. H., Blaustein, J. D., & O'Malley, B. W. (1994). Convergent pathways for steroid hormone- and neurotransmitter-induced rat sexual behavior. *Science, 265*(5176), 1246–1249. Available: www-unix.oit.umass.edu/~blaustei/man1994s.pdf

Manolagas, S. C. (2000). Birth and death of bone cells: Basic regulatory mechanism and implications for the pathogenesis and treatment of osteoporosis. *Endocrine Reviews, 21*(2), 115–137.

Matsumoto, D., & Willingham, B. (2009). Spontaneous facial expressions of emotion of congenitally and noncongenitally blind individuals. *Journal of Personality and Social Psychology, 96*(1), 1–10.

Mauss, I. B., & Robinson, M. D. (2009). Measures of emotion: A review. *Cognition and Emotion, 23*(2), 209–237. Available: www.ncbi.nlm.nih.gov/pmc/articles/PMC2756702/

McDolald, J. W., & Sadowsky, C. (2002). Spinal-cord injury. *Lancet, 359*(9304), 417–425. Available: www.theneuroinstitute.com/research/medref/052%20LIB%20PAPER.pdf

McWilliams, S., & O'Callaghan, E. (2006). Biomedical approaches and the use of drugs to treat adult mental health problems. In A. Carr and M. McNulty (Eds.), *The handbook of adult clinical psychology: An evidence-based approach* (pp. 220–252). Hove: Routledge.

Melzack, R., & Wall, P. D. (1965). Pain mechanisms: A new theory. *Science, 150*(699), 971–979.

Melzack, R., & Wall, P. D. (2008). *The challenges of pain* (updated 2nd ed). London: Penguin Books. (Original work published 1982.)

Meyer, J. S., & Quenzer, L. F. (2004). *Psychopharmacology: Drugs, the brain and behavior.* Sunderland, MA: Sinauer Associates Inc.

Milner, A. D., & Goodale, M. A. (1993).Visual pathways to perception and action. In T. P. Hicks, S. Molotchnikoff, & T. Ono (Eds.), *Progress in brain research, Vol. 95. The visually responsive neuron: From basic neurophysiology to behavior* (pp. 317–337). Amsterdam: Elsevier.

References

Moore, R. Y. (1997). Circadian rhythms: Basic neurobiology and clinical applications. *Annual Review of Medicine, 48,* 253–266.

Mumby, D., Pinel, P. J., & Wood, E. R. (1989). Non-recurring items delayed nonmatching-to-sample in rats: A new paradigm for testing nonspatial working memory. *Psychobiology, 18,* 321–362.

Nadel, L., & Moscovitch, M. (1997). Memory consolidation, retrograde amnesia and the hippocampal complex. *Current Opinions in Neurobiology, 7,* 217–227.

Naya, Y., Yoshida, M., & Miyashita, Y. (2001). Backward spreading of memory-retrieval signals in the primate temporal cortex. *Science, 291*(5504), 661–664.

N'Diaye, K., Sander, D., & Vuilleumier, P. (2009). Self-relevance processing in the human amygdala: Gaze direction, facial expression, and emotional intensity. *Emotion, 9*(6), 798–806. Available: http://kndiaye.free.fr/lab/publications/ndiaye09.pdf

Nguyen, B. H., Pérusse, D., Paquet, J., Petit, D., Boivin, M., Tremblay, R. E., Montplaisir, J. (2008). Sleep terrors in children: A prospective study of twins. *Paediatrics, 122*(6), 1164–1167.

Nicholson, P. J., & D'Auria, D. A. (1999). Shift work, health, the working time regulations and health assessments. *Occupational Medicine, 49*(3), 127–137.

Oatley, K., Keltner, D., & Jenkins, J. M. (2006). *Understanding emotions* (2nd ed.). Malden, MA: Blackwell.

Ongür, D., Drevets, W. D., & Price, J. L. (1998). Glial reduction in the subgenual prefrontal cortex in mood disorders. *Proceedings of the National Academy of Science, 95*(22), 1329–95.

Orwoll, E. S., & Klein, R. F. (1995). Osteoporosis in men. *Endocrine Reviews, 16*(1), 87–116.

Owens, M. J., & Nemeroff, C. B. (1994). Role of serotonin in the parthophysiology of depression: focus on the serotonin transporter. *Clinical Chemistry, 40*(2), 288–295.

Pace-Schott, E., Solms, M., Blagrove, M., & Harnad, S. (Eds.) (2003). *Sleep and dreaming: Scientific advances and reconsiderations.* Cambridge: Cambridge University Press.

Palermo, R., & Rhodes, G. (2007). Are you always on my mind? A review of how face perception and attention interact. *Neuropsychologia, 45*(1), 75–92. Available: www.abdn. ac.uk/~psy423/dept/HomePage/Level_3_Social_Psych_files/Palermo%26Rhodes.pdf

Patterson, F. G. (1978). The gestures of a gorilla: Language acquisition in another pongid. *Brain and Language, 5*(1), 72–97.

Patterson, F. G. (1981). Ape language. *Science, 211*(4477), 86–88.

Penfield, W., & Roberts, L. (1959). *Speech and brain mechanisms.* Princeton: Princeton University Press.

Pepperberg, I. M. (2006a). Ordinality and inferential abilities of a Grey Parrot (*Psittacus erithacus*). *Journal of Comparative Psychology, 120,* 205–216.

Pepperberg, I. M. (2006b). Grey Parrot (*Psittacus erithacus*) numerical abilities: Addition and further experiments on a zero-like concept. *Journal of Comparative Psychology, 120*(1), 1–11.

Petit, D., Touchette, E., Tremblay R. E., Boivin, M., & Montplaisir, J. (2007). Dyssomnias and parasomnias in early childhood. *Pediatrics, 119*(5), 1016–1025.

Phelps, E. A., O'Connor, K. J., Gatenberg, C., Gore, J.C., Grillon, C., & Davis, M. (2001). Activation of the left amygdala to cognitive representation of fear. *Nature Neuroscience, 4*(4), 437–441. Available: http://dionysus.psych.wisc.edu/Lit/Articles/PhelpsE2001a.pdf

Pichon, A., & Chapelot, D. (2010). *Homeostatic role of the parasympathetic nervous systems in human behavior.* New York: Nova Science Publishers.

Pilcher, J. J., & Huffcutt, A. I. (1996). Effects of sleep deprivation on performance: A meta-analysis. *Sleep, 19*(4), 318–326

Pinel, J. P. (2003). *Biopsychology* (5th ed.). New York: Allyn & Bacon.

Pinel, J. P., & Dehaene, S. (2010). Beyond hemispheric dominance: Brain regions underlying joint lateralization of language and arithmetic to the left hemisphere. *Journal of Cognitive Neuroscience, 22*(1), 48–66. Available: www.mitpressjournals.org/doi/pdf/10.1162/jocn.2009.21184

Plomin, R. (1988). The nature and nurture of cognitive abilities. In R. J. Sternberg (Ed.), *Advances in the psychology of human intelligence.* Hillsdale, NJ: Erlbaum.

Potegal, M., Stemmler, G., & Spielberger, C. (Eds.) (2010). *International handbook of anger: Constituent and concomitant biological, psychological and social processes.* New York: Springer.

Premack, D. (1983). Animal cognition. *Annual Review of Psychology, 34,* 351–362.

Proctor, M. R. (2002). Spinal cord injury. *Critical Care Medicine, 30*(11), 489–499. Available: www.sassit.co.za/Journals/Trauma/Paediatrics/spinal%20injury.pdf

Pulvermüller, F., & Fadiga, L. (2010). Active perception: Sensorimotor circuits as a cortical basis for language. *Nature Reviews Neuroscience, 11*(5), 351–360.

QAA (2010). *Quality Assurance Agency benchmark for psychology.* London: Quality Assurance Agency.

Raine, A., Meloy, J. R., Bihrle, S., Stoddard, J., LeCasse, L., & Colletti, P. (2002). Reduced prefrontal gray matter volume and reduced autonomic activity in antisocial personality disorder. *Archives in General Psychiatry, 57*(2), 119–127.

Ranabir, S., & Reetu, K. (2011). Stress and hormones. *Indian Journal of Endocrinology and Metabolism, 15*(1), 18–22.

Rayner, K. (2009). Eye movements and attention in reading, scene perception, and visual search. *The Quarterly Journal of Experimental Psychology, 62*(8), 1457–1506. Available: http://benschweitzer.org/DROPBOX/litreview/rayner-Eye%20movements%20and%20attention%20in%20reading.pdf

Rechschaffen, A., & Bergmann, B. M. (1995). Sleep deprivation in the rat by the disk-over-water method. *Behavioural Brain Research, 69*(1), 55–63.

Rechschaffen, A., Bergmann, B. M., Everson, C. A., Kushida, C. A., & Gilliland, M. A. (1989). Sleep deprivation in the rat: Integration and discussion of the findings. *Sleep, 12,* 68–87.

Rechschaffen, A., Gilliland, M. A., Bergmann, B. M., & Winter, J. B. (1983). Physiological correlates of prolonged sleep deprivation in rats. *Science, 221,* 182–184.

Reilly, T., Atkinson, G., & Waterhouse, J. (1997). Travel fatigue and jet-lag. *Journal of Sports Sciences, 15*(3), 365–369.

Reiter, R. J. (1991). Pineal gland interface between the photoperiodic environment and the endocrine system. *Trends in Endocrinology and Metabolism, 2*(1), 13–19.

Robertson, L. C., Knight, R. T., Rafal, R., & Shimamura, A. P. (1993). Cognitive neuropsychology is more than single-case studies. *Journal of Experimental Psychology: Learning, Memory and Cognition, 19*(3), 710–717. Available: http://istsocrates.berkeley.edu/~shimlab/1993_Robertson_JEPLMC-case.pdf

Rodrigues, S. M., LeDoux, J. E., & Sapolsky, R. M. (2009). The influence of stress hormones on fear circuitry. *Annual Review of Neuroscience, 32*(1), 289–313. Available: http://dionysus.psych.wisc.edu/Lit/Articles/RodriguesS2009a.pdf

Rogalsky, C., & Hickok, G. (2011). The role of Broca's area in sentence comprehension. *Journal of Cognitive Neuroscience, 23*(7), 1664–1680.

Russell, J. A. (2003). Core affect and the psychological construction of emotion. *Psychological Review, 110*(1), 145–172. Available: http://directory.umm.ac.id/articles/psyc-rev2003.pdf

Russell, W. R., & Espir, M. L. E. (1961). *Traumatic aphasia.* Oxford: Oxford University Press.

Sack, R. L., & Lewy, A. J. (1997). Melatonin as a chronobiotic: treatment of circadian desynchrony in night workers and the blind. *Journal of Biological Rhythms; 12*(6), 595–603.

Sacks, O. (1985). *The man who mistook his wife for a hat and other clinical tales.* New York: Summit Books.

Salmon, D. P., & Butters, N. (1995). Neurobiology of skill and habit learning. *Current Opinions in Neurobiology, 152*(1), 1–6.

Saper, C. B., Scammell, T., & Lu, J. (2005). Hypothalamic regulation of sleep and circadian rhythms. *Nature, 437,* 1257–1263.

Sassi, R. B., Nicoletti, M., Brambilla, P., Mallinger, A. G., Frank, E., Kuffer, D. J., Keshavan, M. S., & Soares, J. C. (2002). Increased gray matter volume in Lithium-treated bipolar disorder patients. *Neuroscience Letters, 392*(2), 243–245.

Savage-Rumbaugh, E. S., McDonald, K., Sevcik, R. A., Hopkins, W. D., & Rupert, E. (1986). Spontaneous symbol acquisition and communicative use by pygmy chimpanzees (*Pan paniscus*). *Journal of Experimental Psychology: General, 115,* 211–235.

References

Savage-Rumbaugh, E. S, Rumbaugh, D. M., & McDonald, K. (1985). Language learning in two species of apes. *Neuroscience and Biobehavioral Reviews, 9,* 653–665.

Schommer, N. C., Hellhammer, D. C., & Kirschbaum, C. (2003). Dissociation between reactivity of the hypothalamus–pituitary–adrenal axis and the sympathetic–adrenal–medullary system to repeated psychosocial stress. *Psychosomatic Medicine, 65,* 450–460. Available: www.uni-duesseldorf.de/~ck/_download/3/3_0_0_0/135_schommer---psychosommed-03.pdf

Schwartz, M. F., Kimberg, D. Y., Walker, G. M., Faseyitan, O., Brecher, A., Dell, G. S., & Coslett, H. B. (2010). Anterior temporal involvement in semantic word retrieval: Voxel-based lesion-symptom mapping evidence from aphasia. *Brain, 132*(12), 3411–3427. Available: http://brain.oxfordjournals.org/content/132/12/3411.full

Selye, H. (1975). Confusion and controversy in the stress field. *Journal of Human Stress, 1*(2), 37–44.

Shallice, T., & Warrington, E. K. (1970). Independent functioning of verbal memory stores: A neuropsychological study. *Quarterly Journal of Experimental Psychology, 22,* 261–273.

Shamma, S. A., & Micheyl, C. (2010). Behind the scenes of auditory perception. *Current Opinions in Neurobiology, 20*(3), 361–366.

Shaw, K., Lien, M., Ruthruff, E., & Allen, P.A. (2011). Electrophysiological evidence of emotion perception without central attention. *Journal of Cognitive Psychology,* 23(6), 695–708. Available: http://people.oregonstate.edu/~lienm/ShawLienRuthruffAllenJCP2011.pdf

Shouse, M. N., & Siegel, J. M. (1992). Pontine regulation of REM sleep components in cats: Integrity of the pedunculopontine tegmentum (PPT) is important for phasic events but unnecessary for atonia during REM sleep. *Brain Research, 571*(1), 50–63.

Silver, R., LeSauter, J., Tresco P. A., & Lehman, M. N. (1996). A diffusible coupling signal from transplanted suprachiasmatic nucleus controlling circadian locomotor rhythms. *Nature, 382,* 810–813.

Simon, G. E., Savarino, J., Operskalski, B., & Wang, P. S. (2006). Suicide risk during antidepressant treatment. *American Journal of Psychiatry, 163*(1), 41–47.

Singh, P. B., Iannilli, E., & Hummel, T. (2011). Segregation of gustatory cortex in response to salt and umami taste studied through event-related potentials. *Neuroreport, 22*(6), 299–303.

Smith, E. E. (2000). Neural basis of human working memory. *Current Directions in Psychological Science, 9*(1), 45–49.

Smith, R. (2003). A review of blood–brain barrier transport techniques. *Methods of Molecular Medicine, 89*(3), 193–208.

Soares, C., & Grosjean, F. (1981). Left hemisphere language lateralization in bilinguals and monolinguals. *Attention, Perception and Psychophysics, 26*(6), 599–604.

Somers, M., Neggers, S. F., Diederen, K. M., Boks, M. P., Kahn, R. S., & Sommer, I. (2011). The measurement of language lateralization with functional transcranial Doppler and functional MRI: A critical evaluation. *Frontiers in Human Neuroscience, 5*(1), 1–8. Available: www.frontiersin.org/human_neuroscience/10.3389/fnhum.2011.00031/full

Sotres-Bayon, F., & Quirk, G. (2011). Prefrontal control of fear: More than just extinction. *Current Opinions in Neurobiology, 20*(2), 231–235.

Spanagel, R., & Weiss, F. (1999). The dopamine hypothesis of reward: Past and current status. *Trends in Neurosciences, 22*(11), 521–527. Available: www.psy.fsu.edu/~mnl/CNL/private/DAandReward/SpanagelWeiss.pdf

Sperry, R. W. (1966). Brain bisection and consciousness. In J. Eccles (Ed.), *Brain and Conscious Experience.* New York: Springer-Verlag.

Stabenau, J., & Pollin, W. (1993). Heredity and environment in schizophrenia, revisited: the contribution of twin and high-risk studies. *Journal of Nervous and Mental Disease, 181*(5), 290–297.

Stevens, C., Fanning, J., Coch, D., Sanders, L., & Neville, H. (2008). Neural mechanisms of selective auditory attention are enhanced by computerized training: electrophysiological evidence from language-impaired and typically developing children. *Brain Research, 18*(1205), 55–69.

Stickgold, R. (2005). Sleep-dependent memory consolidation. *Nature, 437*, 1272–1278. Available: www.lemanic-neuroscience.ch/PENSTrainingCenter/articles/stickgold_nature2005.pdf

Swinson, R. P., Antony, M. A., Rachman, S., & Richter, M. (1998). *Obsessive Compulsive Disorder: Theory, Research and Treatment.* New York: Guildford Press.

Taylor, S., & Asmundson, J. G. (2006). Panic disorder and agoraphobia. In A. Carr and M. McNulty, (Eds.), *The handbook of adult clinical psychology: An evidence-based approach* (pp. 458–486). Hove: Routledge.

Terrace, H. S. (1979). *Nim: A chimpanzee who learned sign language.* New York: Knopf.

Thompson, C. K., & Lee, M. (2009). Psych verb production and comprehension in agrammatic Broca's aphasia. *Journal of Neurolinguistics, 22*(4), 354–369. Available: www.ncbi.nlm.nih.gov/pmc/articles/PMC2824436/

Thompson, P. M., Vidal, C. N., Giedd, J. N., Gochmann, P. Blumenthal, J., Nicolson, R., Toga, A. W., & Rapoport, J. L. (2001). Mapping adolescent brain change reveals dynamic wave of accelerated gray matter loss in very early-onset schizophrenia. *Proceedings of the National Academy of Science, 98*(20), 11650–11655.

Tohidian, I. (2009). Examining the linguistic relativity hypothesis as one of the main views on the relationship between language and thought. *Journal of Psycholinguistic Research, 38*(1), 65–74.

Turner, T. H., Drummond, S. P. A., Salamat, J. S., & Brown, G. G. (2007). Effects of 42-hour sleep deprivation on component processes of verbal working memory. *Neuropsychology, 21*, 787–795.

Valentine, E. R. (1992). *Conceptual issues in psychology* (2nd ed.). London: Routledge.

Vergnes, M., Depaulis, A., Boehrer, A., & Kempf, E. (1988). Selective increase of offensive behaviour in the rat following intrahypothalamic 5,7-DHT-induced serotonin depletion. *Brain Research, 29*(1–2), 85–91.

Vitiello, B. (2007). Research in child and adolescent psychopharmacology: Recent accomplishments and new challenges. *Psychopharmacology, 191*(1), 5–13. Available: http://pubget.com/paper/16718480

Voss, J. L., & Paller, K. A. (2008). Brain substrates of implicit and explicit memory: The importance of concurrently acquired neural signals of both memory types. *Neuropsychologia, 46*(13), 3021–3029. Available: www.ncbi.nlm.nih.gov/pmc/articles/PMC2621065/

Wasserman, E. A. (1993). Comparative cognition: Beginning the second century of animal intelligence. *Psychological Bulletin, 113*(2), 211–228. Available: http://www.niu.edu/user/tj0dgw1/pdf/learning/wasserman1993.pdf

Webb, W. B., & Cartwright, R. D. (1978). Sleep and dreams. *Annual Review of Psychology, 29*, 223–252.

Weiskrantz, I. (1987). Residual vision in the scotoma: A follow-up study of 'form' discrimination. *Brain, 110*, 77–92.

Wells, A., & Carter, K. (2006). Generalized anxiety disorder. In A. Carr & M. McNulty (Eds.), *The handbook of adult clinical psychology: An evidence-based approach* (pp. 423–457). Hove: Routledge.

Wheeler-Kingshott, C. M., Hickman, S. J., Parker, J. M., Ciccarelli, O., Symms, M. R., Miller, D. H., & Barker, G. (2001). Investigating cervical spinal cord structure using axial diffusion tensor imaging. *Neuroimage, 16*(1), 93–102. Available: http://spin.ecn.purdue.edu/fmri/PDFLibrary/WheelerKingshottC_NI_2002_16_93_102.pdf

Wilson, M. A., & McNaughton, B. L. (1993). Dynamics of the hippocampal ensemble code for space. *Science, 261*, 1055–1058.

Winson, J. (2002). The meaning of dreams. *Scientific America: The hidden mind – A special edition* (pp. 55–61). New York: Worth Publishers.

Wixted, J. T. (2004) The psychology and neuroscience of forgetting. *Annual Review of Psychology, 55*, 235–269.

Wooltorton, E. (2003). Paroxetine (Paxil, Seroxat): Increased risk of suicide in pediatric patients. *Canadian Medical Association Journal, 169*(5), 446.

References

Wright, I. C., Rabe-Hesketh, S., Woodruff, P. W. R., David, A. S., Murray, R. M., & Bullmore, E. T. (2000). Meta-analysis of regional brain volumes in schizophrenia. *American Journal of Psychiatry*, 157(1), 16–25.

Wundt, W. (1902). *Principles of physiological psychology*. Available: http://psychclassics.yorku.ca/Wundt/Physio/

Yehuda, R. (2001). Biology of posttraumatic stress disorder. *Journal of Clinical Psychiatry*, *62*(17), 41–46.

Zager, A., Anderson, M. L., Ruiz, F. S., Antunes, I. B., & Tufik, S. (2007). Effects of acute and chronic sleep loss on immune modulation of rats. *Regulatory, Integrative and Comparative Psychology*, *293*, 504–509.

Zmigrod, S., & Hommel, B. (2009). Auditory event files: Integrating auditory perception and action planning. *Attention, Perception and Psychophysics*, *71*(2), 352–362. Available: http://home.planet.nl/~homme247/Auditory%20event%20file.pdf

Zuckerman, M. (1991). *Psychobiology of personality*. Cambridge: Cambridge University Press.

Index

Index